PEACE-KEEPING
BY U.N. FORCES

PRINCETON STUDIES IN WORLD POLITICS

Number 4

PRINCETON STUDIES IN WORLD POLITICS

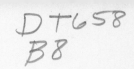

PEACE-KEEPING BY U.N. FORCES

From Suez to the Congo

Arthur Lee Burns
and
Nina Heathcote

Published for the Center of International Studies
Princeton University

by
FREDERICK A. PRAEGER, *Publisher*
New York · London

FREDERICK A. PRAEGER, PUBLISHER
64 UNIVERSITY PLACE, NEW YORK 3, N.Y., U.S.A.
49 GREAT ORMOND STREET, LONDON W.C. 1, ENGLAND

Published in the United States of America in 1963 by
Frederick A. Praeger, Inc., Publisher

© 1963 by Center of International Studies
Library of Congress Catalog Number: 63-15717

Manufactured in the United States of America

Foreword

MANKIND WOULD STAND an excellent chance of suffering unprecedented destruction if the traditional organization of military power on a strictly national basis, and the traditionally weak impediments to the use of military power, were continued in the nuclear age. In fact, both the United States and the Soviet Union have chosen to behave with extraordinary circumspection in international crises that previously would have touched off the chain reaction of military conflict. Yet this unilateral national restraint does not inspire sufficient confidence in man's ability to avoid suicidal warfare—hence the widespread interest in measures, however uncertain, for international arms control and disarmament.

As never before, national security has become dependent on international security and on international arrangements on behalf of international security. In a world saturated with explosives, violence anywhere constitutes a threat dangerous to all, and nations everywhere have an incentive to help contain and speedily extinguish brushfires, no matter how small or remote, and to organize themselves for this purpose. It is far from sure that this incentive will prove strong enough to withstand the pressure of myriad crosspurposes and, by acquiring proper guidance, to engender constructive action and guarantee success. But the urgency of the problem demands that we learn fast and makes any experiments in this direction fascinating to study.

We at the Center of International Studies were therefore delighted to hear of the project that led to this book, and we were glad to lend it our support.

KLAUS KNORR

Princeton University
August 1, 1962

v

Preface

THE USE OF FORCE under international aegis is a much larger subject than that of this monograph, which, omitting to examine the United Nations operation in Korea, concerns the Organization's experience with military and semi-military groups recruited on an international basis and deployed on behalf of the Organization itself by its executive officers. Nor have we attempted an exhaustive account of the United Nations operation in the Congo: The important aspect of nonmilitary technical assistance is not referred to, and even the financial difficulties that the Organization has encountered as a result of its military expenditures in the Congo are merely touched upon. Though several of the UNF's actions in the Congo receive more detailed attention, it is not pretended that this monograph is a military history of the operation. Our intention has been to digest the experience from Suez to the Congo, so as to bring to light some of the limitations and possibilities of the United Nations forces as means for the preservation of international peace and, in the Congo instance, of internal law and order.

Some of the material employed was originally prepared for papers read at the Australian National University in December, 1960, and at the Conference of the Australian and New Zealand Association of Scientists, meeting in Brisbane in May, 1961. The enterprise was discussed at length by one of the authors with members of the Center of International Studies at Princeton University toward the end of 1961. The authors wish particularly to thank Professors Richard A. Falk, Leon Gordenker, and Klaus Knorr; Miss Jean MacLachlan, also of the Center of International Studies, who has undertaken the editing of the manuscript; Miss Catherine Hoskyns of the Royal Institute of International Affairs, Chatham House, London, England; and Professor W. T. R. Fox of the Institute for War and Peace Studies, Columbia University, New York, N.Y.

A. L. B.
N. H.

Australian National University
June 8, 1962

CONTENTS

PEACE-KEEPING
BY U.N. FORCES

I

Introduction

WE HERE STUDY the uses to which the United Nations has put
military force, from the effective employment of the United
Nations Emergency Force (UNEF) at Suez in 1957 to the U.N.'s
joint operation with Congolese Central Government forces against
the Gizengists in January, 1962. We are particularly concerned
with the military force employed by the United Nations Organization Command in the Congo (UNOC). This was the first explicit
deployment of U.N. military power within a reputedly sovereign
independent state (not, as in Korea, power deployed vicariously
through U.S. and other pro-Western forces), the intention at first
being to assist the restoration of internal law and order so that the
troops of Belgium, sent in to protect its nationals and their property, might be withdrawn.

Later innovations were the Security Council's authorization of
the use of force to prevent civil war and to expel mercenaries and
other undesirable aliens; and, more importantly, its outright con-
demnation of Katanga's secessionism. Though the United Nations
Force (UNF) in the Congo was never openly or officially sent to
achieve political ends, it fought in Katanga two actions that produced political effects, and in Orientale during 1962 it was used
to suppress gendarmes who had supported a political nuisance.

Will any of these actions be taken as establishing a precedent for
the U.N.'s using military force for political ends? Do they show
that with the aid of military force the U.N. can smooth the transition from colonialism to independent statehood and prevent bloodshed during it? Above all, do they show that military force in U.N.
hands is an effective instrument for the preservation of peace?

The U.N. was founded as an organization for making and preserving peace; but it does not follow that that is now its principal
function or that the U.N. is now the principal maintainer of peace.

Indeed, it has become evident that peace between the superpowers is maintained by conditions due less to the U.N. than to Providence, and that anyone can use the United Nations for ends quite extraneous to the keeping of peace—to discomfit enemies, to keep allies in line, to reward faithful servants, and so on. A leading notion in this study is that the United Nations has become many things it was not intended to be, but is now, among other things, the institution that *formalizes* and *legitimates* some of the relationships of international politics.

International politics, in our view, is just politics unregulated by containment within the forms of any single state. To be sure, it does not reproduce all the characteristic features of internal politics: Why should it? Its manifestations are sometimes—misleadingly—given the same names as those of internal politics; but a "bloc" and a "caucus" in the General Assembly are, concretely, quite different institutions from those within a national parliament or congress, whose names they have borrowed. But what goes on at the U.N., as in the chambers of any parliamentary institution, is recognizably politics; and is neither warfare, business, nor, in the narrow sense, the administration of government. It is carried on not by "international actors" (though in this study we have recourse to that shorthand mythology) but by persons—representative persons, for the most part, who are compelled to act only in obedience to their government's instructions. External (or "international") politics goes on in other institutions besides the U.N. and outside all institutions. From this viewpoint, the U.N. is merely the formalized part of a largely informal and world-wide "conversation."

Once we see the U.N. in such a light and not as an incipient world government, then we can fairly concede it an ancillary but independent role in actually keeping the peace. Despite Korea, and despite three military actions in the Congo, it does this for the most part not by the exercise of any physical *force:* In ancient terms, it has little *potestas*—even less, perhaps, than the League of Nations had before it; for the League did not labor under the restrictions of the Security Council veto. Insofar as it works to any effect, it does so by virtue of its *auctoritas*—the right that some of the world public thinks it has to represent mankind's conscience and respect for law: by no means the most powerful, direct, or active of our notions, but notions all the same that only a doctrinaire "realism" is likely to disregard.

We may agree that if all the "actors" on the international stage were nation-states or similar, partly mythical, collective entities, there would be little point in referring to "conscience" or "respect for law." But, in fact, international politics is carried on by persons—not, of course, "ordinary people," but persons who are there to represent collectives. It is perhaps a weakness of human nature that very few can sink themselves wholly in the representative role; yet, because they cannot, an international organization such as the U.N. has some hope of affecting the conduct of international affairs. The "representative person" is by no means thrust back upon his own personal conscience only. There is a community of persons —more frequently found in the more or less open societies, yet existing in some measure all over the world—that takes note of the representative person's acts and is prepared to criticize them in moral terms as well as in those of national self-interest. Pragmatic and realistic concessions to the "factor of prestige" are in reality concessions to the efficacy of this international community's conscience. This study's questions ultimately concern the sort of showing that the U.N. has made during the last five years before the bar of that conscience.

II

U.N. Forces in Suez, Lebanon, and Jordan

DURING THE FIRST few years of its existence, the U.N. remained true to the conditions of its origin—that of a wartime alliance. Several analyses[1] have shown how its early meetings were characterized by great unanimity and how later this was destroyed by the pressures of the Cold War.

Our *terminus a quo*, the Suez crisis, was the first occasion for perhaps ten years when the divisive elements in one alliance (the Western) overrode Cold War pressures. None of the subsequent affairs can be understood exclusively in terms of the Cold War alone; all of them reveal divisions and diversities of interest within the blocs. During the Congo crisis there were opening up within the Afro-Asian bloc certain cracks and fissures of interest, like those that had earlier divided first the Western and then the Communist alliances. The remarkable fact is that precisely these divisions allowed the emergence, for the first time since Korea, of a UNF operation, not resulting from the decision of a two-thirds majority of the U.N. General Assembly, but one detailed and sent by the Security Council.

The action at Suez was the first instance of the small-scale but *successful* operation of a U.N. "border patrol." The operation set several precedents for the later and much larger U.N. intervention in the Congo. In order to separate the combatants, the UNEF was dispatched in November, 1956, at the request of Egypt, which was about to be defeated by the joint efforts of invading Anglo-French and Israeli forces.

From the beginning, all the attackers, and particularly Britain, had maintained that they had acted within the framework of in-

6

ternational law and the U.N. Charter. Thus the British claimed that one of the purposes of the expedition was the protection of lives of British nationals allegedly threatened by the Egyptian-Israeli conflict. This, incidentally, was to be the explanation advanced by the United States for its intervention in Lebanon and by Belgium for sending its troops into the Congo. Prime Minister Eden also claimed that the U.N. was as yet an ineffective agency incapable of stopping wars, but that as soon as it was ready to take over, the combatants were willing to let the U.N. do so. The Belgians four years later somewhat delayed their withdrawal by making it conditional upon U.N. effectiveness in restoring law and order.

Because of the British and French veto of a Security Council resolution, the General Assembly was called into emergency special session under the terms of the "Uniting for Peace" resolution. On November 5, 1956, after five days of debate, it ordered a cease-fire and formation of a U.N. force to keep peace between Israel and Egypt.

Lester Pearson of Canada moved the resolution adopted on November 4 (fifty-seven votes to seven, with nineteen abstentions), by which the Assembly requested "the Secretary-General as a matter of priority to submit to it within 48 hours a plan for the setting-up with the consent of the nations concerned of an Emergency International United Nations Force to secure and supervise the cessation of hostilities in accordance with the terms of the above resolution."

In the evening of November 5, another Canadian resolution was adopted, this time incorporating detailed proposals drawn up by the Secretary-General for the setting up of the UNEF. The Assembly also established by resolution an Advisory Committee made up of representatives from Brazil, Canada, Ceylon, Colombia, India, Norway, and Pakistan under the chairmanship of the Secretary-General. The role of the Advisory Committee was to plan the aspects of UNEF functioning not already dealt with by the General Assembly and not falling within the area of direct responsibility of the Chief of Command. This became one of several precedents for the Congo operation. Another was that no nationals of a permanent member of the Security Council should participate in the UNEF.

The U.S.S.R., having abstained from voting on the motion establishing the UNEF, claimed that its composition was not in accord with the U.N. Charter, which provided for the interposition of armed forces of member nations for the maintenance and restoration of peace and international security. The Soviet Union three times offered to place Russian forces at the U.N.'s disposal for that purpose. The United States disapproved of this idea but offered to help with airlifts, shipping transport, and supplies. Selwyn Lloyd in a debate in the House of Commons on November 5, likewise justified Britain's abstention from the motion setting up the UNEF on the grounds that the resolution excluded participation by permanent members of the Security Council. He felt this to be unwise, as the permanent members were the only ones who could effectively contribute to the force. Mr. Eden, however, modified this position on November 9: If it were proposed that the UNEF should consist of small as against great powers, Britain would not object in principle.

The Suez crisis was a clear-cut case of external attack by the armed forces of several countries. Thus the U.N.'s task was to end the conflict and separate the combatants. It managed this with some ease because behind the activities of the UNEF stood all but two or three European members of the U.N.; and, once it became clear that the United States would not tolerate direct intervention by the Soviet Union, the two superpowers were prepared to forgo their immediate interests in the area, in order to avoid a major war. In fact, that was the argument used by the United States in rejecting Russia's proposal that the superpowers jointly intervene.

Another significant fact was that the UNEF did not need to go into the Suez area in order to effect the cease-fire; the resolution of the General Assembly had already accomplished that, along with pressure upon Britain, France, and Israel from both the U.S.S.R. and the United States. Economic sanctions and military intervention alike were threatened. The UNEF had only to police the U.N. mandate.

Thus the clear distinction between internal and external issues, and the virtual resolution of the armed conflict before the UNEF arrived on the scene, distinguished the Suez operation from the later Congo problems. The mission was successful: The size of the force progressively increased until it was made up of 6,000 men from 10 nations (Brazil, Canada, Colombia, Denmark, Finland, India, Indonesia, Norway, Sweden, Yugoslavia)—as compared with 20,000 or so at the height of the Congo operation.[2]

Along with the Suez action, the U.N.'s experience in Lebanon and Jordan was put forward as a precedent by the Secretary-General when the matter of the Congo arose. For that reason, it forms an important background for any study of the U.N. intervention in the Congo.

During May, 1958, there were riots in Lebanon that by June threatened to assume international proportions and to involve the great powers. The United States in May made it known that it was supplying arms to President Chamoun and that it was ready to send in troops as well, should he request their presence. Late in May, NATO exercises were switched from the western to the eastern Mediterranean. The Russians, on the other hand, alleged through Tass that the U.S. naval buildup in the Mediterranean was connected with the crisis and warned against any intervention in Lebanon.[3] Lebanon itself, in a letter dated May 22, 1958, complained to the President of the Security Council against foreign intervention in its affairs by the United Arab Republic, "the continuance of which is likely to endanger the maintenance of international peace and security."[4]

The question was debated by the Security Council on June 6, 10, and 11, the members of the Arab League having failed to resolve the question among themselves.[5] On June 6, Dr. Malik on behalf of Lebanon accused the U.A.R. of intervention in Lebanon's internal affairs, saying that this intervention was aimed at undermining the independence of Lebanon and that the resultant situation could endanger the maintenance of international peace and security. Dr. Malik claimed the U.A.R. was fomenting a rebellion in Lebanon by means of propaganda and by infiltration of men and ammunition across the border from Syria.[6] The representative of the U.A.R., Mr. Loufti, denied these charges and said the disorders were of a purely domestic nature.[7]

On June 10, Sweden presented a draft resolution, by the Operative Paragraph 1 of which the Security Council

1. *Decides* to despatch urgently an observation group to proceed
to Lebanon so as to ensure that there is no illegal infiltration of personnel or supply of arms or other *matériel* across the Lebanese
borders.[8]

The Secretary-General was authorized to implement the decision,
and the group was requested to keep the Security Council "currently informed" through the Secretary-General.[9] The resolution
was adopted on June 11, 1958, by ten votes to none, with Russia
abstaining.[10]

The Secretary-General then told the Council that he envisaged
the operation on two levels: the observation group proper, to be
"composed of highly qualified and experienced men . . . collected
from various corners of the globe"; and "the group servicing the
main group," recruited from the staff of the U.N. Truce Supervi-
sion Organization (UNTSO) in Palestine.[11] At the subsequent
news conference, Hammarskjöld said the group was to be in no way
a "police force" such as the UNEF patrolling the border in Gaza.

The observers (UNOGIL) started arriving in Lebanon on June
12. The largest contingents came from Italy, Denmark, Norway,
Canada, the Netherlands, India, Sweden, and Finland, in that order.[12] The observers at the most numbered 591. As at Suez, the
personnel of the group was recruited from countries that on the
question of Lebanon could be regarded as neutral, so that their
findings would be assumed to be unbiased. The observers, after
some initial difficulties, were deployed on both sides—i.e., in both
the government-held and the rebel-held areas.[13] The results of their
inquiries were published in five reports, dated July 2, 1958 (S/4040
and Corr. 1), July 30 (S/4069), August 14 (S/4085), September
29 (S/4100), and November 17 (S/4114). These reports all agreed
that there was little, if any, evidence of infiltration of arms and
personnel from the outside and that the whole conflict had the
character of a domestic rebellion.

The Lebanese government strongly criticized the findings of the
first report and asked the Secretary-General to circulate its official
comment to this effect, dated July 8, 1958, to all members of the
U.N.[14] At the Security Council meeting on July 15, Lebanon demanded formation of a U.N. police force to seal the border.[15]

In July, the whole situation assumed a more explosive character following a successful coup in Iraq and unrest in Jordan. The United States landed troops in Lebanon at the request of the Lebanese Government on July 15. President Eisenhower in a statement of that day indicated what the current U.S. attitude to the U.N. operations in Lebanon had become. He considered:

> that in the face of the tragic and shocking events that are occurring nearby, more will be required than the team of U.N. observers now in Lebanon.
>
> Therefore the United States will support in the U.N. measures which seem to be adequate to meet the new situation and which will enable the U.S. forces promptly to be withdrawn.[16]

The emergency Security Council meeting that began on July 15 to consider the new situation in the Middle East was remarkable for the number of resolutions introduced, none of which was passed. The United States insisted against the findings of the Observer Group that there were in Lebanon "threats from outside."[17] The U.S. representative, Henry Cabot Lodge, went as far as to claim that "the presence of United States troops in Lebanon will be a constructive contribution to the objectives the Security Council had in mind when it passed the June 11 resolution."[18] Hammarskjöld told the Council on July 15 that, as far as his mandate was concerned, the recent landing in Lebanon of the U.S. troops and the international implications of that action were irrelevant. He also pointed out that under the present mandate he could not change "the observation operation into some kind of police operation" without exceeding his instructions and violating the Charter. "In a police operation," he said, "the participants would in this case need the right, if necessary, to take the initiative in the use of force. Such use of force would, however, have belonged to the sphere of Chapter VII of the Charter and could have been granted only by the Security Council itself."[19] Hammarskjöld thus rejected the plea of Lebanon to turn the operation into a police action and the pretensions of the United States to be acting along with and in lieu of the United Nations.

Various resolutions were then introduced by Russia, the United States, and Sweden. The Russian draft of July 15[20] accused the United States of intervention in the internal affairs of Lebanon and

contravention of the Charter, especially Article 2 (para. 7).[21] It
called for withdrawal of U.S. troops from Lebanon immediately.[22]
At the end of that day, the United States introduced its own resolution.[23] to strengthen the U.N. operation in Lebanon. This was to
be achieved through further development of the Observer Group
and through provision of U.N. contingents to guard the border.
Under those conditions the U.S. troops would be withdrawn.[24]

Sweden on July 16 gave notice that it would introduce a draft
resolution to "suspend until further notice the activities carried on
by the United Nations observers in Lebanon,"[25] on the grounds
that the action taken by the United States in landing troops in
Lebanon was unjustified under Article 51,[26] as claimed, because
there was no armed attack on Lebanon in progress. Further, Sweden considered that the U.S. intervention had altered the conditions under which the Observer Group was initially conceived and
had rendered the operation under these new conditions impractical.[27]

Following the landing of British troops in Jordan, Russia introduced on July 17 a revised draft of its resolution, in which it called
for a speedy withdrawal of British and U.S. troops from Jordan and
Lebanon, respectively.[28]

A revised text of the U.S. draft resolution was also presented that
day.[29] The next day the three resolutions—Russian, American, and
Swedish—were voted on, and all of them were rejected by the
Council. The Russian resolution was rejected by eight votes to one,
with two abstentions. The American resolution was vetoed by Russia, with only Sweden abstaining; and the Swedish resolution failed
to obtain the required seven votes, with only Russia and Sweden
being in favor and nine votes against.[30]

After the voting, three more resolutions were presented. Japan
submitted a draft[31] calling for strengthening and expanding the activities of the Observer Group to permit withdrawal of U.S. troops.[32]
Russia[33] and the United States[34] each submitted a request (S/4057
and S/4056, respectively) for an emergency special session of the
General Assembly.

The Council met to consider these resolutions on July 21. In in-
troducing the Japanese draft, the Japanese representative stressed
that the motion did not aim to empower the Secretary-General to

create a U.N. police force in Lebanon but only to strengthen the already existent Observer Group.[35] The Secretary-General welcomed this suggestion. He was against setting up a U.N. police force in Lebanon along the lines suggested by the United States. He said that under the terms of the U.S. proposal the force would be limited to self-defense and would therefore find it quite difficult to operate outside the government-held territory if, as might well be, such operations should meet with armed resistance. In these circumstances, and while remaining—as it must—strictly within the terms of the Charter, any such force would seem likely to find itself restricted to a rather passive role, which in any case could have been filled by the already existing Observer Group. For this reason, Hammarskjöld was in favor of expanding the functions and powers of the Observer Group as outlined in the Japanese resolution.[36]

The Japanese motion, which was voted on, on July 22, was vetoed by Russia and consequently not adopted.[37] The Secretary-General said, however, that in spite of the fact that the Security Council had failed to take additional action, he would continue to develop UNOGIL so as to give it all the significance it could have, consistent with its basic character as determined in the Security Council resolution of June 11, and with the Charter. The Security Council would be fully informed of the new steps he proposed to take and, were the Council to disapprove of those steps, he would accept the consequences of its judgment.[38]

The Security Council met again on August 7. The meeting had been requested by a letter from the Soviet representative to consider the Russian proposal for the convening of an emergency special session of the U.N. General Assembly.[39] The Security Council, when it met, had before it a Russian resolution of July 18 calling for an emergency session of the U.N. Assembly.[40] The U.S. resolution originally made direct reference to the Lebanese complaints to the Security Council alleging interference by the U.A.R. in that country. Because of Russian objections, the resolution was amended, leaving out the name of Lebanon.[41] The amended U.S. draft resolution was voted on and passed unanimously that day.[42]

The General Assembly met in emergency special session on August 8 and adjourned until August 13 to enable twenty foreign ministers, including those of Britain, Russia, the United States, the

U.A.R., and France, to attend.[43] Hammarskjöld suggested to the meeting that U.N. representation in Lebanon should be maintained after the Observer Group had fulfilled its task.[44]

In an opening address, President Eisenhower argued along the lines of his statement of July 15 that the government of Lebanon, "endangered by civil strife fomented from without," had asked the United States for help and that the United States responded to this appeal.[45] He explained that it was really for the U.N. to aid Lebanon, but that because of U.N. ineffectuality since 1945 the United States had had to carry out this task. However, as he reminded the Assembly, the United States had taken the matter at once to the Security Council and had sought U.N. assistance for Lebanon so as to replace U.S. troops and permit their withdrawal. That this did not come to pass he blamed on the defeat of the two resolutions, those of the U.S. and Japan, by the Russian veto.[46] Mr. Eisenhower then presented the framework of a plan for peace in the Middle East in which the six elements were to be: U.N. concern for Lebanon; measures to preserve peace in Jordan; an end to fomenting from without of civil strife; a U.N. peace force; a regional economic development plan to assist and accelerate improvement in the living standards of the Arab nations; and steps to avoid a new arms-race spiral in the Middle East.[47]

Andrei Gromyko accused Britain and the United States of armed intervention in the domestic affairs of Jordan and Lebanon, challenging the explanations they had offered and particularly their claim that the intervention was compatible with the aims and policies of the U.N. He quoted the UNOGIL reports (S/4069 and S/4085) that refuted the assertion that there had been any interference by the U.A.R. in Lebanon and Jordan and referred to a statement by the Secretary-General, who had been to Lebanon and had come to the same conclusion.[48] Britain's and the United States' justification in terms of Article 51 for landing their troops in the Middle East he therefore considered "extremely far-fetched."[49] Mr. Gromyko then introduced a draft resolution that recommended the withdrawal of U.S. and British troops and suggested that the Secretary-General be instructed to reinforce the Observer Group in Lebanon and to send a similar group to Jordan in order to supervise the withdrawal of U.S. and British troops and to patrol the frontier.[50]

On August 19, Canada, Colombia, Denmark, Liberia, Norway, Panama, and Paraguay introduced a draft resolution calling upon member states to refrain from threats or acts impairing the freedom, independence, and integrity of any state or fomenting civil strife. It referred to formation of a stand-by U.N. peace force and called on the Secretary-General to consult with governments and make suitable arrangements to uphold purposes and principles of the Charter in relation to Lebanon and Jordan. But it made no direct reference to withdrawal of foreign troops, although it mentioned the letters from the United States and Britain[51] that stated conditions under which the troops of these countries would be withdrawn.

On August 21, a resolution sponsored by ten Arab states, including Lebanon and Jordan, was adopted unanimously.[52] Though otherwise framed like the Seven-Power resolution, its Operative Paragraph II referred to withdrawal of foreign troops, and it did not mention a possible U.N. peace force. The Russian and the Seven-Power resolutions were not voted on.

Meanwhile, the internal situation in Lebanon resolved itself. A new president, General Chehab, who was elected on July 31, commanded the support of both the government and the opposition members. On August 1, a new cabinet was formed by Rashid Karami, the former leader of the rebels at Tripoli. On September 27, this government reached an agreement with the United States that the U.S. troops would leave Lebanon by the end of October.[53] The withdrawal was completed on November 2, 1958; and on November 25, the Security Council decided, pursuant to a Lebanese request of November 16, to delete this item from its agenda.[54]

On July 17, 1958, the Security Council adopted as an agenda item a letter from the representative of Jordan to the President of the Security Council concerning a "complaint by the Hashemite Kingdom of Jordan of interference in its domestic affairs by the United Arab Republic" (S/4503).[55] The Council invited the representative of Jordan to participate in the discussion without vote and decided that, after the Jordanian complaint had been heard, the Council should consider the complaints submitted by Lebanon and Jordan simultaneously.[56]

The Jordanian representative, Mr. Toukan, addressed the Council on July 17, leveling a series of accusations against the U.A.R.: that it had instigated the *coup d'état* in Jordan in April, 1957;[57] that since that time the smuggling of men and arms into Jordan had continued; and that inflammatory propaganda, emanating from the U.A.R. incited the people in Jordan to rebellion.[58] He put it to the Council that the recently discovered plot against the government in Jordan, the events in Lebanon and Iraq, and the movement of U.A.R. troops from Syria along Jordan's northern border menaced Jordan's integrity and independence.[59] In reply to these threats to her independence, Jordan had acted in accordance with provisions of Article 51 of the U.N. Charter, requesting military assistance from Britain and the United States. British troops landed in Jordan, responding to her request, on July 17.[60]

Sir Pierson Dixon, for Britain, confirmed that the aim in sending British troops to Jordan was to guard Jordanian integrity and independence against outside threats.[61] However, the U.A.R. representative, Mr. Loufti, denied the charge that the U.A.R. had in any way interfered in the internal affairs of Jordan.[62]

At the Security Council meeting of July 21, Britain gave notice that it proposed to explore urgently with the Secretary-General of the U.N. and in consultation with the government of Jordan, the possibility of effective action by the U.N. to protect Jordan from external interference, so that British troops could be withdrawn.[63] On August 7, the British representative told the Council that his country had already entered into such consultation.[64] However, as we have already seen (see p. 12 above), the Security Council failed to reach any decision and the question of Jordan, along with the question of Lebanon, was referred for debate to the emergency special session of the General Assembly that met on August 13.

The Jordanian representative on August 14 accused the U.A.R. before the Assembly, of indirect aggression that had led to riots in April, 1957, and a planned coup against the king.[65] He reiterated Jordan's charges made in the Security Council, saying that infiltration, smuggling of arms, and inflammatory propaganda from the

U.A.R. were continuing,[66] and that a plot and a network of es-
pionage and saboteurs supported from outside were also discovered
in Amman a few days before the Iraqi events.[67] There was reliable information that a large-scale attack against Jordan from the
U.A.R. was planned to begin on July 17, 1958: This was why
Jordan had asked Britain and the United States for military aid.[68]
The U.N. must adopt practical arrangements to secure effective
international guarantees that would prevent aggression and interference in Jordan's internal affairs.[69] However, he continued,
"Such measures and arrangements must not envisage by any means
the dispatch of United Nations forces or United Nations observers
to be stationed on Jordan territory or to guard the Jordanian
frontiers. My Government will oppose such decisions."[70] Jordan
wanted the United Nations to supply the necessary arms and funds
to repel aggressors and guard its independence.

As we have seen (see p. 15), the General Assembly, after debating the questions of Lebanon and Jordan, on August 21 passed
a resolution whose sponsors included Lebanon and Jordan.[71] In
conformity with this resolution, the Secretary-General presented his
first report on September 29, 1958. The report said that Jordan had
stated its willingness to be the host country for a special representative of the Secretary-General with adequate staff, who might "assist
in the implementation of the resolution, specifically with a view
to help in upholding the purposes and principles of the Charter in
relation to Jordan in the present circumstances."[72] The governments of Lebanon and the U.A.R. undertook to grant all the facilities necessary for establishing a line of communication for the Special Representative stationed in Jordan, including liaison officers in
Beirut and Damascus.[73]

The U.N. Special Representative, Ambassador Spinelli, had gone
to Amman on September 27.[74] The report added that consideration was being given to the appointment of a high-level U.N. representative for diplomatic action that might be required in other capi-
tals in the Middle East area, to be stationed at the U.N. headquarters in New York.[75] The function of the Special Representative in
Jordan would be to follow any departures from the principles of
the resolution and to report to the Secretary-General, for further
action,[76] any findings of a serious nature that could be regarded as

indicating a threat to peace and security in the sense of Article 99, which the Secretary-General would then report to the U.N.[77]

However, the situation in Jordan, as in Lebanon, became stabilized and by November 2, 1958, the withdrawal of British troops was completed.[78]

Secretary-General Hammarskjöld gave the General Assembly his views on the Middle East precedents in a "summary study" (A/3943) of October 9, 1958, that he was later to invoke for the Congo operation. Using the U.N. interventions in Suez, Lebanon, and Jordan as guides, he considered the use of a U.N. police force in future circumstances.

In Suez, the setting up of a police force had been, in his view, appropriate because the force "could be interposed between regular, national military forces which were subject to a cease-fire agreed to by the opposing parties"; and it "functioned under a clear-cut mandate which has entirely detached it from involvement in any internal or local problems, and also has enabled it to maintain its neutrality in relation to international political issues."[79] Considering the Lebanon and Jordan actions, he argued against establishing a U.N. police force in similar situations, which on the basis of the Observer Group reports he described as "domestic conflict": "Neither in Lebanon nor in Jordan would it have been possible to interpose a United Nations force between conflicting parties. Nor would it have been possible in either of these situations to preserve a natural distinction between the presence and functions in various areas of any United Nations force and the presence and functions of government troops."[80]

It should be noted, as background for the legal problems of the Congo situation, that Hammarskjöld maintained this view in spite of the fact that the conflict in Lebanon threatened to assume international proportions. Another of his arguments against setting up a U.N. force in Lebanon was absence of enforcement measures in the U.S. proposal (S/4050, Rev. 1) of July 17, 1958, which would have permitted the force to develop military initiative. Hammarskjöld thought that in Jordan the government would have regarded the presence of a United Nations force as irreconcilable with its exercise of full sovereignty.[81]

After a comparison of situations appropriate and inappropriate

for the use of a U.N. police force, the summary study then set out
a list of basic principles applicable to future operations, the following of which were drawn from the experience of Lebanon and Jordan, as well as of Suez:

In situations where the force was established without enforcement measures envisaged under Chapter VII of the Charter, the
U.N. should not station its units on the territory of a state without
consent of the host government.[82] This meant that there must be
guarantees protecting the U.N. from unilateral actions by the host
government that might put the U.N. in a questionable position
"either administratively or in relation to contributing governments."[83] Thus there should be a status agreement with the host
government regarding the presence of the U.N. units. Such an
agreement had been made with the Egyptian Government, declaring that, when exercising its sovereign right with regard to the
presence of the Force, the government would be guided by good
faith in the interpretation of the purposes of the force. The U.N.
made a corresponding declaration that it would also be guided by
similar good faith in the interpretation of the purposes of the force.
An agreement had been signed with the Lebanese Government regarding the presence of UNOGIL in Lebanon, although it was
much less elaborate than that with the Egyptian Government because of the modest size of the operation. Among other rights, it
conferred on most of the U.N. personnel an immunity from being
tried by local courts—a rule that, according to the Secretary-General, was a necessary condition for any UNF operation.[84]

To ensure neutrality of the force, units from the permanent
members of the Security Council, and from any country having
special interest in the situation, should be excluded.[85]

Another vital principle ensured freedom of movement within
the area of the U.N. operation, including all such facilities for access and communications as would be necessary for successful completion of the task. These principles were retained in the case of
UNOGIL.[86] Directly relevant to the experience in Lebanon and
Jordan was the conclusion that the authority granted to the U.N.
group could not be exercised either in competition with or in cooperation with the host government on the basis of any joint operation. In Hammarskjöld's words: "a U.N. operation must be sep-

arate and distinct from activities by national authorities." This
was an especially important consideration where, as in Egypt, the
UNEF was a "police force"; otherwise, the U.N. would become a
party to internal conflicts, which was against the Charter.[87]

The mandate was a strict limitation on the powers of the Secretary-General, and the U.N. units were directly responsible to the
mandating body—i.e., the General Assembly or the Security Council—although the administrative responsibility rested with the person nominated by these bodies to carry out the operation. In Egypt
the General Assembly had appointed a Commander of the Force
responsible to the Assembly but under instructions from the Secretary-General as executive authority. In the case of UNOGIL, the
Security Council delegated the responsibility for setting up the
group to the Secretary-General, but the group was responsible for
the conduct of its business to the Security Council. A basically similar pattern was followed in Jordan.[88]

In each operation thus far, the U.N. had delegated authority in
terms that set limits to the Secretary-General's authority. Thus the
decision establishing the UNEF qualified the operation as "para-
military," but the absence of an explicit authorization to use offensive action and the legal basis on which the General Assembly
took its decision restricted the Secretary-General to equipping the
force for self-defense only.[89]

The terms of the mandate for establishing UNOGIL were strictly
defined in the resolution of June 11 (S/4023). The Security Council characterized the kind of operation that the Secretary-General
was authorized to organize by the very name—Observer Group—
given to the unit to be established. It excluded the creation of a
paramilitary force and imposed severe limitations on the arming of
the unit and its right of self-defense.[90]

The General Assembly decision on Jordan[91] was in such broad
terms as to permit organization of any kind of operation short of
that permitted only under the "enforcement measures" of Chapter
VII of the Charter. But, in this case of UNEF, a certain incom-
pleteness in the terminology of the decision was covered by the conclusions following from the legal basis on which the decision was
taken.[92]

Hammarskjöld's report then defined the conditions within which

U.N. units should operate. The matter of self-defense could be open, in his view, to a variety of interpretations. He thought, however, that

> A reasonable definition seems to have been established in the case of UNEF, where the rule is applied that men engaged in the operation may never take the initiative in the use of armed force, but are entitled to respond with force to an attack with arms, including attempts to use force to make them withdraw from positions which they occupy under orders from the Commander, acting under the authority of the Assembly and within the scope of its resolutions. The basic element involved is clearly the prohibition against any *initiative* in the use of armed force.[93]

Setting up an Advisory Committee under the chairmanship of the Secretary-General, he felt, was commendable as a precedent for the future but should not lead to division of responsibility or diminished effectiveness of the operation.[94] As to financing, he suggested that the costs should be allocated in accordance with the normal scale of contributions.[95]

The operations in the Middle East had turned out to be neat examples of when and how U.N. units might be used and, particularly, where the use of a U.N. police force was appropriate. That it was possible so to categorize the cases of Lebanon, Jordan, and Suez was due, we suggest, to the limited character of those operations.

However, it was already clear that limited operations could be of only limited effectiveness in preserving peace. In Lebanon, the deployment of an Observer Group precluded from military activity could not forestall the influx of U.S. troops at the invitation of the Lebanese Government. Permanent members of the Security Council may, if they choose to exercise their right of veto, enjoy an immunity in deploying their forces to support allied governments against insurgents. Nothing in any of the U.N.'s Middle East operations had shown that even a General Assembly proposal for the deployment of forces by its Uniting for Peace procedure could by itself deprive a determined permanent member of this privilege; for—as we saw—the cease-fire at Suez was brought about, not by interposition of the UNEF, but by a prior General Assembly resolution merely expressive of a united international disapproval that

France and Britain, with Israel, were unwilling to withstand. In the light of later Congo experience, we may of course speculate whether a persistent campaign in the Assembly might have brought it around to resolving that the United States be ordered to leave Lebanon—and the United Kingdom, Jordan—and that some kind of U.N. policing be used to ensure this; but internal change terminated both incidents before practice could test that hypothesis.

The Congo operation, in its later stages, enlisted the UNF on the side of the Central Government against a dissident movement in Orientale, and in Katanga the U.N. exerted pressure to bring Tshombe to meet with Adoula in December, 1961. But in Lebanon, and a fortiori in Jordan and Suez, no U.N. force was employed *within* any state to preserve *internal* order and peace. The Lebanon operation did, nevertheless, set the precedent of intrastate deployment of a "semimilitary" U.N. body, perhaps making easier the subsequent mission of the UNF in the Congo.

Most important of all, the Secretary-General by his summary study tried to bring continuity and direction for the future employment of military forces and observer corps by the U.N. out of the successive and disparate experiences of Suez and of Lebanon-Jordan. United Nations action in both cases had been made possible by his initiatives and preparatory actions, the resolutions of Council and Assembly chiefly giving direction (as subsequently in the early stages of the Congo operation) to instrumentalities that Hammarskjöld had contrived and set moving. A crucial step had been taken at Suez when the UNEF, despite Soviet and British demur, had been constituted without permanent-member participation and of course without the adoption of "enforcement" measures. If the U.N. could now use its "own" uniformed troops for achievement of the ends enjoined by the Charter, this was because the Secretary-Generalship had become a highly effective office, and because its incumbent had profoundly concerned himself with the U.N.'s use of force. The Congo operation was to produce a crisis for the Secretary-Generalship that may yet turn out to have undone much of Hammarskjöld's painful building-up of the office.

III

The First Phase of the Congo
Operation: Deployment

DURING 1960 and 1961, it became a commonplace in the editorial columns of the world's press that the U.N. was somehow "on trial" in the Congo. If it should fail there—so the U.N. was admonished—it would decline into fatuity as the League of Nations declined during the last few years before World War II.

The terms of this trial were somewhat hard upon the U.N., for the mutiny of Congolese security forces, Katanga's attempted secession, and, in general, the breakdown of effective control by the Central Government created a type of danger to international security with which the Organization was not formally equipped to deal. The notions of a "threat to the peace" under Chapter VII of the Charter, Article 39, and to "international peace and security" under Chapter XV, Article 99,[1] seem to presuppose that all of the world's populated territories are wholly, clearly, and definitely under the sovereign sway of one or another nation-state, and that it is only between those nation-states that there may occur such breaches of the peace as the U.N. may properly take cognizance of.

The President and the Prime Minister of the Republic of the Congo had, however, refused to regard their nation's crisis as in any way internal. Kasavubu and Lumumba, in their request for U.N. military assistance telegraphed to the Secretary-General on July 12, 1960, had accused the Belgians of preparing the secession of Katanga for colonialist purposes and had stated that "The essential purpose of the requested military aid is to protect the national territory of the Congo against the present external aggression which is a threat to international peace."[2]

The following day they telegraphed a clarification to the Secre-

23

tary-General which, had it been addressed to the Security Council, could have been interpreted as an invitation to that body to act under the rubric of Article 39:

> The purpose of the aid requested is not to restore the internal situation in Congo but rather to protect the national territory against act of aggression posed by Belgian metropolitan troops.
>
> The request for assistance relates only to a U.N. force consisting of military personnel of neutral countries and not of the U.S. as reported by certain radio stations.
>
> If the requested assistance is not received without delay the Republic of the Congo will be obliged to appeal to the Bandung Treaty Powers.
>
> The aid has been requested by the Republic of the Congo in the exercise of its sovereign rights and not in agreement with Belgium as reported.[3]

The representative of the U.S.S.R., Mr. Sobolev, in fact opened the proceedings of the Security Council's first session on the Congo issue (July 13–14, 1960) with the recommendation that the first telegram—with its reference to "external aggression" suggesting the pertinence of Article 39—be formally included as an agenda item. But after an explanation by the Secretary-General and something of a rebuke from Mr. Lodge of the United States, the Soviet representative stated that he would not press the proposal.[4]

If the first telegram had been made an agenda item, or if the Congolese complaint of Belgian aggression had been addressed to the Council, that body might at the outset have had to consider whether to determine that Belgium had committed an act of aggression. One or another of the Western powers could have been expected to veto a positive determination, since that would have been apt to lead on under Chapter VII to "enforcement measures" against Belgium—either sanctions under Article 41 or military measures under Article 42.[5] A negative determination or a Western veto, on the other hand, might have compelled the Security Council to refuse all assistance to the Republic of the Congo. Either course would have suited the U.S.S.R. Evidently, the Secretary-General sought, instead, to have the Council deliberate in the terms of Chapter XV, Article 99, which empowers the Secretary-General himself to bring to the attention of the Security Council "any matter which in his opinion may threaten the maintenance of international peace and security"—terms that are not apt to lead on immediately to "enforcement measures" under Chapter VII.

He had asked for an immediate meeting of the Security Council under Article 99,[6] and in his statement of July 13 to that meeting he suggested that the military assistance to be sent to the Congo was to hold the ring "during the period which may have to pass before, through the efforts of the Government and with the technical assistance of the United Nations, the national security forces [of the Central Government of the Congo] are able to fully meet their tasks." He further circumvented recourse to Articles 39, 41, or 42 by recommending that the Council "authorize the Secretary-General to take the necessary steps, in consultation with the Government of the Congo, to provide the Government with military assistance"[7] and by adding that, if U.N. forces were sent, the Belgian Government would see its way to the withdrawal of its own forces.

Hammarskjöld now characteristically offered the Security Council certain guidelines of his own making. The conduct of the U.N. forces, he said, should be based on the principles set out in his own report of October 9, 1958, to the General Assembly, based on conclusions drawn from previous experiences in the field. Acceptance of this summary study (A/3943) as a precedent should ensure that U.N. forces would not be authorized to take any action beyond self-defense and not become party to internal conflicts; and that the sources of the military assistance so provided would be African nations in the first place, the forces of permanent members of the Security Council being explicitly excluded.[8]

By this device, Hammarskjöld produced a remarkable innovation under a precedent. He enabled a United Nations force to be deployed within a member state and yet, in virtue of Chapter I, Article 2 (para. 7) of the Charter, precluded that force from intervening in the state's internal affairs.[9] Article 2 (para. 7) provides that

Nothing contained in the present Charter shall authorize the United Nations to intervene in matters which are essentially within the domestic jurisdiction of any state or shall require the Members to submit such matters to settlement under the present Charter; *but this principle shall not prejudice the application of enforcement measures under Chapter VII* (italics added).

Such enforcement measures could, nevertheless, have been set in train if the representative of the U.S.S.R. had managed to have the Security Council adopt—of his proposed amendments to the eventually accepted Tunisian resolution—at least the operative paragraph that would have condemned "the armed aggression by Belgium against the Republic of the Congo."[10]

Neither then nor afterwards did any U.N. body affirm that there had been armed aggression by Belgium or any other power against the Republic of the Congo; nor did the Council ever declare that U.N. action in the Congo had been taken under other provisions of Article 39, or a fortiori under Article 41 or 42. (Article 49 of Chapter VII, later invoked in a General Assembly resolution,[11] does not of itself imply "enforcement measures." Article 40, which in later Security Council and General Assembly debates the Secretary-General and others were sometimes to suggest to have been implicitly invoked by the various resolutions in the Congo, was never specifically invoked in any resolution or any communication of the Secretary-General.[12] In any case, the "provisional measures" set forth in Article 40 appear to be *alternatives* either to a determination of aggression, or the like, under Article 39, or to consequent "enforcement measures" under Articles 41 and 42.) Instead, the Congo issue was simply brought "to the attention of the Security Council" by the Secretary-General under Article 99.

In his "Summary study of the experience derived from the establishment and operation of the Force" (A/3943, October 9, 1958)[13] the Secretary-General had ready to hand an instrument for the interpreting of mandates for any *non*-enforcing military task laid upon him by the Organization, and from the start he cited it in Security Council meetings, in his own reports, and in instructions to his assistants and memoranda to the Central and other governments of the Congo. The summary study was not formally adopted, as such, by the Security Council;[14] but in the Council's resolution of July 22, 1960,[15] the Secretary-General's "first report" of July 18 was declared to have been "considered" by the Council; and that report explicitly set out for the Council's consideration and approval those principles—most of them derived and many of them directly cited from the summary study—by which the Secretary-General proposed to be guided in the operation, insofar as the Security Council resolution was not detailed or explicit.

The character of the principles of the summary study, as the Secretary-General applied them to the Congo operation, was epitomized in a sentence of his "first report":

> The authority granted to the United Nations Force cannot be exercised within the Congo either in competition with representatives of the host Government or in co-operation with them in any joint operation. This naturally applies *a fortiori* to representatives and military units of other Governments than the host Government. Thus the United Nations operation must be separate and distinct from activities by other national authorities.[16]

This was to prove a serious restriction upon a U.N. *military* force employed to restore order *within* the Congo state. The summary study drew principally upon the experience of the UNEF in Egypt, where restoration of internal order was not in question; but it also referred extensively to the Jordan operation, and—more pertinently for the Congo action—to the U.N. operation in the Lebanon, UNOGIL, where the Observer Group of 500 officers had been described explicitly as *not* "paramilitary" (which UNEF had been) and where "internal conflicts" were causing the trouble. The summary study stated: "In Lebanon, it is unlikely that a United Nations force could have operated without soon becoming a party to the internal conflicts among nationals of the country."[17] But the Secretary-General was proposing to base his interpretation of operations in the Congo upon principles derived from UNEF. This should have presupposed that internal conflicts would not be significant in the Congo—and, indeed, at the outset in July, 1960, they were much less serious than they afterwards became. Yet many of the subsequent dilemmas had their seeds in Hammarskjöld's first bold application of UNEF experience to a situation that took its departure from the mutinies of the Congolese Force Publique, and in which, therefore, ill-controlled and inexperienced national forces and provincial gendarmerie were to confront a mixed international military force rigorously prohibited from "any *initiative in the use of armed force*" (the emphasis is Hammarskjöld's).[18] This prohibition of military initiative by the U.N. was essential to what we shall call Hammarskjöld's "noninterventional" policy. The reader will understand that "nonintervention," in this particular context, refers to the Organization's not intervening in the domestic and internal political concerns of its members, except when "enforcement measures" have been invoked—i.e., a restriction that Article 2 (para. 7) of the Charter imposed and that the Secretary-General endeavored to comply with in spirit as well as in letter. "Nonintervening" does not here relate in any way to the well-known controversies about *national* policies of nonintervention or intervention that bedeviled the participants in the Spanish Civil War. We emphasize this distinction because we shall sometimes have to refer in the same paragraph both to Hammarskjöld's "noninterventional" policy under Article 2 (para. 7) and to issues of open or tacit intervention in the Congo by nations and by other interested parties.

With the advantages of hindsight, we might judge that the UNF's position in the Congo was almost bound to be untenable. The Secretary-General indeed must have realized, in the light of his own contrast in the summary study of the Suez with the Lebanese and Jordanian experiences, that his creative extension of UNEF precedents placed UNOC and the U.N. as a whole at some hazard. Success alone would vindicate so bold a throw; but before success came, another Secretary-General had to permit the UNF a military initiative, allowing it to seek victory over the Katanga forces in December, 1961.

The legal basis for deployment of a UNF, thus restricted, within a sovereign state was to be an agreement or bilateral declaration modeled on the one that the U.N. had made with the government of Egypt with respect to UNEF. Hammarskjöld judged it unlikely that any government in the future would be willing to go beyond such terms. In his words:

> when exercising its sovereign right with regard to the presence of the Force, it would be guarded by good faith in the interpretation of the purposes of the Force. This declaration was balanced by a declaration by the United Nations to the effect that the mainte-

nance of the Force by the United Nations would be determined by similar good faith in the interpretation of the purposes.[19]

The Congolese Government did initial such a basic agreement in late July and thereby also agreed "that it will ensure the freedom of movement of the Force in the interior of the country and will accord the requisite privileges and immunities to all personnel associated with the activities of the Force."[20] "Freedom of movement" was to prove a contentious and politically significant right of the UNF; but at least this clause of the agreement was clear and unambiguous. Otherwise, the significance of "good faith" and of the distinction between the U.N.'s being obliged by the Security Council's resolution of July 14 to "consult with" and "assist" the Congolese government and its being, nevertheless, forbidden to co-operate with the representatives of that government "in any joint operation,"[21] though unmistakable guides to experienced statesmen and international functionaries, might well seem confusing entanglements to an inspired national revolutionist such as Lumumba.

So, whereas the purposes of the UNEF operation in Egypt had always been discernible, it was not easy to say at any stage exactly why the UNF was in the Congo.

In July and August of 1960, however, part of the answer clearly was: to create conditions that would facilitate the withdrawal of the troops of the government of Belgium. (The Belgian Government formally supported the Secretary-General's proposal for U.N. intervention and declared its wish to be rid of the responsibility for intervention.[22]) By adopting the above-mentioned Tunisian resolution, the Security Council (1) called upon the government of Belgium so to withdraw its troops and (2) gave the Secretary-General, almost in his own words, the authorization he had asked for:

> to take the necessary steps, in consultation with the Government of the Republic of the Congo, to provide the Government with such military assistance as may be necessary, until, through the efforts of the Congolese Government with the technical assistance of the United Nations, the national security forces may be able, in the opinion of the Government, to meet fully their tasks.[23]

The kind of assistance envisaged resembles in part that "action in support of the civil power" that national forces have on occasions afforded their own civil authorities when the threat was riot or anarchy rather than civil war. Hammarskjöld's innovation was to put the U.N. into that line of business, with the immediate purpose of forestalling an interventionary war that might have ranged Belgium and other colonial powers against some of the new African states and behind them, perhaps, the U.S.S.R. And we may read back into the situation of July, 1960, his long-term ambitions for the U.N. as he expressed them a year later—that, as a "dynamic instrument of government," it should be ever ready to ensure that "the liquidation of the colonial system" and the ex-colonial nations' "development toward full self-government and independence" should in general proceed peacefully and without involvement in the conflict between the great power blocs.[24]

The exercise of that function requires the removal of anomalies such as disagreement between *de jure* and *de facto* authority. In mid-July, 1960, the Central Government had *de jure* authority but not, in all parts of the Congo, *de facto* authority. From mid-September of that year, when the Belgian Government had withdrawn all but a handful of the forces that it had officially deployed in the Congo, until the formation of the Adoula Government in August of the following year, the "Central Government of the Republic of the Congo *de jure*" could not be located or discerned beyond doubt. And even the Adoula Government did not at once exercise authority over the whole of the Congo *de facto*.

Katanga, the most effective challenger of the *de facto* authority of Léopoldville, had also been its earliest challenger *de jure*. Moise Tshombe, the Provincial President, had announced Katanga's secession from the Republic of the Congo on July 11, 1960. Katanga never acquired the marks of sovereignty; e.g., no other state ever entered into treaty with it as a sovereign power. The United Kingdom, refusing it military assistance, referred to it as "an authority other than the lawfully constituted Central Government."[25] Even the Belgian representative referred to Tshombe simply as "the head of the provincial government" and implicitly acknowledged Lumumba's authority either to object to or to countersign requests for military assistance from any provincial government, whether at Elisabethville or in Kasai.[26]

But Belgian commercial interests, especially the Union Minière du Haut Katanga, which continued to provide the staple of Katanga's finances, were of course rejoiced at the news of secession. Katanga shares at once rose sharply on the Brussels Bourse. But there seems to be no evidence that the Belgian Government at any stage tried to re-extend its sovereignty over any part of the Congo, though it was certainly willing to aid Katanga in some of its pretensions to independence from the Congo Central Government. Belgium seems to have hoped to retain the economic benefit of its former position by demonstrating that Belgian administrators, technicians, and other experts were indispensable throughout the new state; while later, as a second best, the hope was to build up a solid and friendly government in Elisabethville as a counterweight to Lumumbist forces, which the Belgians knew to be "unitarian" and believed to be pro-Soviet. Belgian troops were reinforced in Katanga, as well as elsewhere in the Congo, ostensibly for the protection of Belgian nationals—a course of action that, at least until the signing of the United Nations Charter and probably thereafter, has been the legal right of any nation to take.

On July 18, the Secretary-General reported to the Security Council on his implementation of its resolution of July 14 sending U.N. forces to the Congo. He said that the only "sound and lasting solution" was to re-establish the instruments of the Congolese Government for the maintenance of order. It was the breakdown of these instruments that had created a situation with threat to peace and security justifying U.N. action under the Charter. In his view the question whether or not the U.N. also faced a conflict between two parties—the Belgians and the Congolese—was not legally essential for the justification of the action; but the Belgians, in accordance with the Security Council resolution, must withdraw their troops.[27]

This "first report" by the Secretary-General enshrined, in his considered opinion of a year later, "the basic rules which guide the United Nations activities in such situations."[28] Being unanimously commended in the Security Council resolution of July 22,[29] its rules and their originals in the Secretary-General's summary study of October, 1958, are worth recording:

Though "serving as an arm of the Government for the maintenance of order and protection of life . . . the Force is necessarily under the exclusive command of the United Nations, vested in the Secretary-General under the control of the Security Council."[30]

The report provided for a "good faith" agreement with the host government, which in turn ensured the UNF's freedom of movement (as mentioned above, p. 29).

The U.N. alone was to decide on the national composition of the military elements in UNF but with full consideration of the host's view—any resulting conflict to be resolved "on a political rather than a legal basis." The contingents were to be obtained "in the first place" from African nations, but from others also for the sake of "universality."[31]

The UNF's authority was to be exercised neither in competition nor in cooperation with Congolese Government representatives, and could not be used to enforce political solutions or influence the internal political balance (see above, p. 27).[32] The UNF could act only in self-defense and must never take the military initiative (see above, p. 28).[33]

Until the Security Council's use-of-force resolution of February 20–21, 1961, nothing was enacted either by the Council or by the General Assembly that might have been considered even prima facie a breach of any of these principles. The Secretary-General deemed himself fully warranted in having them govern his implementation of the Security Council's mandate; and indeed, considering the generality and vagueness of that mandate despite his renewed plea to have it made more specific, it was as well that he had the guidance—largely negative though it was—of his own principles and interpretations.

As such, the operations of the UNF from mid-July, 1960, to mid-February, 1961, may be considered as a fair trial of the hypothesis that a "nonintervening" UNF can maintain sufficient intrastate order to make the host state viable and to deter international intervention in its conflicts. Our estimates of the results of that trial will be set out below.

United Nations forces were moved into the Congo with a speed that owed something to the Secretary-General's prior contacts with nine African delegations whom he had convened for briefing about the Congo's need of U.N. assistance (a telegram to him from the

Congolese Government requesting technical assistance with special regards to needs of security administration had preceded those requesting military action).³⁴ By July 17, troops from Ethiopia (460), Ghana (770), Morocco (1,250), and Tunisia (1,020) had arrived in Léopoldville.³⁵ Other offers had been accepted from Guinea, Mali, and the Swedish battalion of UNEF.³⁶

Major-General Carl von Horn of Sweden had been appointed Supreme Commander of UNF.³⁷ Airlift had been provided by the United States and the United Kingdom. From July 15, Ralph J. Bunche, the Secretary-General's Special Representative in the Congo, had been appointed Commander of the Force ad interim and had begun to deploy UNF units to such points as the radio station of Léopoldville.³⁸ General von Horn, the Supreme Commander-elect, continued deployment from July 18.³⁹ By July 26, UNF strength in the Congo was more than 8,000, deployed in all provinces but Katanga. By the end of the month, the strength was greater than 11,000, and included Ghanaians, Irish, and Liberians.⁴⁰ Belgian troops had begun to evacuate Léopoldville before July 20.⁴¹

On July 17, the President and the Prime Minister of the Republic of the Congo dispatched to the Secretary-General's Special Representative a letter concluding with the "ultimatum" that unless the U.N. should seem to be able to effect the evacuation of Belgian troops by July 20 they would regretfully be compelled to request the Soviet Union to intervene.⁴² On July 19, the representative of the U.S.S.R. demanded circulation as a Security Council document of a letter to the Secretary-General complaining of the arrival at Léopoldville on July 17 of a detachment of U.S. Army communications troops that were supposed to be cooperating in the evacuation of refugees. Replying during the Security Council meetings of July 20–21, the U.S. representative derided this charge and at the same time indicated that his government had had a request in the first week of the U.N. operation for U.S. military aid from the government of the Congo. He resolved to help prevent "the intrusion of any military forces not requested by the United Nations."⁴³ In an indignant reply, the Soviet delegate divulged that Lumumba as Congolese Prime Minister had written to the chairman of the Council of Ministers of the U.S.S.R. on July 14, saying it was possible that his government might be forced to request the intervention of the Soviet Union, and that the chairman had replied sympathetically.[44]

These letters from the Congolese Government, together with the U.S.S.R.'s replies, comments, and *tu quoque* accusations against the United States, undoubtedly aroused suspicions about Lumumba and his entourage among the Western powers, and especially so in the United States. Soviet representatives continued to stand upon their nation's right to assist the Congo, as one sovereign state to another, and at the same time to support the policies of those African states—in particular, Mali, Guinea and, with many reservations, Ghana and the United Arab Republic—that were most insistent upon an all-African UNF in the Congo. Cold war was already beginning to obtrude itself. Tunisia through its representative, Mongi Slim, continued to work for a policy that all members of the Security Council might accept, and together with Ceylon proposed the resolution eventually adopted by the Security Council on July 22. Significant provisions as yet unmentioned were the authorizing of the Secretary-General to take steps for the withdrawal of Belgian troops,[45] and requests to all states to refrain from impeding the restoration of law and order in the Congo and from undermining its territorial integrity and political independence.[46]

The Soviet bloc had opposed utterly and consistently Hammarskjöld's apparent intention to foster through the setting of precedents a growth in the authority and power of United Nations forces to preserve external peace and internal law and order. Mr. Kuznetsov, the delegate of the U.S.S.R., explaining his affirmative vote on the resolution of July 22, took care to add:

> The resolution of 14 July and that adopted today should not . . . be considered as a precedent for the future.
> We feel unable to subscribe to certain aspects of the interpretation given by the Secretary-General to the Security Council resolution of 14 July. We cannot regard that resolution, and the ensuing action for its implementation, as endowing the United Nations with the right to interfere in the domestic affairs of a State and to assume responsibility for a country's domestic laws and regulations. . . . The fundamental purpose of the resolution is to be found in its demand for the withdrawal of the Belgian forces. . . .

The United Nations Force must also be entrusted with the task of safeguarding the territorial integrity of the Republic of the Congo.[47]

The last clause was to become the accepted Soviet euphemism for "The UNF must subdue secessionist movements at the behest of the Central government." (Later, Afro-Asian powers used it to refer to dissuading as well as to subduing of secessionists.) The earlier paragraphs mean that the Soviet bloc will always oppose the U.N.'s reorganizing or disarming a state's military forces or attempting to preserve law and order within it by the mere presence of a UNF, or helping the state to consolidate effective sovereignty and control by lending it trained administrators along with technical and other civilian help. Further, they propose to stop any long-run movements for developing a supposedly impartial policing agency under U.N. aegis. Mr. Kuznetsov thus announced intentions of a piece with Mr. Khrushchev's later Troika proposals and readily understandable from the Soviet viewpoint—that of a power which by the practice of political warfare and encouragement to nationalist revolt is revolutionary in effect, but which also conservatively insists upon the maintenance of sovereign prerogatives, and fears the rise of supranational institutions. This, indeed, has been the one possible outcome of the Congo affair that the Soviet bloc might consider something of a defeat. Otherwise, they could not lose: Either they would put a new and radical nationalist government—with prospects of great mineral wealth—under obligation to them, or they could be sure that disorders would ensue most discreditable to Belgium and the other colonial powers.

IV

The Second Phase: Katangese Resistance
and Lumumba's Dissatisfactions

From July 24 through July 26, 1960, Prime Minister Lumumba, accompanied by other Congolese ministers, conferred in New York with the Secretary-General and U.N. officials. A communiqué reported satisfactory discussions about immediate technical assistance in the Congo in fields including administration and security, as well as Lumumba's insistence that Belgian troops withdraw at once.[1] But events were to show that the meeting failed to establish mutual trust between Lumumba and Hammarskjöld.

In the storm center of Luluabourg, 3,000 of the Force Publique laid down their arms as Tunisian troops of the UNF moved in.[2] Though that may seem to have been compliance with the mandate to restore law and order, the representative of the U.S.S.R. complained on August 8 that the U.N. troops had been disarming Congolese forces.[3] In fact, the Central Government was at this stage supporting the disarmament of the Force Publique where U.N. troops were present.[4] Only a thorough and rapid reorganization of Congolese forces could have met the requirements of the Security Council mandate and allowed a withdrawal of the UNF early in 1961; but, equally with the Katangese defection, their continued indiscipline prolonged a crisis that was to overtax the international credit of the organization.

Ending Katanga's secession became the first concern of the Central Government, while the government of Belgium, by concentrating 1,700 Belgian troops in Elisabethville and by frequent references in the U.N. to the 20,000 Belgian civilians in the province,[5] revealed its determination to preserve intact the great Belgian-Katangese economic complex exploiting the area's mineral

wealth. The crux of the matter was and remains a dispute over
who should have the power to collect taxes and, if need be, dispose
of property rights in Katanga's vast sources of wealth.

Tshombe and his supporters continued to speak of Katanga's
"sovereignty" and supported a "confederal" constitution for the
Congo as a whole. Lumumba, who before independence had opposed against any confederal solution a "federal" one, now had
attributed to him a "unitarian" intention. Anglo-Saxon concepts
of unitary, federal, and confederal constitutions have no very en-
lightening application in the Congo case.

Exacerbating the dispute between Lumumba and Tshombe were
conflicts of international allegiance: Lumumba, by his association
with Nkrumah, was identified with that faction of African states
that later came to be known as the "Casablanca" group, in opposition to the Brazzaville (later, "Monrovia") faction; and Tshombe
enjoyed the partisan sympathy of English Tories, Belgians, and
Northern Rhodesians who hoped for Katangese solidarity with
their "multiracial" and "anti-Communist" grouping. Even more
embittering to Congolese party conflict were the ancient traditions
of tribal authority and fierce independence, themselves compli-
cated during the colonial era by Belgian importations of the competent Baluba into Katanga from Kasai.

Two criticisms of the UNOC disposition toward Katanga are
advanced that we are not yet in a position to adjudicate. One is
that Belgian intervention alone generated the separatist sentiments
of the southern Katangese. The other is that if UNOC had allowed Lumumba a "free hand" before the end of July, 1960, he
would have succeeded, with Central Government troops alone, in
subjugating Katanga.

However that may be, Lumumba was by the end of July concerned rather to urge UNF entry into Katanga, claiming that "The
Belgian Government would surely have demonstrated a modicum
of good will in the execution of the United Nations resolutions if
it had proceeded to evacuate Katanga before all other areas."[6] The
Secretary-General had already determined on UNF entry. On
August 2, he told the Congolese Cabinet Committee for Cooperation with the U.N. that his Special Representative, Dr. Bunche,
was to be sent to Elisabethville on August 8 to initiate negotiations

for the withdrawal of Belgian troops (Bunche was in fact able to go on August 4), to be followed the next day by UNF units, and that the Belgian Government in no way opposed execution of the Security Council resolutions.[7] When on August 3 Tshombe had registered a "determination to resist by every means the Lumumba Government," the Secretary-General warned him of the application of Articles 25 and 49 of the Charter and of his own intention to request the convocation of the Security Council should Tshombe maintain his refusal to accept its decisions—specifically, those affirming the principles of UNF autonomy, of noninvolvement in the balance of political forces, and of limitation to self-defense.[8]

On similar grounds Hammarskjöld refused to allow three Central Government representatives, supported by twenty Ghanaian soldiers, to accompany Dr. Bunche,[9] whom he briefed carefully on August 4: Bunche might contact Tshombe and the Belgians in order to secure the withdrawal of Belgian troops. If he considered that Katangese resistance would be a serious risk and should therefore advise against UNF entry, the Secretary-General would immediately seek convention of the Security Council.[10]

Dr. Bunche, returning to Léopoldville, reported on August 5 that such a risk was very serious, and the Secretary-General therefore countermanded UNF entry into Katanga. The Security Council met on August 8 to receive the Secretary-General's "second report," which asked for clarification of the Council's views. It read in part:

> If the Council . . . wishes to maintain its objectives [*inter alia*, Belgian withdrawal and therefore UNF entry into Katanga], it must . . . either change the character of the Force, which appears to me to be impossible, both for constitutional reasons and in view of the commitments to the contributing governments, or otherwise resort to other methods which would enable me to carry through the implementation of its resolution without going beyond my instructions as regards the Force.[11]

Speaking to his report, Hammarskjöld referred to Articles 40 and 41 of the Charter, which license Security Council measures "not involving the use of armed force," but the Council did not in the event take action under these articles. He referred to the "submission" of the Belgian Government concerning withdrawal from Katanga, though reading that to mean only "absence of active resistance"; and he referred to the "great impatience" of the Central Government and to "support from other quarters outside the Congo" for the generating of that "distrust."[12]

The representative of the U.S.S.R. during the debate significantly reconstrued Paragraph 15 of the Secretary-General's first report (S/4389), which had allowed the soldiers of the UNF to resist forcible attempts to make them withdraw from occupied positions: "if in the course of their operation for entering the province of Katanga the United Nations troops should meet with armed resistance, then, in accordance with the Security Council's decision . . . they are entitled to eliminate such resistance by any means available to them." The Soviet representative further argued that if national contingents currently deployed by the U.N. were unwilling so to act, "troops of countries which are ready to participate" must be sent to the Congo.[13] The latter Soviet suggestion was in line with a policy already proposed by the representative of Ghana.

On August 9, the Security Council adopted a draft resolution of Ceylon and Tunisia. While invoking Articles 25 and 49 to secure Belgian withdrawal from Katanga, and endorsing UNF entry there, the resolution reaffirmed that "the United Nations Force in the Congo will not be a party to or in any way intervene in or be used to influence the outcome of any internal conflict, constitutional or otherwise."[14] This paragraph, though formally in complete accord with the Charter and with the Secretary-General's doctrine for a UNF, intensified a substantive discord with those paragraphs of the resolution of July 14 that enjoined on the U.N. a consultative relationship to the *government* of the Republic of the Congo. Undoubtedly the Secretary-General and other UNOC authorities could in their administrative practice incline a little either to the "noninterventionist" aspects of the mandate or to that enjoining consultation with and assistance to the government. In August and September of 1960, they inclined to the former. A year later, some of them, if not the Secretary-General himself, took action in Katanga that in effect supported the then Central Government against Tshombe. But in 1960 the balance of Congolese military power made it likely that strict nonintervention by the U.N. would tend inadvertently to assist Tshombe, by giving him time to build up *de facto* authority and power within Katanga.

Clashes of personality much affected matters. Hammarskjöld, supported by the resolution of August 9, expounded it to Lumumba and Tshombe in correct but somewhat schoolmasterish terms. Lumumba, an activist in a hurry, already revealed his Jacobin impatience with opposition, "legitimate" as well as secessionist. In a statement to the press on August 10, he warned that

> we have been quite tolerant; we have allowed certain persons deliberately and without justification to attack the authorities, the national institutions, and the nation as a whole. . . . freedom[s] of opinion, expression and action . . . however, have certain limits. . . . Today . . . these limits are being grossly exceeded and we are discovering that more and more intrigues are being hatched behind the scenes. The legal Government . . . can no longer tolerate such a state of affairs.[15]

In mid-August, he came into direct conflict with the Secretary-General and his representatives over the U.N.'s entry into Katanga.

Having exchanged cables with Tshombe on August 10 concerning his forthcoming entry into Elisabethville, and having conferred with the Central Government's delegation in New York, Hammarskjöld flew to Léopoldville on August 11, and thence immediately on the twelfth to Elisabethville with Afro-Asian commanders of the UNF, civilian U.N. advisers, and two companies of the Swedish battalion from the UNEF. It was at this date that he sent to Lumumba and Tshombe his memorandum interpreting Paragraph 4 of the resolution of August 9.[16] That closely argued document cited precedents from the Lebanese and Hungarian cases. Paragraph 8 declared in detail that the UNF could in no way be used either to help or to hinder the Central Government in attempts against the Katanga provincial government. Paragraph 9 stated that this interpretation was unilateral and non-negotiable, but could be contested before the Security Council. Paragraphs 10 and 11 spelled out the objective consequences if either the Central or provincial governments were to challenge the interpretation.[17] There followed on August 14 and 15 a remarkable exchange of six indignant letters between the Secretary-General and the Prime Minister. Lumumba challenged the Secretary-General's interpretation, his failure to consult with him in Léopoldville, his talks with

Tshombe and subsequent press release, and his use of Swedish and Irish troops to enter Katanga. He demanded that only African UNF troops be used in Katanga, that all airfields in the Republic be guarded by the Armée Nationale Congolaise (ANC) and Congolese troops, and that arms distributed by the Belgians in Katanga be seized and handed over to the Central Government. Later in the correspondence he declared that "the Government and people of the Congo" had lost their confidence in the Secretary-General and that a group of Afro-Asian observers should be sent to the Congo. The Secretary-General refused to take a Congolese delegation in his aircraft to New York, though giving assurance that the Council would not meet to discuss the Secretary-General's memorandum and the correspondence before the delegation had arrived.[18]

No UNF operation—however hedged about by agreements with the host government and however empowered, short of the provisions of Articles 39 to 42—can be guaranteed against this kind of incident. One is at a loss to think what Hammarskjöld did that he should not have done, or left undone that he should. Evidently, it was the correctness and impartiality that Lumumba objected to.

Two further incidents brought to light on the other hand, the existence of a serious and perhaps avoidable difficulty within UNOC itself—a civilian-military misunderstanding revealed through anti-UNOC incidents. On August 17, two U.N. officials were arrested, robbed, threatened, and detained by gendarmes of the Central Government, despite allegedly tardy intervention by Ghanaian UNF troops. On the following day, Congolese soldiers arrested and disarmed fourteen Canadians of the UNF at Ndjili airport. Commanding officers of the UNF threatened to withdraw it from the airport if such activities continued. On the nineteenth, Lumumba at a press conference accused Hammarskjöld and his representative of "deliberately magnifying" the Ndjili incident to further their interests before the Security Council meeting. At the same time Mobutu, then Chief of Staff of the Congolese Army, apologized for the incident to the Secretary-General's Special Representative.[19] The Secretary-General meanwhile raised with the representative of Ghana at U.N. headquarters questions about the conduct of Ghanaian troops in both incidents and asked for assurances of President Nkrumah's "unreserved support" under Article 49. The reply elicited from Nkrumah contained a report from his Chief of Defense Staff, Major-General H. T. Alexander. This report, repudiating the charges against Ghanaian troops, advanced criticisms of the orders given (or lack of them) by some senior officers of UNF—"nor did they give U.N. troops any liberty of action even for the use of minimum force." Under the restriction of noninterference, the General complained, U.N. personnel could not be effectively protected. He had urged the firm handling and disarmament of the Force Publique and was sure such a policy could be made effective.[20]

Dr. Bunche, the Secretary-General's Special Representative and —as he said—"the responsible United Nations official for interpreting to the Command of the Force the resolutions of the Security Council and the directives of the Secretary General," replied that, though "a reorganized and disciplined Congolese National Army is a most, perhaps the most, vital problem," yet the UNF could not use force to disarm it. He cited the operations directive issued to the UNF to the effect that

> On no account are weapons to be used unless in cases of great and sudden emergency and for the purpose of self-defense. . . . The principal purpose of the United Nations Force in the Congo . . . is to assist the Government in maintaining law and order. . . . [It] should exhaust all peaceful means of keeping order before any resort to force. Every effort should be exerted to avoid harm to anyone, since public reaction to the employment of force by United Nations personnel might well prove disastrous to the success of the entire United Nations operation. . . . Any effort to disarm members of the United Nations Force is to be regarded as a legitimate cause for self-defense.

He referred to the Tunisian contingent in Kasai, which was involved in "severe intertribal conflict and has had to resort to rifle-fire in self-defense when it has come under attack while escorting unarmed refugees." To his military colleagues, he had always described the UNF as a "peace force, not a fighting force."[21]

Though—it must be confessed—a most natural one, so marked a discrepancy of views about restrictions upon the UNF's powers and functions should not have been allowed to develop between the chief civilian and a leading military officer. Dr. Bunche's insistence upon the restriction to self-defense was a correct and proper translation of the Security Council's resolutions and of the Secretary-General's interpretation of them. But that type of negative injunction would be strange enough in soldiers' ears—even for those trained in antiriot action—to warrant also spelling it out in specific positive orders and, more importantly still, in a specific, though peaceable, plan of campaign. As General Alexander had objected, "No soldier can carry out orders if they are not given."

Yet what is the plan of campaign appropriate to such a mandate and such operations directives? The grand object was not a particular one, such as victory over definite hostile forces, nor could it be achieved simply by the routine patrol duty of an ordinary police squad. The UNF had to restore and not merely maintain law and order, and to do so with recourse to less violence than is employed by many a police force in the civilized world. Further, the idea of "law and order" itself bears connotations that vary from society to society. For General Alexander it meant, among other things, the disarming of mutinous soldiery. For most of the U.N. civilian officers and agencies, it rather involved persuading them to return to discipline or—if the Central government ordered them to disarm—providing a "presence" that might awe them into doing so.

For the representatives of Soviet-bloc countries, understandably, "law and order" means just "enforcement of the decisions of a central government"; and apparently Lumumba and his followers had come to understand it in somewhat the same sense—a source of much later misunderstanding between him and UNOC. The notion of an impersonal orderliness involving an impersonal law is not found everywhere: Dr. Bunche and General Alexander, who shared it, nevertheless differed about its practical application.

The presence of Belgian military personnel in the Congo was, by the end of August, causing two quite distinct problems. One was the delay in departure of various bodies of *national troops of the Belgian Government*. The latter had confirmed its representatives' assurances that all its troops would be out of the Congo by August 30. In fact, because of difficulties with transport and misunderstandings—of which some sound rather willful—the Secretary-General had to complain on September 4 and 5 that some Belgian troops were still at Kamina and Elisabethville. In themselves these delays, apart from the publicity given them, were of little impor-

tance and were in fact overcome in the second week of September—
no more than two months after the beginning of the U.N. operation and so, compared with similar evacuations in the past, with
passable punctuality. Incidentally, however, the delaying of the
national troops' departure from Elisabethville contributed to the
second of the problems that might have been avoided.[22]

This was the use made by the Katangese provincial government
of Belgian "advisers" and "technical assistants" not officially seconded by the Belgian Government or, if so, seconded for other purposes. Formally considered, the provincial gendarmerie in which
Belgian officers were enlisted was not usable against troops of the
Central Government but was a "technical" body for preserving
order. In practice, it later provided the core of Tshombe's aggressive forces. Most of the enlistees had been officering the Force Publique, under the Belgian-Congolese General Treaty, and they
moved into the gendarmerie on their own initiative without official
Belgian secondment. They were not entitled to automatic reinstate-
ment in the Belgian Army but seemed likely enough to get it. The
Belgian Government's communications on the matter were quite
disingenuous.[23] It had also admitted to the importing of one load
of Belgian arms into Katanga, contending that this had been arranged under the previous dispensation and that through the error
of an ill-informed official the delivery had not been canceled.[24]

If the present study refers less frequently to the Belgian than to
other forms of intervention or other sources of disorder in the
Congo, it is not because we think it to have been less damaging
than they, but rather because after September, 1960, it was difficult
to lay much at the *official* Belgian door, and as easy to see the hands
of other Belgian and other European groups—and even perhaps of
some other "Western" governments—at work in Katanga.

Kasai, another would-be breakaway province, was meanwhile the
scene of further discord, originating in tribal conflict but almost at
once involving ANC troops and probably implicating, with calam-
itous results, the Prime Minister of the Republic of the Congo.

By August 20, as we have seen, an ANC contingent sent by the
Central Government to build up forces for operations against Katanga[25] and probably out of its Command's control, had opened fire
on unarmed civilians being escorted by a U.N. contingent. An old

quarrel between the Lulua and the Baluba tribes revived, and disorganized ANC units joined in against the Baluba.[26] That this intervention was ordered or permitted by the Prime Minister is not at all clear, but Baluba tribesmen evidently held him responsible for it.[27] Hundreds of Baluba were reported killed on August 29 and 30, as the Secretary-General later informed the Security Council. He also reported "The massacre on August 31, 1960, by troops from the ANC, using machetes, of 70 Balubas including women and children. . . . United Nations officials were informed that unarmed persons were deliberately killed simply on the ground that they were Balubas."[28] Meanwhile, he had protested to the delegation of the U.S.S.R. in a *note verbale* of September 5 concerning, *inter alia*, a report from Luluabourg of the same day that ten Ilyushin-14 aircraft, "coming from Stanleyville, arrived at Luluabourg carrying Congolese troops to reinforce the Congolese force, in the Bakwanga area. According to the report, the troops carried amounted to 200, the planes returning to Stanleyville supposedly in order to transport further reinforcements." In its reply of September 10, the Soviet delegation denied that any Security Council enactment forbade the rendering of such assistance, independent of UNOC, to the Congolese Government by any other sovereign power.[29]

Lumumba thus appeared to the UNOC officials as bent upon unification of the Congo—and, especially, the reintegration of Katanga—by force and, if necessary, with the assistance of other powers independently of the U.N. His government also had an unresolved dispute with UNOC over control of airports, Lumumba wanting them under the ANC, and the U.N. insisting on its own control in order to ensure freedom of movement for the UNF.[30] The Prime Minister must also have seemed less concerned about massacre in such places as Bakwanga than about Katanga's secession. At the same time, Hammarskjöld was evidently disturbed at the prospect of a Soviet intervention against which he could find no absolutely unequivocal or insuperable objections of principle and law; for while Lumumba was prime minister, his government could not be expected to complain of Russian, as they had of Belgian, intervention. Was Hammarskjöld's judgment sound when he saw in this constellation of national interests the makings of an interventionary war on the Korean or the Spanish model? If such an *international* war did not appear possible, UNOC—so a case could be made—should perhaps have become simply a technical assistance operation, the UNF withdrawing since officially the Belgians were all but withdrawn. The mandate could be interpreted as making, of both the restoration of order and the U.N's enabling the government's security forces to meet their tasks, merely means to the end of the Belgians' withdrawal. To assist in the maintaining of internal law and order was, as we have seen, a new and possibly unchartered course for the United Nations.

Hammarskjöld, in fact, seems to have had the termination of UNOC's military activities in view even before that time. On August 21, he had told the Security Council that, following the Belgian withdrawal, and

> with the resulting vacuum filled by the United Nations, we should be entitled to regard the chapter of the Congo story which describes the situation as one of a threat to international peace and security as being close to an end. This is said in the firm expectation, of course, that we need not envisage a risk from any new developments in the Congo outside the framework firmly established by the Security Council. . . . It is said also in the firm expectation that the Government of the Republic will take such measures as are within its power to assist the United Nations Force in carrying out the Council's decision and, thus, helping to bring about the order and stability necessary to avoid future eruptions.[31]

But this was not to be. On September 5, Kasavubu, as chief of state, dismissed Lumumba from the prime ministership. The grounds were that he had "betrayed his office by provoking discord within the Government, depriving citizens of their fundamental liberties and plunging the country into a fratricidal civil war."[32]

At that date and later, the Secretary-General contended that the Chief of State had constitutional right so to dismiss a prime minister (though, when first two and then three rival "Central governments" emerged in Léopoldville, UNOC was instructed to act so as not to imply a U.N. verdict between the disputants). The Chief of State requested Joseph Ileo to form a new government, but on the evening of the fifth, Lumumba declared that Kasavubu was no longer chief of state and called upon the people to rise.

The UNOC promptly closed all airports to other than U.N.

traffic and temporarily closed the radio station. It did so partly as a measure of self-defense for the UNF and partly to avert civil strife. The action has some historical significance as the first initiative—call it "military" or not—taken by or with the UNF in an internal situation where the locus of governmental authority was divided or in doubt. Again, the U.N. posture seems to have been intended to be impartial, yet Lumumba's advocates might claim that without U.N. intervention he would have rallied enough support in Léopoldville to overthrow the Chief of State and re-establish his own *de facto* authority.

For the UNF, the situation's novelty—unprovided for in the Secretary-General's summary study of previous experience—consisted in its having to go on acting despite the schism in the host government. One may think that the proper and obvious course at this point would have been for the Secretary-General to ask for a mandate that would establish the UNF as the sole legitimate police and military force in the Congo, with authority to search for, distrain, arrest, and extradite unauthorized foreign personnel and matériel until such time as a clearly legitimate and effective new government emerged, or until a new constitutional arrangement had evident and overwhelming public support. In reality, the U.S.S.R. would almost certainly have prevented such a mandate, and indeed UNOC proceeded as before, but with an important exception. Deprived of a clearly defined host government, the UNF was effectively limited even further in the degree of armed force it could employ. In its residual mission of maintaining and restoring order, its chief office was to be "present." Never before so strong militarily, its military tasks were less patent than ever. The prime diplomatic objective of UNOC came to be the fostering of a new and, if possible, nationally unifying Central government.

V

The Third Phase: Internal Stagnation
and External Partisanship

TO ADJUDICATE THE RIGHTS and wrongs of the struggle—following Kasavubu's dismissal of Lumumba—to become the legitimate Central government would be beyond the scope of this study. (Succinct accounts of the events in Léopoldville from Lumumba's dismissal on September 5 to General Mobutu's announcement of his "government" on September 20 are readily available.[1]) Apparently the dismissal was constitutionally valid, but not Kasavubu's subsequent appointment of Ileo—not, at least, for certain, once Parliament had voted its confidence in Lumumba. Mobutu and his militarily established Collège d'universitaires have the distinction of being the sole plainly unconstitutional group of pretenders. Much of the world press suggested that Lumumba commanded popular support; and, indeed, unlike all other Congolese leaders he had partisans in every province. But he certainly was no more able than any others to maintain government *de facto* throughout the Congo.

Neither could the ANC be made the instrument of a *de facto* national government. As the Secretary-General later pointed out, the disintegration of these September days "was accompanied by, and is perhaps even a result of, the emergence of the units within the ANC loyal to individual political leaders who began to feud with each other."[2] Mobutu's coup was therefore bound to be ineffectual and impermanent.

It became UNOC practice in these circumstances to deal with any Congolese civilian authority who could be found "in his chair." Of these, Kasavubu, the Chief of State, displayed considerable powers of survival, though for months his effective authority hardly ran beyond the Central province and, in the beginning, Kivu. The

48

activities of UNOC, if in practice they favored any faction, favored his.

The tendency of Afro-Asian and of Soviet criticism was that, in the crisis of September 5, UNOC should have openly supported Lumumba. From UNOC's viewpoint, however, there seems to have been no date at which this would have been practicable. Though Lumumba's following in the ANC was later estimated as the second largest of the various factions (for Lumumba, under General Lundula, 7,000; for Kasavubu-Mobutu, 9,000; for Kalonji, 3,000; for Tshombe, 5,000[3]), even a combination of it with UNF would not necessarily have been irresistible; and it might have precipitated the later military understanding among Ileo, Kalonji, and Tshombe. Moreover, social groupings of considerable vitality—the tribes— underlay the ANC's divisions and made them even more combative. If Kasavubu's decision to dismiss Lumumba could have been foreseen, perhaps the most hopeful course would have been to dissuade him from it, guaranteeing him security against Lumumba's already evident mistrust of him.[4] That, though a quite serious departure from the U.N.'s nonintervening principles, might have maintained some semblance of unity in the Central Government. By the evening of the fifth, Lumumba had several times declared Kasavubu no longer chief of state and had called on the workers and the army to rise.[5] In contrast to Kasavubu's action, this was not even prima facie constitutional.

More importantly, Lumumba's and Kasavubu's factions were now too deeply divided for any remedy but a fundamental reconciliation (which the General Assembly Resolution of September 19, Paragraph 3, calling for a group of Afro-Asians to be appointed by the Advisory Committee on the Congo,[6] was intended to effect). During the next few weeks there appeared numerous documents— later included in those which Kasavubu and Kasongo (President of the Chamber of Representatives) handed over to the Conciliation Commission[7]—which purported to emanate from Lumumba, and which, if all were genuine, would have revealed him as a crypto-Communist, tribal gangster, torturer, and would-be dictator. Since the present authors cannot hope to determine which documents were forgeries, we propose to accept as genuine only the letters of September 12 from Nkrumah to Lumumba. These, together with

official U.N. documents, indicate that, at least after September 5,
Lumumba proposed to "get rid of his opponents forthwith," "make
a new constitution," and call in military aid from Ghana and from
the U.S.S.R. and Communist China to establish his regime and
"throw out the U.N. forces."

Even the actions of Kasavubu could not be squared with the *loi
fondamentale* after October 14, at which date he ought in law to
have allowed Parliament to reconvene, since he had recessed it a
month before. Thus the absence of any clearly lawful central authority in the Congo altered the terms of the "test" that, so we
have supposed, Hammarskjöld's policy of a noninterventionary
UNF deployment was undergoing: Now, the terms were whether a
force deployed under those conditions could function in a partial
anarchy. Even the use-of-force resolution of February 21, 1961, was
to make only one further alteration in the UNF's conditions of
operation, by enabling it to use force in the last resort to prevent
civil war. Readers may be interested to compare the UNF's record
of preserving peace in the Congo during the phase under discussion
with that after February 21, 1961.

By mid-September UNF had more than 16,000 troops, of whom
more than three-quarters were African, deployed throughout the
Congo including Katanga. About 3,000 more, 1,144 Indonesians
among them, were imminently expected. Headquarters were at
Léopoldville, with a Katanga-Kivu subcommand at Elisabethville.
Communications, previously sketchy, were improving. Aircraft
were used entirely for transport.[8] The pattern of deployment was
unmistakably for policing, not for fighting or coercing governments. One cannot see how—without grossly infringing Congolese
sovereignty and exceeding the Security Council mandate—any
more "active" UNF strategy would have been possible.

The Secretariat evidently intended that UNOC would provide
positive "therapy" through its civilian operation. This has been
extensively documented and discussed: In the present monograph,
we will notice only that U.N. officials, unlike some African leaders,
saw the military aspect as merely secondary and supplementary to
the work of social and economic reconstruction. For that work the
Belgians of the former regime had left durable scaffolding—an
economy wealthier than those of most ex-colonial states in Africa

and, as infrastructure to the economy, a complex and efficient transport system that, almost alone, gave the Congo some concrete unity. But, just because of that, the African leaders with their ideological prepossessions about national unity may have been nearer the mark in requiring first for the Congo a strong, effective Central government in control of a unified armed force. They, however, advocated supporting one favored faction in the internal struggle, so that it might overcome the "rebels" and establish unity. The Secretariat, more chary of civil war and bloodshed, sought unity no less diligently, though rather through reconciliation—a preference it has on the whole maintained, despite the apparent exception of UNOC's first excursion into Katanga after a new, lawful government had been established at the beginning of August, 1961.

Indeed, most Congolese leaders were in favor of a unified Central government. Sometimes they tried to bring it about by obtaining U.N. intervention, sometimes by proposals for consultation—Kasavubu and Ileo, for instance, proposed a round-table conference on September 27 and 28. The UNOC could not of course intervene to support any particular faction.[9] Its general practice was to preserve life and liberty where it could, citing the best legal grounds available in order to avoid partisan action. Thus on October 10 it refused to facilitate the ANC's arresting Lumumba, on the ground that the purported warrant flouted Parliamentary responsibility. The newly constituted College of Commissioners-General accordingly threatened UNOC with an "ultimatum."[10] From this time until mid-April of the following year, the U.N. could count on help from no Congolese party.[11]

We shall not follow the parties' ineffective maneuverings at this time, or the well-meaning adjurations to political unity addressed to them by the Secretary-General's Special Representative.[12] More significant and equally troublesome for the UNF were unresolved contentions in the Security Council meetings of September 10–17 and in the General Assembly emergency session, September 17–19. The Secretary-General and his colleagues in UNOC had, as a result of near-anarchy within the Congo and fatuity in the U.N.'s decision-making bodies, to extemporize policy for six months within the Congo despite rigorous limitations upon their power and authority.

The Security Council's meetings of September 16 and 17 were remarkable for the lining up of influential Afro-Asian countries against the U.S.S.R.'s unilateral rendering of military assistance to the Congolese forces under the control, more or less, of Lumumba. All Afro-Asian speakers bitterly denounced Belgian interference in Katanga, and none denounced the Soviet Union by name. But the Ghanaian representative—while seeing considerable difficulties in the UNF's continuing to apply the principle of nonintervention, openly supporting the Lumumba Administration, and sympathizing with its attempts to "seek help from outside"—recognized that "such help can be dangerous" and that "the protagonists of the cold war should not be prompted to enter the Congo area."[13]

The Guinean representative hewed close to the line of the Soviet bloc; but Mr. Asha of the U.A.R. also wanted to prevent introduction of the cold war.[14] The Moroccan delegate held the Security Council responsible for inadequate measures that had allowed Belgian neo-colonialism a free hand in the Congo but, significantly, he did not join the Soviet bloc in attacking the Secretary-General. Yugoslavia believed that U.N. actions, previously "correct," and U.N. interpretations of nonintervention now required revision; yet its representative also spoke of excluding the cold war from Africa.[15]

Sir Claude Corea of Ceylon moved with Tunisia a resolution that for the most part reiterated former ones, but included, as the second sentence in Operative Paragraph 5(a): "and decides that no assistance for military purposes be sent to the Congo except as part of the United Nations action."[16] Mr. Zorin of the U.S.S.R. and Mr. Lewandowski of Poland took this clause to be directed against the Soviet policy of helping Lumumba; and the Tunisian representative, though he took care to point Paragraph 5(a) against Belgium also, left no doubt in a carefully worded speech that the movers of the resolution had the Soviet Union in mind.[17]

Zorin moved amendments, including one for deletion of the offending clause, invoking "sovereign right," as Soviet statesmen will do when pushed to an extreme.[18] Slim of Tunisia politely refused to accept the amendment; the U.S.S.R.'s own resolution was defeated, with only Poland in support, as were its more important amendments, including that to 5(a); and, finally, the U.S.S.R. had to veto the Ceylonese-Tunisian resolution.[19]

Quickly exploiting the rout of the Soviet bloc, Mr. Wadsworth of the United States proposed and succeeded in having accepted a resolution referring the question of "international peace and security" to an emergency session of the General Assembly, under the Uniting for Peace resolution so offensive to the Soviet Union.[20] Mr. Zorin seemed to take this grave diplomatic reversal very hard.[21] As he could rather easily have avoided it by accepting Paragraph 5(a) of the Two-Power resolution, it may be supposed that the Soviet Government was most anxious that the UNF operation should prove a failure. In a historic moment, several Afro-Asian powers had combined to try to make it succeed.

Even those powers, however, by their penchant for Lumumba's Administration and for the unitarian nationalism he represented, differed somewhat from the Secretary-General in their view of what might constitute success for UNOC. This appeared at the special emergency session of the General Assembly, which, following the United States' request, met upon the evening of the Security Council's adjournment. A resolution proposed by seventeen Afro-Asian powers on September 18 (much like Ceylon's and Tunisia's to the previous Council meeting) requested the Secretary-General, in its second clause, to "assist the Central Government of the Congo in the restoration and maintenance of law and order,"[22] strongly suggesting thereby that this Central Government included Lumumba as prime minister. Otherwise, the resolution followed Secretariat policy quite closely. It was opposed by the representative of the U.S.S.R. on several grounds, the most novel being that its provision for conciliatory negotiations by an Advisory Committee referred to a body that had no basis in Security Council resolutions and would be without the consent of the Central (Lumumbist) Government.[23]

The Soviet bloc's own resolution reiterated its position at Security Council meetings, but in the last stages of the session was not pressed to a vote, at the request of the Ghanaian representative.[24]

The Soviet position was further weakened by an attack by the

U.S. representative, who accused the U.S.S.R. of sending to the Congo hundreds of "so-called" technicians with aircraft and motor vehicles.[25] Though the military character of this Soviet group was later denied by the Russian representative,[26] the charge had circumstantial support, as Wadsworth of the United States pointed out, in the stand taken by the Soviet Union at the previous Security Council meeting, asserting its right to furnish unilateral military assistance to other sovereign governments such as the Congo's.[27] The most important paragraph of the Seventeen-Power Assembly resolution, 5(a), administered a scarcely concealed rebuke to the U.S.S.R. by calling on all members "to refrain from direct and indirect provisions of arms or other materials of war and military personnel and other assistance for military purposes in the Congo" while the U.N. was there. When in the following month the Secretary-General accused the Belgian Government of continuing to maintain gendarmerie and political advisers in Katanga, the representative of Belgium was able, in respect of its *civilian* representatives in Katanga, to reply that "paragraph 5(a) of the recommendation adopted by the General Assembly . . . on the 20th September in no way justifies a request for the withdrawal of all officials of Belgian nationality who are working under the orders of the Congolese Government."[28] Soviet strategy had depended upon the existence of a friendly Central government in the Congo, and the measures it had had to take to defend its position afforded loopholes for other powers when political changes within the Congo had frustrated Soviet hopes of effective intervention.

In the general debate of the 15th Session of the General Assembly that followed, Mr. Khrushchev and other Soviet-bloc representatives had their revenge upon the Secretary-General in a debate otherwise notorious for bitter East-West disagreements. No resolution was adopted and, as far as concerns UNF, the principal result was a rallying of financially useful Western support behind the Secretariat.

On December 20, the General Assembly, by deciding to admit to U.N. membership the Republic of the Congo (Léopoldville), began a complex and prolonged debate as to which Congolese delegation should be seated. The two months of discussion need not concern us in any detail. The representative of Argentina—a country which, like a number of South American states, has a tradition of expertise in international law—was able to show that representation in the United Nations is determinable by "effective and stable tenure of power . . . and the ability to fulfill international obligations." Thus, it was agreed, discussions about legitimacy (however important and determinative they might be considered in UNOC's relations to the Congolese Government inside the Congo) should not be allowed to determine the question of representation in the United Nations Organization. (It may be recalled that precisely this line of argument has been advanced by Soviet and other powers to support the claim to accreditation made on behalf of the Chinese Peoples' Republic.[29]) After a dispute on December 9 and 10 in the Credentials Committee, the Committee adopted (by six to one) a draft resolution that the Assembly should accept the credentials granted by the Chief of State of the Republic of the Congo —i.e., President Kasavubu.[30] A fortnight later the recommendation was approved by the General Assembly by only fifty-three votes to twenty-four, with nineteen abstentions.

Technically, this did not settle the question of the legitimate Central government in the Congo; but, conjoined with the continuing *de facto* authority of Kasavubu and Bomboko, at least in and around the Republic's capital, it did assist the position of those two, if only by affording readier access for their appeals to United Nations bodies in New York.

During the month of October, UNF began to acquire the reputation for "passivity" that it retained until the rude shock of events in August and September, 1961. There was little the Force could do at the time—some of its members were considering withdrawal —and at the end of the month, in a debate in the Fifth Committee of the General Assembly, the Soviet Union made it finally clear that it would not contribute to the cost of maintaining the UNF, though it consented not to claim reimbursement for the expense of transporting Ghanaian troops to the Congo in its Ilyushin aircraft. The cost, said the Soviet representative, "should be borne by the chief culprits—the Belgian colonisers."[31]

The Special Representative's "second progress report," for the six weeks concluding October 31, is notable for the indignation it provoked in both Léopoldville and Belgium. Mr. Dayal's remarks on the return of Belgians to the Congo, which had set in during the month of October, implied an act of policy on the part of the Belgian Government—in his words, "A gradual but purposeful return is being staged by Belgian nationals."[32] His description of the U.N.'s military operations as being on a minor scale, but ranging through all the provinces of the Congo, record familiar policing actions in the face of tribal and subpolitical rioting. The section on air operations, though reporting establishment of U.N. scheduled flights for UNF communications and generally improved air services, pointed up the difficulties of a heterogeneously collected air transport service, some of which was going out of operation through lack of spare parts.

The still undisciplined ANC preoccupied the attention of the small and widely distributed UNF detachments. Sometimes the UNF had to protect Mobutu from his own troops,[33] and it was frequently called on to protect many other Congolese officials. Two local operations are worth mentioning as characteristic of UNOC procedure.

Kasavubu had agreed with the U.N. on September 23 to withdraw ANC troops from an area of South Kasai, which was then established as no-man's-land. It was under constant threat both from Katangese gendarmerie and from the Baluba of South Kasai, who had opposed the Léopoldville Government under Lumumba's administration. Kalonji, the self-proclaimed monarch of the "Diamond State" (Kasai), then moved troops led by European commanders into the neighboring Bakwanga area where, though the U.N. tried to turn them into a peace-preserving police force, they and the Baluba alarmed and clashed with Basonga and—more seriously—with Kanioka tribesmen on October 25. At the end of October the UNF had to take into custody four European irregular leaders who had attempted to cross their lines in contravention of the cease-fire.[34]

In North Katanga, where gendarmerie from Elisabethville had brutally repressed the other (anti-Tshombe) branch of the Baluba, another area was established as a United Nations' protected zone, though not before tribesmen made desperate by disorder and threat of Katangese attack had surrounded the town of Kabalo on

October 19³⁵ and dispersed only after "protracted negotiations" conducted by the U.N.

Measures such as these must be set down to the credit of UNF, against earlier and later cases where lives were lost and brutalities perpetrated despite U.N. intervention (e.g., the attack on Albert Ndele, Vice-President of the College of Commissioners-General). In recording the lessons of the Congo operation, we must note that, for the prevention of strife involving such intertribal conflict, one requisite is quick deployment of sufficient and appropriately trained U.N. troops, under the command or with the assistance of skilled administrators of the "District Officer" type; but care should be taken to avoid the misleading "colonialist" associations of that kind of title.

Numbers and *concentration* of troops are more necessary for a UNF than for imperial forces in analagous colonial situations, since an imperial power has in reserve an ability to conduct punitive expeditions if any of its thin-spread forces are attacked. But when, for instance, nine of an eleven-man Irish patrol were killed from ambush in North Katanga on November 8,³⁶ it was unthinkable that UNOC should take steps to avenge them. Proportionately, U.N. forces need for their own safety to be deployed in larger groups; and this entails that they will often not be present to deal with small-scale and localized trouble.

A further difficulty characteristic of the task of a UNF arose when ANC forces, allegedly incensed at the U.N.'s protection of Lumumba, attacked UNF units guarding the Ghanaian embassy on November 22 and 23, killing a Tunisian soldier. President Nkrumah protested to the Secretary-General about the suggestion, attributed to U.N. representatives in the Congo, that protection might not continue to be provided for the Ghanaian embassy and police in Léopoldville.³⁷ Though U.N. officials have throughout the operation commended the Ghanaian contingent for its loyalty to UNOC orders and principles, Ghanaian political and diplomatic representatives were, understandably, less circumspect than their troops and, because Ghana was so closely identified with the Lumumbist cause, put an especial strain upon UNOC and, indeed, upon their own contingent in UNF. Some commentators have argued, reviewing the Congo experience, that the principle of

"universality" in recruitment of troops for UNF should be abridged
so as to *avoid* contribution from the host country's region, as well
as from the Security Council powers and other interested parties.
This seems politically impracticable; but, if so, some other procedures are called for to offset the disadvantages of recruitment from
neighbors who, like Ghana, have generalized political ambitions in
the region.

Anti-Lumumbist troops had ringed Lumumba's home since their
unsuccessful attempt to arrest him on October 11. Within that
ring, the UNF had established a guard (as it had for Kasavubu's
residence, and others) that prevented arbitrary action against him
but in no sense made him a prisoner; he was free to come and go,
although advised by U.N. officials against putting himself in jeop-
ardy. On the night of November 27, a car carrying him left his
home, though it was not until the following day that U.N. and
Léopoldville authorities discovered his absence. ANC troops arrested him near Port-Francqui on December 2, and the Léopoldville Administration retrieved him and imprisoned him at Thysville, where the Special Representative of the Secretary-General
tried to get him Red Cross assistance. Kasavubu and Bomboko
maintained that Lumumba would be brought to trial under the
previous regime's penal code.[38]

The Secretary-General had, nevertheless, to record protests from
many member states against Lumumba's treatment. He urged
President Kasavubu to see that due process was observed in the
proposed actions at law against him.[39]

At this point in the narrative, it may be appropriate to consider
whether in future intrastate operations the U.N. should seek an
agreement with the host government that would govern arrests and
legal action. For example, the U.N. might require: (1) discretion
to issue warrants when prima facie cases could be made out against
individuals, and permission to apprehend them upon such warrants; (2) the right to inspect warrants for arrest made out by
host authorities; (3) the right and duty to recognize and to enforce writs of habeas corpus in respect of persons apprehended by
itself or by the host authorities; and (4) the right to be legally
represented as a third party in legal procedures against persons
charged under these terms. Such an agreement would go far be-

yond the paradigm agreement set forth by Hammarskjöld in his summary study of October, 1958;[40] but it would serve to prevent threats to peace like those that followed Lumumba's arrest and assassination, and it would enable the UNF to prevent or deter illicit entry of arms and personnel—for example, mercenaries—into host countries where public order was in danger of collapsing. This issue is further discussed below (pp. 166–68, 190).

The Afro-Asian states' concern with Lumumba's sufferings had immediate consequences for the UNF. Ceylon, Guinea, Indonesia, the U.A.R. and Yugoslavia announced their intention of withdrawing their contingents, since these events indicated a failure to implement the Council's and Assembly's Congo resolutions. Morocco declared it would initiate discussions on the subject with other African states.[41] By December 13, it was withdrawing its 3,240 troops.[42] It seems likely that the vacillations of the major Afro-Asian, India, had had much to do with these withdrawals: it had been contemplating withdrawal itself, so Prime Minister Nehru told the world on December 12. He regarded the U.N. and UNF as having taken too passive a role in the Congo; he attacked a "new kind of Belgian imperialism" in the region; he wanted General Mobutu overruled and the Congolese Parliament recalled; he demanded the release of Lumumba.[43]

It is not unfair to remark that Dayal's reports to the Secretary-General, though unexceptionable in their content, expressed an attitude that followed Nehru's mind of mid-December. When later the United Kingdom and the United States moved a motion in the General Assembly meeting of December 20 to strengthen the hand of the Secretary-General, it was alleged that Krishna Menon had been, in measure, responsible for the loss of their resolution.[44] Six weeks afterwards, the Secretary-General expressed alarm at the weakening of UNF by withdrawal of Afro-Asian contingents and warned of the consequent possibility of civil war.[45] It required no great acumen on the part of the West to point out that new Afro-Asian states, especially poor ones, stood most to gain or lose by the fate of the U.N. and its instrumentalities.

At a Security Council meeting on December 7, the Secretary-General reviewed the entire U.N. operation in the Congo. His statement amounted to a revision, in important respects, of

UNOC's objectives, and his own paraphrase of the speech is worth
quoting at length:

> the initial aim of the United Nations had been to protect human
> life and property within the Congo, in order to eliminate the reasons
> for the Belgian military intervention and to reduce what had to be
> regarded as a threat to peace. In pursuit of that aim the United Na-
> tions had had to maintain a position of strict neutrality. There had
> been no shifts in policy and no deviation from its principles, nor had
> servility been shown to any interest. Obviously those who found that
> such a line of conduct obstructed them in the pursuit of their own
> objectives had not failed to criticize the activities of the United Na-
> tions. In that connection the Secretary-General expressed his grave
> concern at the way in which the United Nations had been abused in
> words, and abused as an instrument for purposes contrary to the
> Charter.
>
> Reviewing the various phases of United Nations action in the
> Congo, the Secretary-General repeatedly drew attention to the pre-
> cise terms of the mandate of the United Nations Force, as laid
> down in the Council resolution of 14 July. Although that resolution
> had not specifically stated that the Force was to maintain law and
> order, it was clear from the context that that would be its essential
> function. At the initial stage, which had been characterized by the
> progressive withdrawal of the Belgian troops, the United Nations had
> not concerned itself with the constitutional issues or political institu-
> tions of the Congo. It had been made clear at that time that the
> Force could not take any action that would make it a party to internal
> conflict in the country.
>
> After the adoption of the Council's first two resolutions, the in-
> ternal conflicts and political rivalry had increased; competing politi-
> cal groups had asked the Force to take action in their favor, on the
> basis of constitutional provisions.

At this point, the Secretary-General cited the Resolution of August
9 to endorse his following the principle of U.N. impartiality at that
time.[46] His paraphrase continues:

> The United Nations, which could not become involved in coercive
> action against political factions without violating Article 2 of the
> Charter, had exercised its military power to protect political leaders
> of various factions from outright violence; it had also protected all
> major installations vital to the maintenance of minimum civilian ac-

tivities, as well as those installations which were vital to the security both of the Congolese and of the United Nations.

On the one hand, the United Nations had been accused of not intervening in internal conflicts of a constitutional nature and of not creating a stable government within the framework of the constitution—measures that would have represented infringements of the sovereignty of a Member State. Others had tried to discredit the United Nations by innuendos to the effect that it was trying to do something which in fact it had no desire to do: namely, to establish some kind of international trusteeship in the Congo. In particular, it had been said that it was the duty of the United Nations and of the Secretary-General to liberate Mr. Lumumba; yet any use of force for the purpose of liberating Mr. Lumumba would have meant overriding the authority of the Chief of State, who had certainly endorsed the warrant for his arrest. The same applied to the demand that Colonel Mobutu's "illegal armies" should be disarmed by force: in the case in point it was a matter of the Congolese National Army, under the supreme authority of the Chief of State, who was actually one of the two signatories of the initial request made to the United Nations on which the United Nations action was based.

He laid responsibility for continued misuse of the ANC at the doors of those Security Council members who had made much of the sovereign rights of the first Congolese Government, and asked, "Why were the critics not, at an earlier stage, interested in widening the mandate, as their comments now indicate, including a disarming of the ANC?"[47] His speech, in paraphrase, concluded:

Through combined military and diplomatic efforts, the United Nations had, during that difficult period characterized by wide-spread political breakdown, intense political rivalry and tribal conflicts, achieved a pacification which was far preferable to repression and it had laid a very valuable foundation for technical assistance to the Congo. Hence it was not possible to speak of a failure of that phase of the United Nations operation, which had been conducted in a new framework, different from that in which it had successfully carried out its first objective, namely the evacuation of the Belgian troops and the restoration of law and order.

Developments had shown, however, that the means available to the United Nations had been insufficient for the creation of a stable political life in the Congo. It was now a matter of determining what were the true functions of the United Nations in the changed situation. The situation with regard to the *cadres* of the ANC was not very different from what it had been at the time of the July crisis; the need for reorganization which had existed then had not disappeared. Similarly, it was still necessary to maintain the United Nations military presence in order to avoid anarchy, which would make the technical assistance activities and normal political leadership impossible. If the United Nations Forces were withdrawn, everything would crumble, unless denationalized multilateral assistance were replaced by bilateral assistance, with all that that meant. The Force should not be withdrawn until it could leave to the people of the Congo a legacy of order with which they could maintain a peaceful life.[48]

The "real problem," as Hammarskjöld had pointed out, concerned "the true functions . . . of the United Nations in the changed situation."

The inadequacy of describing the UNF as "an international police force" should now be evident to us. Civil police purportedly act to prevent clearly impending breaches of the peace or to apprehend those who appear to have committed offenses. The UNF had now become an instrument for much more than that: broadly, a political instrument. But the political objectives it was now being used to achieve were not *particular*—they were not, for instance, equivalent to purposes of conservative or of revolutionary nations sending armies of order or of liberation to subject-territories. In an era of emergence from colonial status, one political objective common to many states with otherwise conflicting particular interests was the *general* wish for a stable transition from colonialism, in which loss of life would be minimized and new nations would arise capable of doing their internal and external jobs. In referring to a general will to stability, we do not mean to imply that all nations hope that colonialism will be liquidated in peace—states that make a policy of promoting revolutionary movements have, perhaps, an interest in chaos that they can exploit. Nor do we suppose that particular interests of some nations sharing the general purpose of stable transition will never be hindered by the fulfilling of the general purpose. There is some analogy here with the aim of ironing out fluctuations of boom and depression within a national economy; a few (necessarily no more than a few) competent speculators may expect through economic stability to lose opportunities for gain; and many particular interests, without having been singled out for punishment, should in fact expect to suffer damage from ironing-out measures. But, these qualifications admitted, we can refer in a guarded way to a general interest in economic stability. Similarly, there may be a "general" purpose of international stabilization. At least, we can establish the logically distinct concept of a political interest or purpose that is general and not the particular and peculiar interest of some nation or group of nations; that, nevertheless, a nation may promote, either against its immediate and particular interest or in order to further some particular interest; and that, finally, can also be distinguished from the particular interest of U.N. officials considered as individuals or as a social group. Without such a distinction we could not discuss coherently the opposition between this general interest and a revolutionary power's particular interest in chaos, or the *status quo* powers' perception that by promoting a U.N. interest they might incidentally thwart the interests of revolutionary powers.

We have called this general U.N. purpose or objective a political one, in contrast to a policing objective, to indicate that it characteristically persists through great changes of situation and that usually it must be furthered through activities properly described as political—including a carefully qualified employment of military forces. The study of the United Nations is assigned to the academic field of "international organization": Developments in the Congo are among those that suggest it should also be studied as an aspect of "world politics."

The issue also raised questions of possibly conflicting responsibilities. From September, hundreds of Belgian men, women, and children had been returning to the Congo. Dayal's "second report" had suggested that "a gradual but purposeful return is being staged by Belgian nationals."[49] The Belgian Government angrily repudiated this suggestion, maintaining that those who had returned, and many who had stayed in official positions with provincial (i.e., Katangese) authorities and elsewhere, had done so as private citizens but under bilateral arrangements with the various Congolese governments. The Belgian Government had suggested on October 28 that it should send a special envoy to New York to "clear up

misunderstanding" with the Secretary-General.[50] Addressing the
Security Council on December 13, Hammarskjöld pointed out the
difficulties of that suggestion: If the Belgians had returned "on the
basis of individual arrangements," the matter had nothing to do
with the Belgian Government but was for Congolese-U.N. negotiation. If, on the other hand, the Belgian Government recognized
even indirect responsibility for their return, then there was relevance in the Secretariat's insistence that all technical and other aid
should be channeled through the United Nations, and the Belgian
Government might be held answerable under the various U.N.
resolutions for the presence of Belgians in the Congo.[51] Hammarskjöld, one must observe, had been persisting in his attempt to
"eliminate the Belgian factor" in Katanga and even elsewhere,
despite the evident practical assistance that many of the experienced Belgian civilians might have rendered in the Congo if only
they could have been persuaded to abjure Congolese politics.

A second issue of responsibility involving Belgians also bore upon
UNF policy. Though at the beginning of the month both the
Secretary-General and his Special Representative had protested the
ANC's arrest of Lumumba, doubting the validity of a warrant that
seemed to disregard parliamentary immunity, the Secretary-General
had stated on various occasions during the Security Council debate
that he was not legally entitled to use the UNF to liberate Lumumba. On December 9, the Special Representative reported that
Bernard Salamu, District Commissioner of Stanleyville, had declared he would arrest all Belgians in Orientale and kill some if
Lumumba were not released within forty-eight hours. After Manzi-
kala, the Acting Prime Minister of Orientale, had endorsed it,
Salamu extended the threat to all Europeans, of whom there were
nearly 1,000 in the province. The UNOC responded by establishing a place of refuge at Stanleyville, and sent thither the Chief of
Staff of UNF and two senior civilian officials.

In a long speech on December 13, the Soviet representative
chided Hammarskjöld for manifesting partiality:

> When it is a question of the defense of the Belgians, his mandate
> from the Security Council is sufficient for him, he does not seek for
> further instructions, he acts on his own initiative. But when it is a

question of ensuring the safety of the Head of the national Government of the Congo, that same mandate is insufficient for the Secretary-General to take any action.[52]

The Secretary-General allowed himself a blunt reply:

> If Mr. Zorin does not see the difference between using the normal means at our disposal, mainly diplomatic, in order to forestall a move about which we had, generously, been pre-warned; a move to the effect that what Mr. Zorin called "the legitimate provincial authorities," within forty-eight hours intended to take some 1,000 or more hostages and perhaps execute a few of them unless we met certain demands of theirs—I say, if he does not see the difference between that and the use of military initiative to liberate somebody who has been arrested, then I find it difficult to discuss, because it is then obvious we do not speak exactly the same language.[53]

Many parties to the Congo situation indeed did not speak the same language as the Secretary-General: Some Congolese officials and Afro-Asian representatives seem to have had genuine difficulty in grasping the kinds of distinctions that the Secretary-General was familiar with, while Soviet-bloc representatives, who understood such concepts very well, could by no means be prevented from ignoring and trying to obscure them. Yet matters of much greater legal complexity were arising from day to day and induced the Secretary-General to ask in this debate for a kind of assistance he was never to receive—a group representing the Security Council and General Assembly that would shoulder on their behalf a "fair share of the responsibility of those organs for current interpretations of the mandate."[54]

This proposal foreshadowed, perhaps, the kind of "second-echelon" advisers whom the present Acting Secretary-General has incorporated into his office. Certainly, in any future Congo-like operation, the Secretary-General has every right to demand that some such "Cabinet committee" of the U.N. organs should share his legal and moral responsibilities.

A third question of powers and responsibilities was raised in this Security Council debate. As usual, several speakers had called for armed intervention by the UNF in various intra-Congo affairs. The Secretary-General reiterated that, as Articles 41 and 42 had not been invoked, no enforcement measures overriding the domestic jurisdiction limitation of Article 2 (para. 7) would be proper:

> My own view, which I have expressed to the Council, is that the resolutions may be considered as implicitly taken under Article 40, and, in that sense, as based on an implicit finding under Article 39. But . . . neither the Council nor the Assembly has ever endorsed this interpretation, much less put such endorsement in a resolution. What is even more certain is that the Council in no way directed that we go beyond the legal basis of Article 40 and into the coercive action covered by Articles 41 and 42.[55]

To look ahead, we may notice that even the later resolutions of the Council (February 21 and November 24, 1961), which were apparently to extend the mandate by making so much of "the use of force," did not formally invoke Article 39, 41, or 42, and thus did not enjoin "enforcement measures." But there certainly has been a change—more than anything, a change of atmosphere. With Hammarskjöld dead, there also departed a degree of scruple about respect for the Charter. Furthermore, the new United States Administration and its representatives at the United Nations were to be rather more concerned than their predecessors in office with getting results—primarily, in late 1961, a defeat of the remaining Lumumbists, whom they regarded as Communist cat's-paws, and, secondarily, a peaceful settlement of the Congo affair. Both the interests and the legal and statesmanly scruples of the United Kingdom were overcome by a fear of disagreeing too openly with the United States. The new Acting Secretary-General has settled to practical business without, like his predecessor, expending the superfluity of his energies in lectures on law to the members of the Organization.

Nothing came of the Security Council's December sessions: East and West vetoed each other's resolutions.[56] The sole matter arising that concerned UNF was the entry of ANC under Léopoldville control into the Kitona base on December 13. The Secretary-General referred to Article 40 as governing the provisional measure by which Kitona was temporarily to be under the exclusive authority of the U.N. and its military forces, while the resolution of August 9, by virtue of Articles 25 and 44, obliged the Congolese Government, like that of any other member, to comply.[57]

Once again the General Assembly, meeting from December 16–20, was able to achieve no more than had the previous meeting of the Security Council. President Nkrumah of Ghana again attempted an initiative supporting Lumumba and offering the services of "an African High Command to take immediate action to restore law and order so that the legal government, headed by Premier Lumumba, can operate." He urged such a step if UNOC should prove unable to disarm the ANC under Mobutu, release Lumumba, reconvene Parliament, and evacuate all Belgian military and official personnel.[58] Nkrumah had urged in a letter of December 7 that the command of the UNF be changed immediately.[59] There was in fact a change on December 20 when Major-General von Horn returned to UNTSO in Jerusalem and Major-General Sean McKeown replaced him. Ghana continued to play its peculiar role in the Congo affair, supporting Lumumba and criticizing many aspects of UNOC, but tactfully opposing the Soviet line, and alone of the Casablanca group, continuing to maintain a contingent with UNF. The U.N. authorities have praised the riot squads supplied by Ghana and also Nigeria, arguing that in situations like the Congo these specialist forces can be more helpful than the best of assault troops.

Eight powers of the Casablanca group, but including India, proposed a resolution much along the lines they had contended for in the General Assembly since September.[60] The United Kingdom and the United States proposed an inflated version of their defeated resolution of the previous Security Council meeting.[61] They and the Canadian representative turned the tables on the eight powers by suggesting that that group's resolution might "give rise to a kind of U.N. Trusteeship over the Congo": A Standing Delegation appointed by the General Assembly might hamper the Secretary-General and his Special Representative; further, it would be beyond the legal competence of the United Nations to release prisoners, disarm the ANC, convoke Parliament, and reactivate the "lawful government"—whatever might be said for any of these measures on their own merits. Within the framework of the

Charter, the Congolese authorities should be encouraged to take these steps themselves.

The Secretary-General reaffirmed his views about the absence of enforcement measures in the Congo mandate. He advocated "the normal political and diplomatic means of persuasion and advice rather than the use of force." When, two months later, the assassination of Lumumba provoked an extension of the mandate by the Security Council, that did not represent the clarification of the existing mandate and the provision of appropriate legal means that he had continued to ask for at the December meeting of the General Assembly.

Both resolutions before the Assembly were defeated, failing to gain the two-thirds majority. This again was due primarily to a split among the Afro-Asians, along lines subsequently formalized by the division of African states into Casablanca and Monrovia factions. An Austrian resolution to keep the Congo item on the Assembly's agenda was adopted.

As we have seen, a process began in December that suggested the possibility of a characteristic disorder in any nonpermanent U.N. force: The Afro-Asian participants began to withdraw their contingents. This made the Secretary-General's situation rather like that of a twelfth-century English monarch, except that the U.N. has no patrimony of its own to live off. During the first week of the month, it was Ceylon and the U.A.R.;[62] in the second week, Indonesia, Morocco, and Guinea[63]—all powers that had seen themselves as representing anti-colonialism. On December 21, Yugoslavia urgently required the withdrawal of its technical personnel.[64]

These withdrawals were motivated by political disagreement with the UNOC policy of neutrality in the struggle for control of the Central Government. Another kind of politically motivated obstruction was shown to be possible when in December, 1961, the "Katanga lobby" and other English Conservatives objected to the British Government's offering 1,000-pound bombs to the U.N. The Congo experience indicates that ability to withdraw military assistance is in fact a more effective instrument for limiting the scope of U.N. political action than is raising difficulties about finding the money for it. The operation can go on even though bankruptcy threatens: but it halts without troops and weapons, or when supporting aircraft cannot get clearance to fly in.

The difficulty will probably be acute whenever a U.N. operation is designed to ease the transfer from colonial status. Those in charge of the operation may be tempted to accept contingents only from those countries likely to be enthusiastic for the U.N. policy in question: If the officials succumb, they will be transforming an apparently impartial operation in the "general interest" into the maneuver of a coalition, like the Korean effort. Since the United Nations began as a wartime coalition, the Charter has empowered the Security Council to undertake "Korean" operations, and the Uniting for Peace resolution enabled the Assembly to recommend to similar effect, so that not all U.N. operations purport to be in the "general interest." Hammarskjöld, by maintaining the policy of UNOC despite threats of withdrawal from many sides, sometimes at the cost of immediate effectiveness, preserved the character of objectivity and impartiality that he had begun to establish for the U.N. at Suez.

He had to practice a patient diplomacy to do so. In mid-January, the Casablanca powers issued a joint declaration of withdrawal because the purposes justifying a UNF presence in the Congo were not being realized.[65] The Secretary-General replied with messages to some of their members—Ceylon, Guinea, Indonesia, Morocco, the U.A.R., and Yugoslavia—emphasizing the serious consequences of their withdrawal.[66] The UNOC had reached its nadir.

Within the Congo, events of December and January proceeded from the Stanleyville schism. Gizenga, claiming to lead as acting prime minister the rightful Lumumbist Central Government of the Congo, established forces at Stanleyville, where the provincial government was Lumumbist. On Christmas Day, sixty members of the Stanleyville ANC arrested at Bukavu the president, three ministers, and the local ANC commander of the neighboring Kivu Province, the Commander of the UNF having been informed that they did not want U.N. protection.[67] Even granting the pretensions of the Gizengist regime, these actions seem to have been quite illegal; but UNF, having no mandate at this stage to prevent civil war and no request for protection, would do nothing. President Kasavubu, for whom the Stanleyville section represented rebellion and now, by its invasion of Kivu, usurpation, approached the Belgian authorities in nearby Ruanda-Urundi on December 30 for permission to land his ANC forces at their Usumbura airport on the way to liberate Kivu. The Secretary-General promptly warned both the Belgians and the Congo President that ANC transit through the trust territory of Ruanda-Urundi would violate the General Assembly's Resolution 1474 (ES-IV). In this the Ruanda-Urundi authorities acquiesced,[68] yet on New Year's Day Mobutu managed to land his troops at Usumbura and have them "ejected" from Ruanda-Urundi at a point convenient to him on the Kivu border, where, so it appears, many of them were promptly captured by Lumumbist troops.[69]

The Secretary-General reacted sharply and appropriately. As trustees, the Belgians were peculiarly liable to U.N. reproof. Hammarskjöld announced his intention of going at once to the Congo, and warned Kasavubu, as well as the Belgians, that if there were civil war in the Congo, U.N. forces would have to be *withdrawn*.[70]

Meanwhile, a Stanleyville Lumumbist minister, Anicet Kashamuru, installed himself as administrator at Bukavu on January 2. At the same time, talks began at U.N. headquarters in New York about the future of the Ruanda-Urundi trust territory[71] and thus Belgium was in some measure brought to book for conniving at Mobutu's transfer of forces. The new over-all Commander of UNF, the Irishman, Major-General McKeown, also reached Léopoldville at this time, which has been supposed to have strengthened the command.[72] The Soviet Union meanwhile, had asked for a Security Council meeting to condemn Belgian aggression via Ruanda-Urundi.[73] On January 14, the Security Council rejected an anti-Belgian resolution proposed by Ceylon, Liberia, and the U.A.R.,[74] and a few days later two battalions of Belgian troops were flown into the trust territory in order to "guard the Congo border." A suggestion, subsequently denied by Belgium, was reported to the effect that if the U.N. were incapable of protecting European civilians in Kivu and Orientale provinces, these troops would cross the border to do so.[75] Yet Dayal had to protest against the arrest of twelve Belgians in Orientale, and even these arrests called forth no Belgian military reprisals. Finally, Belgians were advised to leave Kivu and Orientale.

A controversy between President Kasavubu and the Secretary-General in regard to the latter's Special Representative occupied the first fortnight of January. It reminds one of Lumumba's quarrel with Bunche in mid-August of the previous year over the Katanga issue. The President complained of U.N. passivity about Gizenga's usurpation in Kivu, about Dayal's alleged partiality, and about the unauthorized landing of a U.A.R. Ilyushin at Lisala on December 31. In reply, Dayal and Hammarskjöld justified UNOC reactions by the Security Council mandate of August 9, and the latter refused on the basis of Articles 100 and 101 to withdraw Dayal.[76]

The Conciliation Commission, appointed by the Secretary-General's Advisory Committee in accordance with the Assembly resolution of September 20, had convened in Léopoldville at the beginning of January, and was interviewing as many Congolese political leaders as it could obtain access to. In particular, it had persistently asked the President to enable it to interview Lumumba. He, with his associates, Mpolo and Okito, were transferred in circumstances of considerable brutality from Thysville to Elisabethville on January 18, 1961—the day on which the Nigerian chairman of the Conciliation Commission at a press conference was advocating the reconvention of the Congolese Parliament. One wonders if the President had decided to remove his prisoners from these enquirers and, indeed, whether the Conciliation Commission's further and even more determined attempts in Elisabethville to see Lumumba precipitated his assassination. The Secretary-General protested to the President and to Tshombe against Lumumba's transfer as a further interference with his right to defend himself, and as a hindrance to attempts at reconciliation and reunification.[77] Tshombe was astonished that the U.N. should agitate itself because of the transfer by President Kasavubu of one "recognized as guilty of genocide"—a reference to Hammarskjöld's comment on the Bakwanga massacres of August, 1960.[78]

During the January days, the actions of Kasavubu and Bomboko strangely resembled Lumumba's former conduct. On the twenty-fourth they protested at the U.A.R.'s interference in Congolese internal affairs;[79] and four days later the President threatened to call in outside military assistance if the U.N. refused to intervene against violence in Orientale and Kivu or to restore the legal au-

thorities there.[80] Without friends inside or outside the Congo,
UNOC was almost a pariah when the U.S.S.R. asked on January
30 for a meeting of the Security Council to discuss "new acts of
Belgian aggression against the Congo."

At the resultant Security Council meeting, the Secretary-
General's intervention in the debate of February 1, 1961, included
an early expression of his conviction that the hand of UNOC
should be strengthened, even through measures that "by some
might be felt as coming close to a kind of interference."[81] The
sources of this conviction were principally two: the reinforcement
of Congolese factions from outside with arms and with foreign
soldiers; and the forcible intervention by parts of the ANC in factional and local conflicts. He suggested that the Security Council
should provide "a basis for arrangements which would eliminate
the present threat from the army."[82] But he counterbalanced this
with a warning of the problems that would arise were the mandate
to be widened so as to permit the UNF to take the "military initiative"; requests for armed U.N. intervention had already come, he
pointed out, from four competing sources—from Kasavubu, from
the Belgian Government, from members of the U.N. seeking the
liberation of Lumumba, and from the Central Government seeking
aid against Tshombe.[83] Quite apart from this, the growing difficulty
of its tasks were in any case such that, if the UNF continued to be
weakened by repatriations—he again reminded them—he might be
obliged to put the possibility of its liquidation before the Council
or the Assembly.[84]

In short, the Secretary-General already contemplated new kinds
of measures for the removal of mercenaries and prevention of sales
of arms, and new powers to control, if not to disarm, the ANC—
but nothing that would remove the long-standing and apparently
well-advised prohibition upon a UNF military initiative. He had
not "so far found" any "sufficient legal basis in the resolutions"
that would have enabled "countermeasures by the U.N." against
the influx of men and arms. And we may infer that, whatever "legal
basis" he was seeking, it was not an empowering of the UNF to use
force, whether under Article 41 or 42 or by other authorizations.
We may learn the nature of the new powers he was contemplating
by considering his later remarks to the Security Council on Febru-

ary 15. (Though these followed the announcement on February 13 of the deaths of Lumumba and his associates, there is no evidence that those otherwise epoch-making events had altered the Secretary-General's views about the impropriety of the UNF's using force to expel mercenaries and other foreign soldiers.) On February 15, he distinguished five points—investigation into the assassination of Lumumba,[85] protection of the civilian population against attacks from armed units,[86] the forestalling of clashes between armed units (what were later called "civil-war risks"), reorganization of the ANC, and elimination of "the Belgian political element in the Congo" (specifically, in Katanga)[87]—on all of which he had already "taken action," and for which he felt no new legal mandate was required; and he marked them off sharply from three other points "on which it is for this Council and only for this Council to decide what it feels entitled to do and what it wants to do."[88] These were: the reconvening of Parliament (which would require the Council "to override the sovereign rights of the Republic of the Congo"),[89] prevention of the transfer of funds into the Congo when not for "economic" or "humanitarian" purposes,[90] and the right to inspect trains and aircraft coming to the Congo" for imported arms. On the third of these issues (which seems incidentally to imply that a new legal mandate would also have been needed to prevent the incursion—and a fortiori to license the apprehension and expulsion—of mercenaries), the Secretary-General averred: "The legal advice I have sought and obtained indicates that we may have no such right of search."[91] Thus, the UNF was not empowered to prevent arms shipments such as had been alleged to have come from Belgium, the U.S.S.R., and the U.A.R.; nor, indeed, did the later use-of-force resolution of February 20–21 (S/4741) so empower it. For these three issues, he specifically laid the responsibility upon the Security Council "to determine the ends and to decide on the means, in full awareness of its responsibility for the maintenance of peace and security, but also of its duty to respect the sovereignty of a Member nation. It cannot shirk its responsibility by expecting from the Secretariat action on which it is not prepared to take decisions itself."[92]

In discussing the third of the five points already mandated—the preventing of clashes between armed units and thereby the remov-

ing of "civil-war risks"—it is notable that the Secretary-General
spoke of having given instructions that "the United Nations should
use all means, *short of force* . . ." [italics added].[93] In this respect
alone did the Three-Power use-of-force draft resolution, published
on February 17[94] and carried by the Security Council on February
21, extend the mandate of the UNF to use force. On and before
February 15, the Secretary-General had been so little inclined to go
beyond the mandate that, as he had stated, "were clashes between
armed units to develop, the United Nations could not permit itself
to become a third party to such a conflict. But the use of force in
support of cease-fire arrangements should not therefore be excluded."[95] Paradoxically, a chief deterrent to civil warfare in the
Congo was to be the threat that, in such a case, the UNF would be
withdrawn. Earlier in the month the Secretary-General had told
the Security Council: "Were it to break out in spite of the restraining influence of the presence of the United Nations, I consider that
the right thing to do would be for the United Nations Force to
withdraw . . ."[96] But, short of that extreme, a UNF could be an
influence, proportionate to its size and by virtue of its mere presence, for the preventing of civil war: "Negotiations to those ends
can be conducted on the basis of the military force at the disposal
of the United Nations. The chance of success is greater the bigger
is the force."[97]

We may pause here to notice, in these pronouncements of Dag
Hammarskjöld of February 1 and 15, 1961, a fully developed and
perhaps a final version of the doctrine of a UNF as a "nonintervening" presence *within* a member nation—to preserve *internal* peace.
We say "perhaps" a final version, because the Three-Power resolution of February 21 was to empower the UNF to use force in the
last resort for the prevention of civil war, and may thus have set a
precedent that in future could be invoked at the beginning of any
intranational U.N. operation.

Had the doctrine been successful? The vast expanse of the
Congo, its tribal divisions and savagery, its political conflicts exacerbated by the embattled interests, economic ambitions, and ideolo-
gies of the world powers, its government's lack of experience in
sovereign rule and, above all, its mutinous and divided ANC had
combined to set the severest of tests. Hammarskjöld evidently be-

lieved that the Force had not been big and strong enough, and he could well have claimed that, lacking also the right to search for imported arms, the UNF had been unreasonably tried. Certainly, the politically and tribally motivated massacres, Mobutu's coup d'état, the armed support for Katangese and Kasaian secession and for Stanleyville's claims to legitimate succession must be counted against the "nonintervening" doctrine. On the other hand, these had been civil *battles* and shows of force: They had not amounted to sustained campaigns of civil *war*.

More importantly, official intervention by other powers had ceased, or had been prevented. In mid-twentieth-century conditions, this may have been of less moment than the unofficial but actual involvement of Western commercial interests, of resurgent African movements, and of Soviet Communist subversives and provocateurs (the Spanish Civil War had set a gruesome precedent for informal intervention). Nor can we know whether the use-of-force resolution of February 21 did not forestall unmistakable civil war. Experience, then, seems to have pronounced its usual verdict, "Unproven."

The whole doctrine was to be challenged in an interesting but little-noticed speech of the Pakistani delegate, Mr. Hasan, on February 20:

> The weakness of the current operation, as it has been conceived in this Council so far, is that it alternately faces and refuses to face, the fact that the United Nations, by the very instigation of this operation, has assumed a jurisdiction over the Congo which exceeds the provisions of the Charter if too legalistically interpreted. . . . a consensus has already emerged that the situation in the Congo is incapable of correction through means which are conventionally within the Charter. . . . we believe that the solution of the problem created by the present situation . . . can be sought only in the administration of the country by United Nations assistance, to the end that, in the resulting conditions of peace and stability, the Congolese people may be enabled to achieve their own political settlement, unhampered by outside interference, military or political—and both are important. . . .[98]

Mr. Hasan went on to suggest, among other measures, the absorption of the ANC under U.N. command, a U.N. take-over of the entire civil administration control, a "moratorium" on disorderly party activity, and reinstitution of constitutional processes only after a constitutional referendum. Though the Security Council could hardly be expected to follow deliberately so *ultra vires* a path then and there, the courses to which UNOC was subsequently driven established precedents—as we shall suggest—that may embolden the Organization, if called upon in the future for intra-national UNF assistance, to require from the host government much broader rights of access and operation than those that Hammarskjöld delimited in July, 1960 (A/3943), on the basis of Suez and Lebanon experiences. Before adoption of the Three-Power resolution on February 21, he could justifiably complain that "those who have established the mandate and those who have decided on the means by which the mandate should be fulfilled attack the representatives of the Organization because they have not exceeded the mandate, thus established, or acted against it, and because they have not used means which have never been put at their disposal . . ."[99] And, indeed, there was only one aspect of the mandate that he could have been accused of not complying with. The Soviet delegate had not failed to make the most of this: "Almost from the beginning of the operation in the Congo, the lawful government of the country was forced to draw the Security Council's attention to the fact that the Secretary-General was not taking the views of the Government into account. . . ."[100]

By February, perhaps the United States alone supported whole-heartedly both of the elements—"noninterference" coupled with "dynamic U.N. action"—that distinguished Hammarskjöld's policy for UNF operations. From the beginning of the Congo venture, citing his own summary study (A/3943) of previous experience with U.N. forces,[101] he had fought for his policy in tacit opposition to Kasavubu's and Lumumba's telegraphed demand, and to their interpretation of the first Congo resolution's second paragraph, which—in Hammarskjöld's own words—had enjoined "military assistance" to and "consultation" with the Central Government.[102] Nevertheless, it was not to the United States but to the African states that the Secretary-General paid tribute for having helped UNOC—by "African solidarity"—to avoid "drift into a war . . . of the Korean or Spanish type";[103] for he desperately needed African contingents and, even more, African political support on the Advisory Committee and the Conciliation Commission. But now African solidarity was lost. It had split between proponents of different Congolese governments. For instance, Ghana's sympathy with the Lumumbist faction[104] slowly waned during Gizenga's leadership of it; and her ambitions for a pan-African take-over of UNOC and of Congolese arrangements for internal security, expressed as late as February 18,[105] were frustrated by Hammarskjöld's new agreements intended to implement the Three-Power resolution of February 21, itself the fruit of the Casablanca powers' deliberations.[106]

Mention of pan-Africanism and of the Casablancans who support it suggests that this may be an appropriate place for discussing regionalism: in our context, the possibility that operations—and especially intranational operations—of the UNF might be organized and managed on a regional basis. Two kinds of future context may be conceived of as plausible for such regional actions: (1) If measures of arms control—e.g., disengagement, nuclear-free zones—are ever implemented by the U.N. through the kind of regional institution envisaged in the Charter, Articles 52–54, a regional UNF may be called upon to enforce inspection and control. (2) If the U.N. is again called to act within or between ex-colonial nations of Africa, pleas may again be raised for an Africans-only UNF and for some "Organization of African States" to manage it. The pros and cons of regional UNF's will be discussed below; here we need only call attention to the principle of "universality" by which, as early as July 18, 1960, the Secretary-General had qualified his request for a largely African UNF in the Congo;[107] and to the savage mutual recrimination with which African states filled the Security Council debates of mid-February.[108] It is not too much to say that the Congo affair occasioned the introduction to Africa of cold-war-by-proxy between Mali and Guinea, on the one hand, and some of the Brazzaville powers, on the other.

The first draft resolution submitted on February 17 to the Security Council by Ceylon, Liberia, and the U.A.R., and adopted on February 21,[109] offered a commendably balanced program of action for the U.N.—calling for investigation of Lumumba's assassination, proposing the restoration of parliamentary institutions, the reorgan-

ization of the ANC, and pre-eminently the taking of measures to
prevent civil war—a calamity that had been imminent in the report
of February 12[110] by the Secretary-General's Special Representative,
Dayal. The Special Representative's report referred to violations of
the North Katanga zone (neutralized by a U.N.-Katangese agreement of October, 1960) by Katangese gendarmerie under the Belgian, Colonel Crève-Coeur. A village had been burned and action
begun against the Baluba that eventually involved 2,000 of the
Katangese gendarmerie.

Tshombe evidently believed that these gendarmes were essential
for Katanga's security. In a letter to the Secretary-General dated
February 7, he had taken issue with the U.N.'s "disarming the
regular forces of the ex-Belgian Congo" on the ground that it
would be "practically impossible to disarm the rebels, the outlaws,
and the Lumumbist youth organization."[111] Tshombe's press had
also complained of UNF incapacity to stop the "continuous ex-
cursions of Baluba rebels."[112]

The provincial gendarmerie of the Congo constituted a special
problem. They were distinct from the ANC, and became, in effect,
the private armies of dissident leaders in the provinces. As late as
January, 1962, gendarmerie at Stanleyville, no longer recognizing
the authority of the provincial president, formed a militia at the
command of Gizenga alone.[113] By February, 1961, the Katangese
gendarmerie disposed of "planes capable of small aerial raids" and
"military trucks and vehicles."[114]

Among the strongest arguments for insistence that in any future
intranational U.N. operations the UNF be assigned a monopoly of
the lawful use of arms is that founded on the practice—common in
many unsettled states—of maintaining several distinct and independent groups of men-at-arms. While a UNF could not with
propriety proclaim martial law, there is a case for requiring any
government that invites the UNF in to agree to put all its forces
under U.N. command and to grant authority to the UNF for ap-
prehending all who unlawfully bear arms and for seizing unlicensed
imports or stores of weapons. Provided such an agreement were
terminable either at a fixed date or by mutual consent of the U.N.
authority and the host government, such practices might not infringe or require the amendment of Charter provisions respecting

domestic jurisdiction.[115] The law thus enforced by a UNF would be, normally, that of the host state. More difficult cases would arise in stateless areas or those in which no effective writ were running. The lack of any recognized U.N. procedure in such situations could well be vexatious for peace-preserving actions in the future.

The above-mentioned Three-Power draft resolution, by reaffirming all relevant previous resolutions of the Security Council and the General Assembly[116] and by its operative paragraphs, presupposed the indeterminate continuation of UNOC and its UNF. The U.S.S.R., on the other hand, had earlier (February 15) introduced its own draft resolution[117] which—while calling for application, under Article 41, of sanctions against Belgium as an aggressor, and for (1) arrest of Tshombe and Mobutu, (2) disarming all military units and gendarmerie under their control, and (3) disarming and removal of all Belgians from the Congo, by "the command of the troops that are in the Congo pursuant to the decision of the Security Council"—directed that "the 'United Nations Operation' in the Congo shall be discontinued within one month and all foreign troops withdrawn from there so as to enable the Congolese people to decide its own internal affairs."[118] The Soviet representative evidently expected his draft resolution to be vetoed, for its effect, had it been carried, would have been to establish the Lumumbists in power, either directly, or more probably after a civil war waged with the help of "volunteers" from the Soviet bloc and from the few Afro-Asian powers who hoped for a similar issue.

Nevertheless, the U.S.S.R. did not itself veto, though it abstained on,[119] the Three-Power draft resolution. The latter, however remarkable its provision for the use of force to prevent civil war, in no way authorized U.N. operations either against the ANC forces under Mobutu or in support of efforts explicitly directed to end the secession of Katanga. Indeed, the second part of the Three-Power draft resolution expressed a conviction that "the imposition of any solution, including the formation of any government not based on genuine conciliation would, far from settling any issues, greatly enhance the dangers of conflict within the Congo and threat to international peace and security."[120]

However, the resolution contained three operative paragraphs later to be construed by some as enjoining measures that might through their incidental effects induce Tshombe to abandon the Katangese pretensions to sovereignty. Of these paragraphs, B-2 urged that "Congolese armed units and personnel should be reorganized and brought under discipline and control, and arrangements be made on impartial and equitable bases to that end and with a view to the elimination of any possibility of interference by such units and personnel in the political life of the Congo." (This paragraph did not specifically empower UNOC authorities, but in the event of an agreement between them and a recognized Central government it could have been cited as some warrant for the "reorganization" of gendarmeries.) Secondly, A-2 urged that "measures be taken for the immediate withdrawal and evacuation from the Congo of all Belgian and other foreign military and paramilitary personnel and political advisers not under the United Nations Command, and mercenaries"—an injunction that was to be followed with far-reaching consequences in the Katanga operation of August–September, 1961. Lastly, Paragraph A-1 urged that "the United Nations take immediately all appropriate measures to prevent the occurrence of civil war in the Congo, including arrangements for cease-fires, the halting of all military operations, the prevention of clashes, and the use of force, if necessary, in the last resort." Now, this could be taken to mean that if a secessionist province were to use its forces to wage civil war, the U.N. Command could "in the last resort" take the military initiative against it—with all the consequences, presumably, that can follow upon such action in the heat of battle.

We shall see that, after the government of the United Kingdom in August and September, 1961, had taken exception to some aspects of the U.N. operation in Katanga, Dr. O'Brien[121] asserted that the United Kingdom should have vetoed the Three-Power resolution rather than have sought later to obstruct it.

There was this much justice in Dr. O'Brien's strictures: In the debate of February 20–21, Sir Patrick Dean, the U.K. representative, had been uncomfortable about the breaching of the careful restrictions on the use of force the Secretary-General—and, through its acquiescence, the Security Council—had initially imposed on the UNOC. He had said:

I would draw attention to Part A, operative paragraphs 1 and 4 [4 required both an investigation of the circumstances of Lumumba's death and punishment of "the perpetrators of these crimes"], and part B, operative paragraph 2. Each of these paragraphs, if taken in isolation could, it seems to me, mean that the U.N. would take action in the Congo by force without appropriate consultation with the representatives of the Congolese people. . . .

Specifically as regards paragraph 1 of Part A, I must explain that the interpretation which my delegation put upon the words at the end of that paragraph, namely "and the use of force, if necessary, in the last resort," is that force will only be used by the United Nations to prevent a clash between hostile Congolese troops. There can be no question of empowering the United Nations to use its forces to impose a political settlement.[122]

So interpreted, Paragraph A-1 meant no more than a strictly limited modification of the previously established Hammarskjöld doctrine,[123] the "use of force" being firmly built into Paragraph A-1 and inapplicable to the resolution's other operative paragraphs.

Sir Patrick Dean's stand of February 20–21 was upon two distinct principles—firstly, that the U.N. should not take action by force (except in self-defense) without consultation with the host government; and, secondly, that it should not use its forces to impose a political settlement. Together, the two could be quite constricting, since the only uses of force that might have been approved by a host government in the days of Lumumba's prime ministership would have also imposed a political settlement.

The second principle by itself, on the other hand, does seem compatible with the course of action advocated by the Pakistani delegate on February 20, and with that which we have described above as "UNF monopoly of the lawful use of arms." Intranational order can be preserved and illicit forces disarmed without deliberately imposing any *particular* political solution; e.g., Katangese and Orientale gendarmeries, Lumumbist youth and white mercenaries, can be dealt with according to *general* rules of conduct formulated beforehand—and in that sense, dealt with impartially. But even impartial U.N. action can in practice cause changes, perhaps foreseeable, in the internal political balance—e.g., in parliamentary states,

a rearrangement of electoral boundaries, impartial so far as it de-
rives from some general demographic principle, but foreseeably
damaging the prospects of some political party. Inaction, even
more, can inadvertently affect the balance of power.

At a different level of analysis, U.N. action as such can be regarded as favoring "bourgeois democracy." A UNF with policing
powers, which observes a code of behavior approximating to the
laws that govern police actions in constitutional states, tends to
cooperate with other constitutional authorities, and, on the other
hand, to inhibit political movements impatient of constitutional
and legal restrictions. Broadly, this is because organizations governed by general rules readily establish relations with each other,
but do not readily adapt to movements directed to particular objectives. Further, since a UNF policing action must look toward
eventual withdrawal and handing over to some local authority,
U.N. officialdom will tend to look for a constitutional authority. It
is hard to envisage U.N. bodies agreeing to hand over to a blatant
dictatorship or a totalitarian and would-be monolithic party. Soviet
states therefore mistrust UNF policing, so that Khrushchev's dis-
belief in "neutral men" makes sense insofar as he has in mind the
constitutionalist bias of the U.N. and its administrators. The code
of impartiality and objectivity can be interpreted by Marxists as
"bourgeois ideology."

The United States, France, China, Turkey, and the United Kingdom combined by their abstentions to defeat on February 21 a *second* Three-Power draft resolution[124] chiefly because it particu-
larized about "atrocities and assassinations" in Léopoldville, Katanga, and South Kasai. The United States had sought to amend
this exclusive direction of the charge against the anti-Lumumbist
strongholds, seeking to replace it with "in various parts of the
Congo," but had been defeated therein by the vote of the U.S.S.R.
Five Western abstentions and China's adverse vote had also deleted a further licensing of "force as a last resort" to be used to prevent outrages in the Congo such as atrocities and assassinations. In
the small hours of February 21, the Secretary-General based an important argument upon that deleted clause's having been proposed
at all. In the course of defending himself from accusations of re-

sponsibility for Lumumba's imprisonment and deliverance to the Katangese authorities, he said:

It had always been clearly recognized that the resolutions of the Security Council, authorizing the United Nations Force to assist in the maintenance of law and order, did not constitute an "enforcement" measure calling for coercive military action against governmental authorities. The fact that the Council did not take any action under Articles 41 and 42 of the Charter had been expressly pointed out to the Council at an earlier stage, and no Government expressed any dissent.

It is telling that in the second three-Power draft resolution (S/4733/Rev. 1) considered by the Council today, there was a reference to the use of force which obviously was regarded by the sponsors as a new departure giving new rights, presumably with Article 42 as a basis. That being so, it is clear *a contrario* that such a right to military intervention to liberate prisoners detained by local authorities *de facto* or *de jure*, was not considered as having existed in previous resolutions, and the draft thus confirmed the interpretation maintained so far.[125]

Several important consequences follow from that argument. The *first* Three-Power resolution's licensing of the use of force to prevent civil war did not invoke Article 42 (the Secretary-General thus implicitly confirming Sir Patrick Dean's interpretation of it). Further, the U.N. Command had not yet been empowered to use force to override "local authorities *de facto*," which would include the Katanga provincial government so long as the Central Government was unable to exercise effective control over it. Therefore, presumably, the UNF was not entitled to apprehend mercenaries or others under the protection of local authorities by virtue of its own unsupported authority alone.

This may help to explain why it was not until mid-August, 1961, after the formation of the Adoula Government and President Kasavubu's proclamation of Ordinance 70,[126] that UNOC initiated, with such revolutionary consequences, its operations against the Katanga mercenaries, and even then first sought the cooperation of the Tshombe Administration.

Thus the Secretary-General appeared to have successfully circumscribed the amendment of his original doctrine of delimitation on the UNF, confining the U.N.'s new power of forcibly preventing civil war to a kind of prestigious reserve. (He had failed, we may notice, to get those other new powers for which he hinted so broadly on February 15.[127]) For the reconstituting of parliamentary government and for elimination of non-Congolese interlopers, however, he now commanded the strongest moral support. It may seem, then, that February had brought no new epoch for the operation of United Nations forces.

Yet the three Afro-Asian powers may after all have induced the Organization to take the decisive step. Despite British scruples and against Soviet purposes they had armed the UNF with a potent phrase: "the use of force." Invoked once, it was more easily invoked again, as the Security Council debate of November was to show. Much accepted opinion about international law could now be called in question.

VI

The Re-creation of Constitutional Government: March–August, 1961

A STORM AT ONCE blew up in Léopoldville over the new Security Council resolution: Mr. Dayal was almost the only person there who publicly welcomed it;[1] the Prime Minister, Mr. Ileo, maintained that he was ready to resist the UNF by force if necessary;[2] Tshombe accused the U.N. of declaring war on the Congo.[3] On February 22, Kasavubu cabled the President of the Security Council to the same effect. He affirmed the sovereign right of the Republic of the Congo to prevent civil war, to recruit technicians, to authorize any Security Council investigation of the assassinations, to convene Parliament, and to determine when to seek U.N. assistance for the reorganization of the ANC. The telegram concluded with a detailed defiance of any U.N. attempt to implement the new resolution.[4]

In its opening paragraph, however, the President had referred approvingly to "proposals recently put forward" by the Conciliation Commission. That body had on February 15 recommended to the Secretary-General's Advisory Committee on the Congo that the "basis of the newly formed Provisional Government of Prime Minister Ileo should be broadened so as to make it a government of national unity." It had advised cessation of military operations in Katanga, the reconvention of Parliament, and the convening of a summit meeting of Congolese leaders; and furthermore it suggested that, as things were, only a "federal form of government" could preserve Congolese unity.[5]

The document's chief value lay, on the one hand, in providing the Kasavubu Administration with a more palatable U.N. finding than the resolution of February 21; and, on the other, in assisting

85

the Secretary-General to secure a new agreement with that administration as a step toward reconstitution of an evidently legal Central
Government. His actions of the next few months suggest that this
was what Hammarskjöld envisaged as the first stage in implementing the February 21 resolution—U.N. operations against Katangese
"mercenaries" would have to wait and, meanwhile, representations
should be made to evacuate Belgian and foreign military and political personnel. (The Belgian reply to the Secretary-General foreshadowed an objection later leveled by responsible non-Belgians
against Security Council policy, when it hinted that officers and
noncommissioned officers from the UNF should directly take over
the responsibilities of Belgian members of the Force Publique
placed at the disposal of the Congolese authorities under Article
250 of the *loi fondamentale*.[6] The removal of these Belgian officers
of the Katangese gendarmerie, it has been suggested, opened that
Force to the callous and irresponsible mercenaries and French "ultras" who planned the damaging campaigns against the U.N. of
September and especially of December, 1961. The Secretary-General's rejoinder, however, made it clear that neither he nor his Advisory Committee, whom he consulted on this matter, could see
their way to ignoring the "peremptory" character of the Security
Council's resolution on that subject.)[7]

No immediate military campaign seems to have been expected of
the UNF. Civil war was still rife, as reported by the Special Representative: General McKeown had mediated between Mobutu and
Lundula to avoid hostilities in the Equateur-Orientale sector. In
Kasai, the UNF tried to head off an attack by Stanleyville forces
against the secessionist Kalonji and at the same time to restrain the
latter from joining with Mobutu to attack hostile tribes. Similar
U.N. negotiations with Tshombe had dissuaded him from attacking the UNF direct.[8] The Ileo-Kasavubu Administration rejected
U.N. remonstrances about action against "rebels" from Stanleyville, but by persuasion and well-managed interposition of Ghanaian UNF forces conflict was again halted, and the Stanleyville
troops retreated from Luluabourg. In all three areas, by the end of
March, a mixture of UNF presence, informal staffwork, and military diplomacy had effected an at least temporary patch-up of these
threatening situations. From month to month, much of the UNF's

work was of this sort, undramatic and sometimes apparently less prompt than outside critics would have liked. But, considering the thin spread of UNF units, their peace-preserving achievements at this time were remarkable.[9]

In late February, random outrages by unofficial groups and opposition from official sources were reported in Léopoldville,[10] apparently in response to the use-of-force clauses in the resolution of February 21. The UNF was later unjustly accused of having provoked these, though on the occasion the London *Times* had described it approvingly as behaving with its "customary passivity." [11] India did much by promising a brigade of troops to UNOC, though on condition that it should not be called upon to fight any other nationals of U.N. member states except rebellious Congolese and Belgians.[12] But the Force as a whole was undermanned, according to the Secretary-General: Although by February 24 its numbers had risen to 18,450, he asked for 25 battalions (23,000 men) immediately and estimated that at least 25,000 would be needed for the new tasks laid upon it.[13] These now looked graver than ever: The news of Lumumba's death had increased attacks on persons; and news of the Security Council resolution stimulated resistance to the U.N. by formerly rival Congolese leaders and, more seriously, by the administration in Léopoldville itself.

In Stanleyville, reprisals for Lumumba's death had been taken against Europeans. In Katanga, the Baluba feared attack by the Katangese youth organizations and others. In Luluabourg, the attack from Stanleyville had reawakened tribal conflict. In Léopoldville, Lumumbists feared attack from the presidential faction or at least serious restriction and annoyance. The U.N. therefore followed a practice earlier adopted in Kivu and elsewhere, establishing "protected areas" for political and other refugees.[14] These proved in general a most effective means of preserving law, order, and peace, although in Elisabethville the influx of Baluba created a semipermanent refugee camp of many thousands. The existence of this camp exacerbated the situation there in September and December, placing on the UNF a constricting responsibility—of a kind that United Nations forces are likely to be saddled with in the future.

In opposition to the Lumumbist resurgence in Orientale, a "military protocol" was reported by Tshombe to have been signed by him, Kalonji, and Ileo at Elisabethville on February 28.[15] Though little came of this, the change of atmosphere may have encouraged the Léopoldville ANC in its next ventures against UNOC. These had been officially supported by a demand from the Foreign Ministry of the republic that the U.N. should withdraw from various installations, including Ndjili airport, and should keep out of ANC camps.[16] Also, the "Military Bulletin" of the ANC's Léopoldville headquarters published on March 3 an adjuration to its soldiers to resist the disarmament that, it said, the Security Council's resolution, not content with ordering the expulsion of friendly "foreign technicians" and "specialists," intended to impose on it.[17] Though the Léopoldville Government later disclaimed responsibility for that article, it had been preceded by speeches to the same effect from the President and some of his ministers.[18] There can be little doubt that a principal cause of these misapprehensions had been Nkrumah's reiterated proposal for disarmament of the ANC and introduction into the Congo of an all-African UNF.[19]

At the beginning of March, ANC force seems to have concentrated around the small and lightly armed UNF units guarding the port and staging areas of the Bas-Congo—i.e., Banana and Matadi. Following minor attacks on U.N. personnel, shots were exchanged on March 3 between Sudanese of the UNF and ANC troops at Moanda airport. The ANC shelled the UNF camp at Banana that evening and the following day; and on March 4 and 5, the Sudanese detachment guarding the Canadian Signals unit was attacked. To avoid further conflict and bloodshed, the UNF agreed to withdraw temporarily from Banana and Matadi. Acting Prime Minister Delvaux refused to countenance reoccupation until the U.N. admitted that the Sudanese had fired the first shot (an implausible charge that hardly concealed the fact that the Léopoldville Administration had instigated the ANC buildup and subsequent action). A month-long correspondence ensued between the Secretary-General and his Special Representative, on the one hand, and President Kasavubu and two of his ministers, on the other. Hammarskjöld made the position of the host government, especially under the Security Council resolutions of 1960, quite clear, referring also to the U.N.–Congolese Government "agreement" of July 27.[20] One may infer, however, that this dispute with President Kasavubu's Administration gave him further motives for coming to a new joint agreement, such as was signed on April 17. The whole incident of Banana–Matadi revealed how little a United Nations force may be helped by resolutions to "put might behind it," and how well advised its commanders are in accepting the apparent ignominy of minor retreats instead of reinforcing and counterattacking as an ordinary occupying military force might do. For its pains, the Léopoldville Administration achieved little beyond the expression of its antipathy against African troops and against Dayal, the Secretary-General's representative, who had become the chief object of the Léopoldville Administration's wrath and was "withdrawn for consultations" on March 7.[21] His replacement, Mr. Mekki Abbas, was welcomed to Léopoldville by a brass band.[22] Belgian technicians returned to the Congo in large numbers.[23]

This was not the last time that a bellicose resolution of the Security Council was to enrage Congolese authorities and provoke them to action against a UNF that was not proposing—at least, not immediately—to live up to the bellicosity. At Elisabethville in November and December of 1961, UNOC did not attempt to explain or justify the UNF's military actions by referring to or invoking the new powers mandated it under the Security Council resolution of November 24.

A further outcome of the *rapprochement* between Katanga, Kasai, and Léopoldville had been the calling of the Tananarive Conference. Gizenga, as heir of Lumumba, and his lieutenant, Kashamuru, were to attend the conference. This was made more plausible by the report that Gizenga had recently expelled *Communist* journalists from the area under his control. In the event, they postponed the talks for twenty-four hours while waiting for Gizenga, whose sole excuse was that Madagascar remained French colonial territory and that he would prefer to attend a conference on noncolonial territory.[24] President Kasavubu had on March 9 asked the General Assembly to take no position on the Congo before the results of Tananarive were known.[25] The Tananarive decision, as finally announced, was in favor of a *loose* confederation, each state having autonomy and sovereignty, but all sharing a common foreign policy to be determined by a Council of State.[26] There was otherwise no Central government provided for, and the confederation was to be based on *de facto* territorial power. This was the peak of Tshombe's diplomatic achievement. As is well known, Kasavubu had supported a federal solution for the Congo against the "unitarian" Lumumba. But Tshombe's provision at Tananarive for local autonomy would have in effect eliminated central government—except for a presidency—from the Congo. The later conference at Coquilhatville turned the tables on the Katangese president.

The Tananarive program had a mixed reception at the 5th Session of the General Assembly. It was denounced by the Pakistani delegate as "dismemberment" and by the Byelorussian as the work of "colonialist stooges."[27] Several Afro-Asian powers opposed it in similar terms; but African members of the Brazzaville conference supported it as a well-meaning endeavor at a unity that was not spurious but as far-reaching as the diversity of Congolese society allowed.[28]

The Soviet Union's attack upon the integrity of the Secretary-General was combined at this session with the reiteration of Soviet proposals put forward at the previous Security Council meeting. Gromyko attributed to the Secretary-General the sentiment: "Les Nations-Unies, c'est moi."[29] The representative of the Congo, without endorsing Soviet charges, did claim that the Secretary-General had tried to implement a "more ambitious" mandate than had been determined by the Security Council and the General Assembly. But he also expressed his government's doubts of the wisdom of the use-of-force resolution adopted by the Security Council a month before, regarding it as an infringement upon Congolese sovereignty and apt to generate conflicting interpretations. This speech suggests that Congolese antipathies were turning away from UNOC and the Secretary-General and toward Afro-Asian powers, especially some members of the Casablanca group, whom the new Léopoldville administration had learned to mistrust.[30]

Little that was said in this interminable session of the General Assembly can have much assisted UNOC or the Secretary-General. The resolutions adopted, though numerous and wordy, involved no principle that could have made a significant difference to the operation of the UNF. They chiefly concerned withdrawal of foreign soldiers and political advisers, and re-establishment of constitutional government.

Twenty-one Afro-Asian powers led by India advocated withdrawal of foreign personnel and proposed a time limit of twenty-one days, action in accordance with the Charter being threatened as a sanction. These two latter proposals were deleted when the Assembly adopted the resolution as a whole. Pakistan led sixteen other Afro-Asian nations in a proposal that in effect endorsed the recommendations of the Conciliation Commission (even to recommending the appointment of a new one) and traced out a program already begun upon by the Secretary-General and to be carried further by UNOC during the coming months. This also the Assembly adopted. But it rejected a resolution of the U.S.S.R. which, deploring "dismemberment" of the Congo, urged the convening of Parliament within twenty-one days. A group of four Afro-Asian countries also secured the establishment of a Commission of Investigation to inquire into the deaths of Lumumba and his colleagues. It is perhaps noteworthy that the Assembly as a whole made no concessions to the Soviet viewpoint but in its resolutions supported the policy of the Secretariat.[31]

Katanga's ambitions for reconquest of the North Katanga zone had revived, to be thwarted by deployment of Indian troops at Kamina on April 2. Tshombe and his followers then more or less repeated the recent Bas-Congo agitations against UNOC, adding to them a boycott of UNF troops. It is noteworthy that against such pressures the entitlement to use force has not assisted United Nations forces, whereas the diplomacy of the Secretariat has sometimes reduced opposition at its source.[32]

On April 17, two months of discussion produced an initialed agreement between the representatives of the Secretary-General and the President of the republic. To implement Paragraphs A-2 and B-2 of the resolution of February 21, the U.N. agreed to assist the President to repatriate foreign personnel whom he had not himself recruited or recalled and to help find replacement technicians; the republic in turn agreed to reorganize the National Army with U.N. assistance and under the President's authority, in accordance with proposals he had made on March 5.[33] These were that he should remain in command of it, that armed forces in all the provinces must comply, and that an advisory National Defense Council should be established.[34]

The paragraph concerning repatriation of unwanted foreign personnel was to prove most significant for the tangled events of August, September, and December, 1961:

> the United Nations is to assist the President of the Republic so that all foreign personnel, whether civilian, military or paramilitary and all mercenaries and political advisers who have not been recruited or recalled under the authority of the President, be repatriated from the Congo within the shortest possible period of time. To implement the above and taking into account the recognition of the sovereign rights of the Republic and the constitutional powers which he holds, the President of the Republic will re-examine the appointments of foreign civilian, military and paramilitary personnel made under his authority and will take the necessary decisions compatible with the interests of the Republic of the Congo;[35]

As a whole, the agreement of April 17, though attracting much less notice than the dramatic resolution of February 21, was of capital importance, laying the foundation for future cooperation between the U.N. and the administration, which was beginning to seem more stable, and thus giving promise that it might issue in a new and "legitimate" central government. Evidently, remarkable though undocumented changes in Kasavubu's and Bomboko's attitudes had been brought about by skillful U.N. diplomacy. The President and his ministers must have realized that without U.N. support they could not achieve country-wide authority and in particular could not hope to curb Tshombe or Gizenga.[36] The Secretary-General for his part had recognized that the U.N. had to take cognizance of Congolese domestic politics, if only because without some stable central authority any future U.N. action against the mercenaries would not be feasible. So while leaving as much initiative to the Congolese as possible in composing their differences, the U.N. was now prepared to mediate between the various Congolese factions and the Central Government of the President—indeed, going out of its way to please the latter. For example, since the Central Government continued to object to Dayal (and was as firmly supported in this by the Kennedy as by the Eisenhower Administration),[37] his resignation "at his own request" was announced on May 25.[38]

As a first step toward the unification of the Congo, Kasavubu sponsored a conference of Congolese leaders that was held in Coquilhatville on April 22. Some of its sponsors looked to it to draft a constitution for the Republic of the Congo so that Parliament, suspended since September, could be reconvened.[39] This was in the spirit of the Kasavubu–U.N. agreement of April 17, and would implement the Security Council resolution of February 21 (S/4741), paragraph B-1 of which urges "the convening of the parliament and the taking of necessary protective measures in that connection."

The conference was not particularly successful in getting the quarreling provincial governments to agree. Gizenga did not attend and Tshombe walked out of it the next day, refusing further cooperation until Kasavubu renounced his agreement with the U.N.[40]

Proceeding without Tshombe, the Coquilhatville Conference drafted a new constitution, under which the Congo was to be a federation with Kasavubu as chief of state and with a strong central government.[41] Also, it unanimously endorsed the agreement of April 17, demanding that "all military forces not under the control of the Chief of State be disarmed." This motion seems to have been primarily directed against Katanga, which did not recognize the authority of the Chief of State; and apparently U.N. assistance was being looked for, since only the U.N. had the physical power to attempt the disarming.[42] Tshombe himself was arrested as he was trying to leave from the Coquilhatville airport.[43] The Kasavubu Government announced that he would be tried for high treason and for killing Lumumba and that Katanga would be liberated by force if necessary and all foreign advisers expelled.[44]

The U.N. did in fact begin to arrest Tshombe's advisers and mercenaries. The most spectacular was the arrest in Léopoldville on April 28 of six of Tshombe's Belgian aides,[45] who were subsequently flown to Belgium.[46] The Secretary-General now appeared confident that the danger of civil war in the Congo had lessened considerably,[47] and that the Central Government might reassert its authority over the whole country by relatively peaceful means. This would greatly simplify the task of the U.N., which could then deal with the foreign mercenaries without taking sides in an internal conflict.

The Secretary-General suggested that the resolution would have to be implemented in the above order, when replying to a Soviet enquiry of May 15 about measures taken to implement the resolution of February 21.[48] No immediate steps were taken against mercenaries, only thirty-seven having been apprehended by the middle of May.[49] Instead, the Secretary-General and his representatives applied pressure on the Central Government to cooperate in the unification of the country. On April 26 Hammarskjöld had stated the U.N. intention to provide assistance to the President's Administration, "dependent on your determination to cooperate fully."[50] The President, in turn, notified the Secretary-General on June 7 that the Congo would accept the conditions laid down for reception of substantial economic aid by the U.N., a formal agreement being signed five days later. Hammarskjöld had been outspoken about the distribution of this aid, warning that "Any discrimination in the use of the financial assistance made available to you would be contrary to the spirit in which it is extended and would jeopardize the chances of further action."[51] Diplomatic pressure of this sort was continued by Linner and Khiari to secure the reconvention of Parliament a month later.

The Katangese ministry, shorn of Tshombe, now appeared much more forthcoming,[52] and attempts were being made by the Central Government to reach an understanding with the Stanleyville regime. The U.N. staff closely cooperated with the Central Government in planning for a meeting of Parliament. They mediated between the Kasavubu and the Gizenga factions until on June 19 an agreement was signed that scheduled a meeting of the Congolese National Parliament on June 25.[53] Gizenga agreed that the Parliament be convened in Léopoldville, provided the U.N. gave adequate guarantees for the safety of all members.[54] A U.N. representative also tried to persuade the Katanga provincial government to send Katangese deputies to the meeting of the National Parliament.[55]

The U.N.'s attempt to cooperate with the Congolese revived for its UNOC administrators the troublesome question: Which was the rightful government? The fact that the Kasavubu delegation had been seated at the General Assembly could be used as a rough guide, and U.N. officials acted on the assumption that the Léopoldville authority would become the recognized government; but they were careful not to commit themselves verbally to recognition until Parliament had been called and the government validly chosen. Until then they were hampered by the Soviet bloc's and a number of Afro-Asian countries' regarding Gizenga's regime as the rightful heir of the Lumumba Administration.[56]

Agreement with the Gizenga faction did not remove all obstacles. The real opposition to reconvening of Parliament came from Tshombe,[57] who in this was supported at Léopoldville by Mobutu and Bomboko.[58] Mobutu, annoyed that his army was to be kept out of politics, decided to make common cause with Tshombe, with whom he shared hostility to the April 17 agreement and to the inclusion of Gizenga in the government.[59] On June 22 the General, apparently acting on his own initiative,[60] released Tshombe, who in return signed an agreement on June 24 putting Katangese troops under Mobutu's command "as a common front against communism."[61] Tshombe's unexpected freedom threatened to delay the opening of the Parliament indefinitely; for, closing of the old session and constitution of a new government was the price he exacted from Kasavubu on June 24 in return for a signed promise to end Katanga's secession.[62] Only after it had become obvious that Tshombe had no intention of keeping his promise,[63] and when the U.N. had threatened sanctions hinting at the withdrawal of economic assistance,[64] did Kasavubu order that the Parliament should open on July 15.[65]

The Senate first sat on July 22, and the House of Representatives on July 23; on August 2, Cyrille Adoula, a moderate with no particular tribal or party support, was confirmed prime minister of the Congo by an overwhelming majority—200 out of 221 members of Parliament. Adoula's election was hailed as a major victory for the U.N.,[66] which offered him wholehearted recognition and support. On August 13, Hammarskjöld assured Adoula that the U.N. would deal with his government as the Central Government of the Congo and would render aid to it alone.[67] This recognition of legitimacy had important and inescapable implications for U.N. policy toward the dispute between the Central Government and Katanga. On

August 3, Dr. Sture Linner, the Swedish head of operations for
UNOC, said that "if the Government used military force to impose
its control on the entire national territory, and if resistance by local
authorities led to bloodshed, the 'United Nations would not regard
this as a civil war' and would do nothing to prevent it."[68] *The New
York Times* correspondent assumed that these remarks referred to
Katanga; and the same newspaper concluded on August 16: "In a
shift of policy since last year the UN has indicated that if Mr.
Adoula should use his army against Katanga, the UN would not
intervene to prevent bloodshed."[69] Dr. Linner's pronouncement of
August 3 could be taken as a broad hint to the Central Government to attack Tshombe's regime in Katanga, though its formal
implications are simply that the U.N. would be maintaining its
standards of "noninterference," which otherwise might have
seemed overridden by Paragraph A-1 of the February 21 resolution, enjoining an intervention—forcible, if necessary—to prevent
civil war.

There can be no doubt that it was the Secretary-General's policy
to bring about Katanga's integration into the Republic of the
Congo. The only formal mandate that he had for such a policy
was in the second and third (and possibly the fifth) paragraphs of
the General Assembly's resolution[70] of September 19, 1961:

(2) request the Secretary-General to continue to take vigorous action in accordance with the terms of those resolutions and to assist
the Central government of the Congo in the restoration and maintenance of law and order throughout the territory of the Republic of
the Congo and to safeguard its unity, territorial integrity and political independence in the interests of international peace and security;

(3) appeal to all Congolese within the Republic of the Congo to
seek a speedy solution by peaceful means of all their internal conflicts
for the unity and integrity of the Congo, with the assistance, as appropriate, of Asian and African representatives appointed by the Advisory Committee on the Congo, in consultation with the Secretary-
General, for the purpose of conciliation . . .

(5) request all States to refrain from any action which might tend
to impede the restoration of law and order and the exercise by the
Government of the Republic of the Congo of its authority and also
to refrain from any action which might undermine the unity, territorial and political independence of the Republic of the Congo;

As far as it went, this was a mandate for integration through persuasion, certainly not through force to be employed by the U.N.; and it could not be considered as explicit as, for instance, the instruction to expel mercenaries in Paragraph A-2 of the February 21 resolution, which also failed to license the use of force for its purposes.

It may be asked—as the U.S. representative in the changed situation of November was to ask—why U.N. pressure toward integration should not also have been applied to the other "schismatic" provinces of the Congo. Kalonji's position seems not to have received much attention during the summer of 1961; Gizenga's stand, and that of his regime in Stanleyville, had been somewhat modified. By August there was no longer any color to the charge that he was a secessionist: his regime had on the fifth of that month declared itself officially dissolved in favor of the Adoula Government,[71] and on the eighteenth he had accepted the post of vice-premier in the new ministry and had promised to go to Léopoldville.[72]

Yet Gizenga's position as leader of the Lumumbist faction centered in Stanleyville remained ambiguous, for he maintained many reservations in cooperating with the Central Government and had founded the Lumumbist Congo Party on August 30.[73] When the Parliament was being convened, he had made certain difficulties with the U.N.,[74] and as late as mid-September the Stanleyville contingent of the ANC under General Lundula had still not been integrated into the National Army.[75] Gizenga himself would not appear in Léopoldville until September 3 to join Adoula in leading the Congolese delegation to Belgrade.[76]

The U.N. took in late August an action affecting Gizenga that went rather beyond Hammarskjöld's 1960 policy of scrupulously withholding initiative. On August 27, acting at the request of the Adoula Government, the U.N. impounded a plane flying regularly between Cairo and Stanleyville that was recognized as one of the most important props of the Stanleyville group. This action put the Central Government in a position to announce that no direct flights between Stanleyville and foreign countries would be allowed in the future,[77] and it certainly weakened Gizenga. He at first tried to salvage his position in Stanleyville by arresting at gunpoint Mr. Ingram Englund, the U.N. representative there. After the commander of the UNF garrison had threatened to use mortars against Gizenga's residence, Englund was released.[78]

It is by no means clear that the U.N. was empowered to impound planes or to seize weapons either on its own or on the Central Government's behalf, although, as we shall see, it was beginning to extend its authority in Katanga also. The legal justification for the latter activity was partly derived from an ordinance promulgated by President Kasavubu on August 24.

The new Prime Minister had declared five days before that if Katanga did not end its secession he would use force against Tshombe.[79] In the event, he did not; but in a formal letter to the U.N. Chargé de Mission in the Congo he requested the assistance of the U.N. in implementing Ordinance 70 of August 24 transmitted with the letter.

The ordinance opened with a legally impressive citation of grounds in law, including the *loi fondamentale*, a Belgian decree of June 4, 1956, Paragraph A-2 of the resolution of February 21, and the Congolese-U.N. agreement of April 17, 1961; referred to the "aggressive actions of the Katanga gendarmerie," which were "exclusively attributable to the non-Congolese officers and mercenaries who are commanding and serving in the units of the Katanga Forces"; declared the latter "undesirable aliens"; and ordered their expulsion forthwith from the territory of the Congo. The Ministers of the Interior (Gbenye) and of National Defense (Adoula) were to be responsible for the fulfillment of the ordinance.[80] This ordinance, and the Prime Minister's letter requesting U.N. assistance for its implementation,[81] can be perhaps best regarded as making expulsion of mercenaries and undesirable aliens part of UNOC's mandated duty to preserve *law and order*. It gave the UNF a very broad warrant—probably, however, excluding military initiative—to expel the mercenaries. But it did not provide any legal basis for a direct and explicit attempt to help in ending Katanga's independence.

On August 25, nevertheless, Dr. Linner went so far as to say that the U.N. would support any policy in the Congo that would lead to integration of the secessionist Katanga Province;[82] and on the next day it was reported: "A high United Nations official said today the United Nations was ready to help Premier Cyrille Adoula of the Congo end Katanga's independence with military force if necessary. The statement came from Mr. Conor Cruise O'Brien, chief United Nations representative in secessionist Katanga Province, after his talk with President Moise Tshombe." This statement, however, originated with press sources in Katanga: United Nations sources in New York denied having had any report of it. Dr. O'Brien has since confirmed the statement.[83]

The reporting, if accurate here, would reveal that something went fatefully wrong with UNOC communications. To say that the U.N. was ready to help Adoula end Katanga's secession, while tactless and possibly imprudent, was not to exceed the total mandate of the Secretary-General or to misrepresent his Katanga policy— except in overtones already added, it would seem, by Dr. Linner's statement of the previous day. But to include the phrase "with military force if necessary" was actually to infringe the mandate and to suggest an astonishing ignorance of it. United Nations documentation for this period of late August has so far been quite sparse, and the present writers have discovered no official commentary upon the accounts given by Dr. O'Brien after his resignation.[84]

VII

The First Action at Elisabethville:
August–September, 1961

O N AUGUST 26, MUNONGO, Katangese Minister of the Interior, announced that 1,500 ANC troops were on their way in U.N. planes to attack Elisabethville. The UNF Command there, in response to "an atmosphere of tension" created by "similar false rumors," then took "security precautions." These could be justified by reference both to the UNF's right of "self-defense" and to its instructions under Paragraph A-1 of the February 21 resolution. Their actual purpose, however, was to prepare for the U.N.'s planned implementation of Paragraph A-2 of the same resolution— the evacuation of foreign military personnel and mercenaries.[1]

Official documents and other sources provide conflicting explanations of why the U.N., on August 28, 1961, moved its troops into Katanga, seized the airport, post office, telephone system, and radio station in Elisabethville, raided army headquarters,[2] and began to arrest foreign personnel and mercenaries.

The U.N.'s own official account was that these key posts were taken over as a security precaution to prevent outbreaks of violence. The radio station and other communication centers were occupied in order that "no statements of inflammatory nature likely to lead to an incitement to tribal or civil disturbances in violation of paragraph A-1" (the anti-civil-war and use-of-force paragraph) should be made.[3] Tshombe was nevertheless permitted to broadcast on August 28 that his government had approved of the evacuation of foreign military personnel and that he had dismissed all the foreigners from the Katangese armed forces.[4]

The U.N. then delivered an ultimatum to foreign consuls demanding they turn over by 9 A.M. the following day the white offi-

cers who had sought refuge with them.⁵ The operation, which had
promised to be successful, was frustrated, it was alleged, because
arrangements for evacuation were not "scrupulously observed" by
the Belgian consul in Katanga. He had promised on behalf of himself and his colleagues to be responsible for repatriation of the foreign personnel in Katanga mentioned in the Security Council
resolution. While the U.N. refrained from carrying out search and
deportation, the Belgian consul appeared not to be carrying out
his part of the agreement; and the foreign officers resumed their activities in the army and the police force.⁶

Tension between the U.N. and the Katangese mounted—there
were reports of plots to murder U.N. personnel in Katanga, anti-
U.N. demonstrations were organized in Elisabethville,⁷ the Katangese Parliament called for war against the Organization,⁸ and foreign officers were arming the Katangese gendarmerie. The U.N.
command set September 9 as the deadline by which all foreign
military personnel were to report for repatriation and warned the
consuls that, if their nationals did not immediately depart as instructed, the U.N. would use all possible means to implement the
February 21 resolution. On September 11, after the Deputy U.N.
representative in Elisabethville was arrested on orders of a non-
Congolese officer of the Katanga political police, the U.N. issued an
ultimatum to all foreign officers of the Sûreté to leave Katanga
within forty-eight hours and, in a last-minute bid for conciliation
on September 12, tried to persuade Tshombe to remove the mercenaries and to resolve his differences peacefully with the Central
Government.⁹ All this having failed to influence Tshombe, on September 13 the UNF attempted to repeat the action of August 28,
again preventing inflammatory broadcasts, presumably in accordance with Paragraph A-1 of the February 21 resolution. When the
Katangese resisted, the U.N. responded with force, which began an
eight-day war between the Katangese and the U.N.

Why did UNOC take at Elisabethville this warlike action of
September 13? Neither its mandate nor the Secretary-General's
Katanga policy or general principles evidently extended to so extreme a course. No explanations have been provided by the U.N.,
but a sequence of events can be tentatively reconstructed from
other sources.

A "secret" session of the Congolese Parliament had called, on September 8, for draconic measures against the Tshombe regime. Tshombe himself on September 9 told a press conference that the National Parliament had decided on an invasion of Katanga by the Congolese Army backed by the U.N. and that its plan called for suspension of the Katangese Government, arrest of its ministers, including Tshombe, arrival of a special Léopoldville envoy to take control of Katanga, removal of Katanga's National Assembly, and disarming of Katanga's army by U.N. troops.[10] Another account tells the same story as follows: On September 9, the Congolese Parliament adopted a resolution calling for action by U.N. troops to disarm the Katanga army prior to the occupation of Katanga by forces loyal to the Central Government. The resolution also called for the ouster and arrest of Tshombe and his ministers, dissolution of the Katangese Parliament, and the sending of commissioners to run the provincial government.[11]

The adoption of such a resolution, and its misinterpretation or misrepresentation—by somebody within UNOC—as an officially adopted UNOC directive, would go far to explain Dr. O'Brien's remarkable story of the exceptional instructions given him by Dr. Khiari on September 10; and these in turn would explain many of the actions taken in the following few days. According to Dr. O'Brien:

> On 10 September, Mr. Mahmoud Khiari and Mr. Vladimir Fabry arrived at Elizabethville with instructions for General Raja, Commander of the U.N. forces in Katanga, and myself. Mr. Khiari, a Tunisian, was nominally Head of U.N. Civilian Operations in the Congo, but Dr. Linner had entrusted, or relinquished, to him great authority in the political field in which he had shown enormous ability. He was mainly responsible for the successful meeting of the Congolese parliament, for the Adoula-Gizenga *rapprochement* and for the emergence of a well-balanced Central Government.[12]

O'Brien goes on to say that Khiari had given him his instructions for the operation of August 28, so that "it seemed entirely natural" to accept his *bona fides* on September 10. Khiari then gave the following instructions, according to O'Brien:

to take over the post office, the radio studio and the transmitter; to raid the Sûreté and Ministry of Information offices; to arrest any European officials found there, and seize their files; and to arrest . . . Munongo . . . Kibwe . . . and Kimba. . . . Tshombe was also to be arrested if absolutely necessary. Mr. Fabry, who was then Legal Adviser to the ONUC at Leopoldville . . . produced . . . *Mandats d'amener*—roughly equivalent to warrants for arrest—for Tshombe, Munongo and the others. These warrants bore the seal of the Central Government. . . .

The trouble was that nobody outside Elisabethville, except Mr. Khiari and Mr. Fabry, seems to have known about these instructions.

When I went to Leopoldville several weeks after the close of hostilities, I found to my bewilderment that neither General McKeown nor Mr. Linner knew the instructions I had received. In New York I found that neither Dr. Bunche nor General Rikhye—the Military Adviser—knew about them either. Dr. Bunche believes that Mr. Hammarskjöld did not know about them at all. . . .

Mr. Khiari claims that he had been in personal, direct communication, by a channel unknown to anyone else, with Mr. Hammarskjöld by secret unnumbered telegrams.[13]

Further confirmation that Hammarskjöld knew of no U.N. instruction to implement the whole of the "secret" session's resolution comes from a source then in close touch with the Secretary-General, reporting that only the radio station and the post office in Elisabethville were to be occupied, and the action was authorized in the belief that those points could be taken over with little, if any, bloodshed.[14] On the other hand, Michel Tombelaine, the second-ranking U.N. civilian in Katanga, said on September 25: "It would be wrong to assume that we acted in Katanga without the approval of the Secretary-General. . . . There were so many cables at the time that I could not say who signed the actual go-ahead."[15]

Other evidence supports the hypothesis that some U.N. officials, wittingly or unwittingly, were implementing the resolution of the Congolese Parliament's "secret" meeting as though it had been part of the Security Council mandate. When the Central Government on September 13 sent over a delegation headed by the Commissaire d'état for Katanga, Mr. Egide Davidson-Bocheley, to assist the provincial authorities in a restoration of law and order,[16]

he was brought into Katanga by a U.N. plane[17] and remained
under U.N. protection at the airport until September 19, when he
was allowed to return to Léopoldville.[18] It was also reported on
September 14 that two Katangese ministers had been arrested, but
that Munongo escaped.[19]

Dr. O'Brien himself had seemed in no doubt about the purpose
of the operation. He had told a news conference at 8:30 A.M. on
September 13 that Katanga's secession had ended. *The Times* of
London reported him as follows:

> "It is now a Congolese province run by the Central Government in
> Leopoldville."
> He said United Nations forces would continue to occupy buildings
> and "further measures will be taken in the course of the day." The
> action had been taken to prevent civil war between Katangans and
> Central Government troops who planned an invasion, he said. A
> High Commissioner for Katanga would arrive later today from
> Leopoldville.[20]

One important element of O'Brien's on-the-spot explanation,
however, introduces an extra complication. If the action had been
taken in order to "prevent civil war," it certainly came under Paragraph A-1 of the February 21 resolution, which specifically allowed
the use of force. If, however, that paragraph were being invoked
to justify ending by force the Katangese bid for independence
(since otherwise the Central Government would itself attack),
then Linner's earlier verdict—that action by the Central Government against Katanga was no longer to be regarded as "civil war"—
necessarily conflicted with O'Brien's explanation of the morning of
September 13. At that time, indeed, Linner was offering a quite
different justification of the U.N. attack:

> There is a striking discrepancy between the statements by United
> Nations officials in Elizabethville, who say that they acted to prevent
> a civil war and that Katanga has now been placed under the Central
> Congolese Government, and the explanation given by Dr. Sture C.
> Linner, the officer in charge of the United Nations Congo operation.
> According to Dr. Linner's report . . . the Katanga operations
> were undertaken solely to obtain compliance with a section of the
> Security Council resolution of February 21 calling for "the im-

mediate withdrawal and evacuation . . . of all . . . foreign military and paramilitary personnel.[21]*

"Dr. Linner's report" is that of September 14 (S/4940) with its additions, from which we have quoted parts of Ordinance 70, and it was of course the official explanation of the action of the previous day, the military actions then taken being justified as necessary resultants of a mandated operation; but what O'Brien, as local authority, had said on the subject shows that in emergency situations the man on the spot (and a United Nations force is no exception in this respect) can exercise an incalculable authority. And it may be pleaded in his defense that a successful and bloodless action on September 13 might have produced the result he was seeking—in which case the valid legal objections to a UNF use or threat of force to subdue Katanga might have seemed reactionary pedantry.

Even Linner's report indicates that the UNF had orders to occupy not only the post office and radio station (for which, as

* Dr. O'Brien maintains that this discrepancy was created by a fabrication in Dr. Linner's report, concerning "arson . . . discovered at the U.N. garage" on September 13 (S/4940, issued on September 14, and therefore presumably with Hammarskjold's knowledge). Dr. O'Brien writes:

> If this is an accurate account of what took place in Elisabethville on the morning of September 13, my name is Titus Oates. The fighting started in a quite different way. It had its origin in Katanga-European resistance to a planned action by the United Nations. I have no idea what the source for the "arson" statement may be. No such fire was ever reported by me, or to me, or ever referred to in my presence. . . .
> The version was false militarily because the U.N. forces could not be given a clear mission. Finally it was false politically, for the great political objective of the U.N. was—and necessarily remained—to end the secession of Katanga, and that objective was jeopardized, or at least postponed, by an official version which made it possible for Mr. Tshombe at any moment—by simply saying "I accept a cease-fire"—to come back to Elisabethville and re-establish his secessionist State. (*The Sunday Telegraph* [London], November 11, 1962, p. 4, col. 5.)

Without accepting all of Dr. O'Brien's inferences, we may now conclude that U.N. forces took the military initiative on September 13, but that on September 14 Dr. Linner, probably with the Secretary-General's consent, endeavored to represent the UNF as responding, in the course of their duty, to an attack.

It is also possible that, as Belgian authorities later contended (see below notes 23, 24, 25, Chap. VII), fire had not been opened from a building under Belgian control.

peace-preserving measures, the actions of the UNF in August, 1960, and on September 5, 1960, might have served as a precedent) but also the headquarters of the Katanga gendarmerie, which, surely, could have been gained only by the UNF's taking a "military initiative." Now, abstention from a military initiative had not been enjoined in so many words by any resolution of the Assembly or Council; but it had been an essential of the code for the UNF promulgated by the Secretary-General in his summary study. That this principle was breached by the action of September 13 is a matter of moment for the present study: but it would be a bewildering one if a later report by the London *Observer* were correct:

> The Indian U.N. Force commander in Katanga, Brigadier Raja, was thwarted last September in his attempt to expel Mr. Tshombe's mercenaries quickly and virtually without bloodshed. He made an eminently sound military appreciation of the problem and produced a plan for a night attack on mercenary command posts and billets. This plan was rejected at the U.N. in New York (although Mr. Hammarskjöld and Dr. O'Brien personally favoured it) because its execution suggested a U.N. military intervention and the final downfall of Mr. Tshombe's forces.[22]

It is hard to believe that Hammarskjöld favored such a military initiative. To occupy the gendarmerie headquarters was to offer battle, and for this there was no UNF precedent short of the Korean War —i.e., an "enforcement measure" from the Security Council would have been needed on a strict view of the Charter. But when the whole matter was reviewed by the Security Council in the fourth week of November, there was neither censure for UNOC for having exceeded the mandate, nor, on the other hand, adoption of enforcement measures under Articles 39, 41, and 42. In this way, the inconclusive action of September 13—followed as it was by the death of Dag Hammarskjöld, an exacting and scrupulous observer of legalities—may prove to have broken the bonds of noninvolvement with which he had bound United Nations forces.

The main conclusion to be drawn by this study from the events of August–September, 1961, may be that the United Nations should abstain from any employment of military forces unless it can confidently rely upon its second and third echelons of civilian officials. United Nations civilian control is supreme over its military element.

Though the Secretary-General has a most onerous task in interpreting and implementing the resolutions—often of unmanageable generality but sometimes ineptly specific—promulgated by the Security Council and the General Assembly, he at least is *publicly* answerable to those two bodies. He could not be so did he not maintain his authority to "hire and fire" his immediate civilian subordinates (a powerful objection to the extension of "Troika" recruitment principles into the "field officer" grades of U.N. civilian officials); and, since like a good minister he must stand by and support them publicly, his sole instrument of discipline will be his authority to dismiss those in whom he has lost confidence. However favorable to a "balanced approach" to U.N. problems may seem to be proposals for recruiting U.N. staff with their geographic and ideological affiliations in view, such a practice is likely to make the UNF at best intractable to any policy or directive and at worst unpredictably explosive. Even though appointments remain his alone, the Secretary-General can make mistakes in them, as Hammarskjöld evidently had in one or more instances concerned with the Katanga operation; but present arrangements provide him with the negative advantage of having to consider only competence and reliability.

When the UNF set out to seize the key points on September 13, Katangese resistance took them by surprise, and there has been some dispute whether the shooting was intended or whether again much independent initiative was in fact exercised by the local U.N. command. The official report was that they did not fire first: "As the United Nations troops were proceeding toward the garage premises, fire was opened on them from the building where a number of foreign officers were known to be staying."[23] Moreover, the Indian commander of the UNF company attacking the post office complained of fire from the Belgian consulate,[24] though this became "the building" in the official report, after the Belgians had at once and indignantly rejected the charge.[25]

On September 7, Katanga announced it was building up its forces in Elisabethville,[26] and during the night before the attack Tshombe's troops entrenched themselves. The UNF is thought to have made a mistake in not surrounding the capital,[27] and Elisabethville was soon cut off from other U.N. bases in Katanga. Although they retained the post office, they forwent other points in the city to the Katangese troops. Tshombe's forces threatened the U.N. base at Kamina and took prisoner the Irish garrison at Jadotville.[28] (While the press has exaggerated—if not, indeed, invented—the "defeat" of the UNF at Elisabethville, the capture of the Irish was undeniable, and provided the mercenaries and their "affreux" leadership with hostages for the exaction of cease-fire terms exceedingly embarrassing to the whole UNOC enterprise.) A Fouga jet fighter manned by Europeans had control of the air and was a key factor in the U.N. setback.[29]

The U.N. was reported to have been short of manpower,[30] although General McKeown claimed four intact UNF battalions in Elisabethville against about 1,800 Katangese.[31] Other considerations, however, were mentioned by the press as having given the Katangese temporary but decisive military superiority. There was no directive from the Security Council indicating how much and in what way the U.N. troops could exercise "force" as prescribed in Paragraph A-1 of the February 21 resolution. The troops were still under the restriction to fire only in self-defense[32] and were limited to defensive weapons. General McKeown said that his request for jet fighters and tanks, made to the U.N. before the Katanga action started, was turned down because they were offensive weapons.[33] These considerations add to one's doubts whether a military operation with use of force was ever ordered by Hammarskjöld. The UNF as a military unit was further handicapped by the need to guide its choice of aims and means of attaining them not merely by considerations of military advantage but also by humanitarian principles. General McKeown told a news conference on September 23, 1961, that the U.N. could have won the battle of Katanga at the price of heavy casualties to civilians.[34]

The New York Times summed up these special difficulties:

> In other fighting, when a mortar shell aimed at a military position strikes at a nearby hospital, it is considered a bit of bad luck, but part of the war. For the U.N. it brings a sense of shock undermining the unique and controversial role of the world organization here. It is as if it is permissible for the U.N. to fight a war, but its war should be cleaner and nicer and U.N. soldiers should have better manners than other soldiers.[35]

We may ask ourselves at this point why the shooting was necessary. Would a mere show of force have proved sufficient in mid-September if there had been as much great-power moral support for the UNF's campaign against mercenaries as there was at Suez? But it was anybody's guess at that stage what sanctions, if any, would follow the determined effort of the Katangese to resist the U.N. troops, and the prestige of the Organization failed to deter them.

The U.N. debacle of September made it a reasonable inference that any future attempt to evacuate the mercenaries from Katanga would involve the use of military force; and that if that force were to be used effectively, the terms of the mandate would need to be clarified. The confusion as to what the U.N. was supposed to do and how it was to go about it not only brought military discomfiture but put the U.N. constantly on the defensive. This difficulty persisted long after the operation.

The U.N. authorities had to explain from time to time the true nature of the Organization's mandate in Katanga. A letter from Dr. Bunche appeared on October 15, 1961, in *The New York Times*;[36] a joint communiqué of the Central Government and UNOC, issued on December 9, 1961, assured the world that the objective of the U.N. action in Katanga was the "restoration of law and order and the arrest of mercenaries," that the "U.N. officials have noted with growing concern that the objectives of the U.N. operation in Katanga appeared to have been misinterpreted," and that the U.N. did not seek "to remove from or impose on Katanga any particular political regime."[37]

The mandate should have been more specific. This does not mean that the U.N. should never pursue limited objectives, but that compromise in reaching agreements at the Security Council level should not be allowed to hinder the implementation of the resolutions and their necessary consequences.

Britain and France objected to the U.N.'s using force in Katanga as soon as the UNF went into action in September. This was in line with their objections to and qualifications of parts of the resolution in February when it was being discussed by the Security Council. France, which had abstained in the vote on it, was quite unequivocal in condemning the U.N. On September 15, a French spokesman said the U.N. had exceeded its mandate and had possibly violated the Charter by intervening with force in Katanga.[38] Britain was more restrained, partly because it did not wish to be out of step with the United States, which at once supported the action;[39] but it called for a cease-fire.[40] Britain also objected to the use of force—the government was reported to regard it as an attempt to bring Katanga under Central Government rule by intimidation and violence.[41]

Use of force by a UNF in international disputes is authorized in the Charter only upon recommendation of the Security Council, under Chapter VII, Article 42 (and by provision outside the Charter—in the Uniting for Peace resolution of the General Assembly, from which the U.S.S.R. still dissents). When arguing against military action by the U.N. in Katanga, Britain and France emphasized among other things that use of force is alien to the nature of an organization such as the U.N., whose proper function is prevention of war by means of conciliation and mediation. But they failed to say what should happen when a mandate is resisted with force or where arbitration does not succeed.

In the case of the Congo, the resolutions of July, 1960, through February, 1961, had been so framed as to dissuade uncooperative or dissident Security Council members from using the veto. This vagueness probably allowed the operation to go on and, as it went on, it broadened its scope. But it was hardly surprising that as the resolutions found a more definite shape in concrete situations to which they were applied, Britain and France felt themselves further implicated than they wished to be. They realized that the climate of opinion on the Security Council favored interpretations from which they would differ. Dr. O'Brien considered that Britain and France should have vetoed the February 21 resolution. He criticized "failure by a permanent member [of the Security Council] to vote against—and thereby veto—resolutions to which it is in fact radically opposed," adding: "In this way, the organization becomes committed to tasks the fulfillment of which is obstructed by very powerful members of the organization."[42] British representatives might find an answer to this charge as regards the resolution of February 21 (though not, so we shall suggest, as regards that of November 24). Sir Patrick Dean, explaining (see above, p. 81) before the vote of February 21 the interpretation put upon the phrase "use of force in the last resort" by the British delegation, could not have been accused of having departed from the plain meaning of those words. O'Brien's own account of the September operation entails that either he or Dr. Khiari or both had egregiously and disastrously mistaken their own Organization's policy and instructions; so that if the back bench of the government of the United Kingdom had not included the Katanga lobby, nor its Commonwealth partner's Sir Roy Welensky, informed world opinion might be considered rather in Britain's debt for calling for a cessation of the fire that, on Dr. O'Brien's own showing, had been opened only because of a mistake about U.N. instructions. The United Kingdom, made wary by its few influential right-wing Tories, its numerous colonial and ex-colonial responsibilities, and its relationship with the United States, acted more and more timorously and ineffectually in the Congo affair. The United States, less concerned with long-term issues and the setting of precedents, and more disturbed by the dangers of a pro-Lumumbist (and, as its representatives believed, therefore pro-Communist) coup, could afford to see Katanga handed over without too much nicety, provided Orientale and Kivu were also to be brought within the fold— a policy far more popular with the Afro-Asians.

Considerations of national interest evidently carried weight. Britain and France, along with other colonial powers such as Portugal, were reported to fear that the Congo affair might serve as precedent for a forcible U.N. intervention in their colonial and semi-colonial areas.[43] The United Kingdom, further, was accused of partisanship on behalf of Tshombe and against the U.N. on account of British interests in the Union Minière through Tanganyika Concessions, which held 14.5 per cent of the shares.[44] It certainly set out energetically to stop the march of events as soon as the Katanga operation of September 13 began. The Marquess of Lansdowne, Under-Secretary of State for Foreign Affairs, was sent to Léopoldville on that day, with express instructions from Macmillan to bring about a cease-fire, and held talks with Kasavubu and Hammarskjöld. The British consul in Elisabethville, under orders from the Foreign Office, attempted to bring together Tshombe and the Secretary-General with the officers of the U.N. Command in Katanga.[45] Hammar-

skjöld's sudden death evidently demoralized UNOC officials, especially in the subsequent negotiations. British officials from
Northern Rhodesia, Lord Alport, High Commissioner to the Federation of Rhodesia and Nyasaland, and Sir Evelyn Hone, Governor
of Northern Rhodesia, were present at the cease-fire talks.[46] The
provisional cease-fire agreement was announced on September 20,
1961, to take effect from 12.01 A.M. on the twenty-first.[47] And the
cease-fire terms, at first tolerable to UNOC, became unfavorable
by October 13, when the protocol virtually restored the *status quo
ante* to the Katangese Government.[48]

Tshombe considered and let it be known that he had won a victory over the U.N.[49] Meantime, there was a wave of anti-British
sentiment in the Afro-Asian countries. Britain and the colonialists
were blamed for what was regarded as a defeat of the United Nations at the hands of Tshombe. Britain was particularly unpopular
for its participation in the cease-fire negotiations and also for its refusal at the crucial time of fighting to permit three Ethiopian jet
planes on their way to the U.N. in Katanga to land and refuel in
Uganda,[50] until September 18. The loss of time thus incurred was
said to have tipped the balance in favor of Tshombe's forces. The
anti-British sentiment reached its height in India[51] when the plane
carrying Hammarskjöld and a number of his staff to the peace talks
crashed near Ndola airport, Northern Rhodesia, on September 18
in unexplained circumstances.

At a news conference in India on September 19, Nehru accused
British vested interests of trying to prevent the end of colonialism
in Katanga. He pointed out that the British Prime Minister of the
Federation of Rhodesia and Nyasaland had criticized and condemned the U.N. action and that other British officials had opposed it. Ceylon, Indonesia, and the U.A.R. also saw colonialism
behind supporters of Tshombe.[52] A Ghana newspaper even accused
Britain of being in direct complicity with Tshombe to cause Hammarskjöld's death.[53] In Léopoldville, the Prime Minister, Mr.
Adoula, joined in these accusations against the "capitalist powers,"
and the British and Portuguese embassies there became targets of
demonstrations.[54]

This vehemence of feeling among the Afro-Asians seemed to
guarantee that they would press very soon for putting more teeth

into the UNF to deal with Tshombe. Another war with Katanga
appeared imminent.

By the end of September, there were left in Katanga very few
Belgian officials or military officers for whom the Belgian Government bore responsibility. Through fourteen months, Belgium had
resorted to dubious shifts in ensuring protection for Belgian material interests and for the lives of the many Belgian and former Belgian civilians still living in Katanga. At long last it had proved
possible through pressure on the Belgian Government to rid Katanga of what Hammarskjöld called the "Belgian factor"; but these
officers and officials were—viewing them in the most unfavorable
light—preferable to the irresponsible adventurers and fanatical
"Ultras," the Right International, who after August, 1961, remained as mercenaries in the Katanga forces. Such states of affairs
are almost bound to occur as a by-product of the workings of international politics wherever the U.N. has a commitment similar
to the one in the Congo. It should now be possible to develop
UNOC's primitive code for preserving law and order by adding
authority to police and to adjudicate upon the presence of "undesirable aliens"; the host country needs for its part to provide something like Ordinance 70, together with a system of papers of iden-
tity for peaceable foreign settlers, workers, and businessmen. This
might obviate the need for a United Nations force to contemplate
taking military initiative against patriotic, if misguided, troops led
by rootless and destructive cadres of mercenaries.

In September the future of the Congo operation was hard to fore-
see. Hammarskjöld's death and the truce in Katanga temporarily
deprived the U.N. of much-needed initiative. While in New York,
Russia and America were debating on how to replace the Secretary-
General, conditions in the African state were fast deteriorating. It
was not till after U Thant was elected Acting Secretary-General on
November 3[55] that the Congo question came under review before
the Security Council meeting on the thirteenth.[56]

Until then, the U.N. had been given no further ways and means
to recuperate from the September blow to its strength and prestige.
The mission that had been "sent to the Congo to assist the Central
government to keep order and to prevent chaos and anarchy from
threatening the peace of the world"[57] now seemed powerless to pre-

vent continued, though more covert, foreign interference in Katanga and a civil war between that province and the Central Government, or to cope with renewed riots and excesses in the Congolese Army and revived rumors of a rebellion from Stanleyville.

Yet the fast-changing conditions in the Congo required daily adjustments and inventiveness on the part of the U.N. The day-to-day administration was carried on ably enough, in view of the odds, by the permanent officials of the Secretariat, the so-called Congo Club,[58] assisted by the members of the Congo U.N. mission. But it was impossible to do more than that. In these critical conditions, the numerical strength of the UNF was being depleted. From the 19,825 men in July, it was down to 15,500 at the end of November and was expected to drop further to about 14,400 in December.[59]

The operation was also threatened with insolvency. On October 16, the U.N. revealed that there were only enough funds to continue ONUC for another two weeks.[60] Out of more than a hundred U.N. members, only sixteen had contributed anything during 1961. Most of the expenses of the Organization were borne by the United States which, in addition to its share of $32.2 million, paid in 1961 more than 50 per cent of the assessments of the small powers.[61] The Communist countries, most of the Arab states, France, Belgium, Portugal, and South Africa refused to contribute on political grounds, while a number of Afro-Asian and Latin American countries pleaded poverty.[62] In October imminent disaster was averted only when the General Assembly Budgetary Committee, overriding Russian opposition, voted $10 million a month for November and December, 1961.[63] This was approved by the General Assembly on October 30, 1961.[64]

The mandate was not abandoned—a fact underlined by the Secretariat in the note ratifying the cease-fire[65] handed to the Katangese authorities by Mr. Khiari on October 23, 1961.[66] The conditions were: that the agreement would in no way affect the resolutions of the Security Council, including that of February 21, 1961, and of the General Assembly; that it would not apply outside Katanga; that it was of a strictly military nature, applying solely to the United Nations Force in Katanga and to the armed forces of Katanga; and that it had no political intention or aim. It was stressed that "full compliance with the requirements of para. A-2 of the

Security Council resolution of February 21, 1961, is a condition essential to the effective application of the Protocol."[67] The U.N. representatives told the Katangese authorities that failure to eliminate the mercenaries would amount to breach of the cease-fire, in which case the U.N. might resort to direct action in the matter.[68]

However, at the time this was an empty threat. Such armed action by the U.N. against Katanga was not considered militarily feasible. After the September fighting the UNF did acquire a small air force of jet fighters, bombers, and transport planes,[69] but— according to the estimates in *The New York Times*—it would have had to be equipped with tanks and artillery and to double its numbers for such an action to succeed.[70]

The U.N. was thus left in the Congo with the Katanga problem still unresolved. The U.N. report listed in November, 237 foreign officers still remaining in Katanga (388 had been evacuated, including 317 Belgians). But apparently a number of those evacuated were returning,[71] while many of them, disguised in civilian clothing, had become hard to identify.[72]

Dr. O'Brien said later that "what the U.N. needed was not wider powers on paper, but fuller and more consistent practical, diplomatic and financial support for the Secretariat in carrying out the far-reaching resolutions already voted."[73]

Thus lacking support, confused by the death of the Secretary-General, militarily embarrassed by the Katangan forces, and fearing for their Irish prisoners, the U.N. was compelled to sign a cease-fire without implementing the mandate. The negotiations for a cease-fire agreement were prolonged and difficult,[74] and its provisions strengthened Tshombe, who called it a victory for Katanga.[75] The protocol that implemented the cease-fire agreement signed by the local U.N. authorities and the authorities of Katanga canceled all gains of the September action, requiring the U.N. to give up all the points it occupied during the fighting. In addition, the agreement provided for three mixed Katangese-U.N. commissions to carry out inspections of cease-fire and to handle complaints of violations. The Katanga side promised to assure that no civilians carried weapons. Both sides were to cease hostile propaganda, and the prisoners of war were to be exchanged without delay.[76]

As *The New York Times* correspondent put it, "The agreement in effect completely negates the United Nations' attempted coup."[77] In fact, the ratification of the truce in New York was postponed because the Afro-Asians, supported by Russia, considered the very existence of such an agreement tantamount to capitulation and recognition of Katanga's secession.[78] The three-hour meeting of the eighteen-nation Congo Advisory Committee discussing this question behind closed doors was described as "stormy."[79] When the truce was finally ratified, the decision was apparently made by the Congo Club without reference to all other members of the Congo Advisory Committee.[80]

It was now pertinent to ask what, if any, combinations of mediation and conciliation, mere U.N. military presence, and active U.N. use of military force had "produced results" in the highly publicized Katangese situation. Conciliation and U.N. diplomacy alone had not succeeded either in implementing the mandate or in integrating Katanga with the rest of the Congo (an objective mandated only by suggestion, if at all, in the General Assembly resolution of September 19, 1960, and not to be specifically mandated until November 24, 1961). "Passive" military presence had done no better, although its advocates might plead that the U.N. presence in Katanga had not been numerically overwhelming. The combination of August 28 of negotiation with very circumspect military precautions had at any rate led to the extradition of some Belgian officers and advisers. The taking of active military initiative on September 13 had neither eliminated mercenaries nor ended Katanga's secession (and it should be noticed that even the thoroughgoing Security Council resolution of November 24, 1961, which mandated U.N. action to end the secession, specifically failed to mandate that it should be ended by force). It may be claimed that "military initiative" was not given a fair trial on September 13 because of British and French demands for a negotiated cease-fire and possibly because of Hammarskjöld's own depreciation of the usefulness and appropriateness of force in U.N. affairs. If the objection is that the U.N. had not enough forces present, it can be assented to, given that the same applies to the case for a "passive" military presence. If, however, the objection is that the UNF had to fight with "one hand tied behind its back," we can only reply that that is the nature of U.N. forces. A more determined bid for victory might have been made, but there are many types of military action (e.g., undercover operations, mass bombardment) that, if used by a UNF, would cause mass withdrawals from the Organization and possibly military countermeasures against it. And, as the Jadotville capture of the Irish demonstrated, a UNF is not always favored in the hazard of battle.

The aftermath of the September operation furnished a combination of conciliation with the consequences of an ineffective use of force. As Tshombe considered himself the victor, his declared intention to negotiate could not be taken seriously. His terms included recognition of Katangan independence and repudiation of the U.N.'s intervention; and these the Central Government could not accept. Furthermore, he had sent Katangan aircraft on bombing raids to Kasai against the troops of the Central Government, and this brought to an end negotiations for a *rapprochement* between Katanga and Léopoldville.[81]

Tshombe proved equally intractable on the subject of mercenaries. On September 30 he told a news conference that he no longer wanted them. This was repeated by Kimba two days later. They asserted that the issue of mercenaries had been settled on August 28. On that day the whites in the Katangese Army were paid off, and as far as the Katangese were concerned the issue was dead: It was now entirely the responsibility of the U.N. and the consuls. The cease-fire negotiations, which had been going on for a week, stalled on this issue. The U.N. maintained that there was evidence the mercenaries remained in Tshombe's service.[82] Members of the Central Government considered the U.N. had let them down and that it had signed the cease-fire in order to recover its 190 prisoners,[83] whom Tshombe refused to release until the truce was ratified in New York.[84] Apparently, in the discussions on ratification, the question of the U.N. prisoners emerged as the key issue.[85]

This raises interesting questions. If the U.N. runs into military difficulties, at what point should it abandon its mandate, and how much human life should it be prepared to sacrifice in order to reach its objective?

The cease-fire endangered the good relations between the U.N. and the Central Government that had existed since the signing of the agreement on April 17. On October 21, the Central Govern-

ment tried to take the matter to the Security Council. In his note
to the President of the Council, the Congo's Foreign Minister,
Justin Bomboko, warned that his government might reconsider its
relations with the United Nations in the Congo because of dissatis-
faction over the Katangese cease-fire. The note contained a memorandum from Premier Adoula, dated October 15, warning against
ratification because the agreement could "affect the very continuation of all United Nations operations in the Congo,"[86] and threatening that the Congolese would themselves attack Katanga. ". . . in
the Katanga affair," the memorandum said, "the Government is
bound by obligations of a national order which require it to take its
own steps to put an end to Katanga's secession."[87]

After the agreement was ratified, Congolese troops started mass-
ing along the Katanga border. On October 30, Adoula said that a
"police action" was being taken by the troops of the Central Government "to liquidate the Katanga secession." He pointed out that
the government had exhausted all means to peaceful conciliation.
His statement followed bombing of troops and installations by
Katangese planes along the Katangese-Kasai border.[88] The Congolese then made a show of invading Katanga, technically creating
conditions of civil war, although the invasion was not taken very
seriously elsewhere since it was well known that the Central Government lacked enough military power to get very far with it.[89]
The operation, which General Mobutu reported on November 2,[90]
broke down two days later.[91]

The U.N. was obliged by Paragraph A-1 of the February 21
resolution to prevent civil war, by force if necessary, but the application of the resolution had been qualified by the officers of the
U.N. mission in the Congo in the summer of 1961 when they said
that war between Katanga and Léopoldville would not be considered civil war and therefore the United Nations would not intervene to prevent it.[92] During the November invasion of Katanga
by the Congolese forces, the U.N. gave moral and perhaps some
physical support to the Congolese forces. The Congolese invasion
of Katanga was described by Dr. Linner as "police action" without
further comment.[93] But Katangese bombings of the Central Government troops were referred to as acts of civil war violating Paragraph A-1 and the cease-fire agreement. The U.N., in a strongly

worded note handed to the Katangese authorities on October 31, threatened to destroy any Katangese aircraft engaged in military activities in Kasai and said that failure to heed this warning would cause the U.N. to destroy such aircraft in Katanga on the ground.[94] Five Swedish jet fighters were sent to patrol the Kasai border with instructions to ground Katangese planes if possible or shoot them down if necessary.[95]

The U.N. described these operations as counteraction for self-defense and for protection of its over-all operation in the Congo.[96] Tshombe pointed out that the cease-fire agreement had specified that he could reply to an attack by a third party and that the planes were bombing Mobutu's troop concentrations, which were planning an attack on Katanga. A spokesman for the U.N. Secretariat in New York said the provision cited by Tshombe applied only to attack from outside the Congo.[97]

However, the U.N. did not give the Central Government all the support it wanted. Although the U.N. described Katangese bombings as violations of the cease-fire, its spokesmen were careful to point out that they did not thereby consider the cease-fire to be ended.[98] Thus, the Central Government, which on October 13 proclaimed it would not be bound by the cease-fire,[99] might go ahead and attack Katanga, but the U.N.—except for the action of its jet fighters already described—could not. The action of the jets was probably of some importance. It was said, for instance, that on the day that "no United Nations jets could fly . . . the invading Congolese had no air protection. This was the day the Congolese invaders were bombed in Kaniama."[100] But this was not decisive and not sufficient. The report continued:

> The Congolese, for their part, are demanding ever-increasing air support from the United Nations and attribute the failure of the invasion to the United Nations command's not having backed it up with jet planes.
>
> Now the Congolese are talking of a second invasion. They have officially asked for a joint military command with the United Nations, with all United Nations planes being flown at Congolese command.[101]

Thus, although the United Nations put a different construction on the activities of the government and the rebels, this may have been due partly to the peculiar conditions of the cease-fire, as well as to partiality for the government cause against Katanga.

It seems that much of the U.N. reputation for impartiality was lost during the September fighting in Katanga. On November 7, Tshombe asked for an *impartial* Commission of Inquiry into the fighting between the U.N. and Katanga forces in September.[102] *The New York Times* reflected on "the restoration of the United Nations position as impartial arbiter among the various Congo factions—a position that was prejudiced a month ago by its armed offensive against secessionist Katanga."[103] The U.N. certainly was unable to carry out detailed and accurate observation of the Congolese offensive against Katanga, but it is hard to say why. Some of the difficulties may have been due to local conditions. The U.N. was unable to report when the invasion started,[104] how far the Congolese Army advanced in Katanga, how much bombing was carried out by the Katangese, and whether the mercenaries were engaged, because they were unable to follow the Congolese Army into Katanga.[105] Preparations for invasion brought together large concentrations of Congolese troops. General Mobutu's forces were gathered in Luluabourg and the Luputa area, and General Lundula's in Kindu and Kasongo.

In November, disorders reminiscent of those that had caused the initial entry of the UNF into the Congo occurred in these areas. In Luluabourg, on November 2, fifteen white women were raped by drunken Congolese soldiers.[106] Continued unrest was reported there at least until November 9.[107]

In Albertville in North Katanga, excesses and looting were perpetrated by soldiers and others between November 10 and 13.[108] The worst violence occurred in Kivu. Some connected these disorders with Gizenga, who had left for Stanleyville on October 4 and had failed to return to resume his post as vice-premier.[109] It was thought he was trying to re-establish his following in Stanleyville.[110] On November 11, 2,000 Congolese mutinied (it was said, in Gizenga's favor),[111] and seized thirteen noncombatant Italian airmen flying for the U.N. and murdered them.[112] The incident strikingly illustrated difficulties in the way of controlling the Congolese Army and making it into a disciplined force.

Before it was known that the captured Italians had been murdered, a U.N. delegation conferred with Colonel Pakassa, the commander of the rebellious troops, and presented the following demands: every effort was to be made to find and bring back the Italians, who were said to have escaped; U.N. property, aircraft, armored cars, and so on, were to be returned; all culprits were to be punished. General Lundula and Mr. Gbenye, who came to assist the U.N. delegation on behalf of the Central Government, had, it was found, little authority over these troops, who were hostile to the Léopoldville Government.

When it became known that the Italian flyers had been murdered, Dr. Linner demanded from the Central Government the immediate arrest of the ANC commander at Kindu—Colonel Pakassa —and the establishment of a joint investigating commission to apprehend the supects, with the proviso that the guilty be severely punished. The U.N. informed the Central Government that it would seal off Kindu and disarm the troops there and that U.N. resources in the Congo would be fully employed to this end. The Acting Secretary-General directed that this be carried out with the utmost vigor and dispatch.[113] However, on November 25, in a letter to Prime Minister Adoula, Dr. Linner informed the Central Government that the U.N. would not disarm the Kindu garrison.

The reasons for this were believed to be, firstly, that the UN plan was considered tactically impractical since it might cause widespread bloodshed between the Congolese troops and the U.N. personnel throughout the Congo; and, secondly, that it would lead to a vote of censure in the Congolese Parliament against the government and strengthen the left wing there.[114] Accordingly, the government was reluctant to cooperate. Adoula was reported to have said it would be "impractical" for the U.N. to disarm the garrison and conduct an investigation, and that, as the government knew which soldiers were guilty, it could punish them. By then, however, the murderers had probably escaped into the bush, where it would be almost impossible to find them. "The government apparently feared that an attempt to disarm the garrison would invite other army units to mutiny."[115] As late as November 23, it was reported that the Congolese side had still made no appointment to the Joint investigating Commission because no Congolese wanted to serve. The Commission finally left for Stanleyville on December 3.[116]

The U.N. had its own difficulties. Its contingent in Kindu was too small for the sealing-off operation, and there was a conflict of command between the Malayans and Ethiopians stationed there.[117] The culprits were not apprehended. On January 10, the Joint Commission interrogated twenty-nine soldiers handed over as suspects by their commanders, who were, it was found, completely innocent and, it was thought, had probably been used as decoys. The U.N. was reported to be contemplating the arrest of top officials, including Colonel Pakassa. The issue then merged with general political difficulties in the area. The Commission itself was said to have narrowly escaped arrest that day on the order of Gizenga.[118]

When Gizenga fell, his close friend, Colonel Pakassa, was apprehended and placed under arrest by General Lundula on behalf of the Central Government.[119] The Kivu murderers, however, were never punished, and armed units of the ANC were not disarmed, as the U.N. had initially planned. Lack of discipline in the Congolese Army remained, like Katanga, a major unsolved problem.

As reported in *The New York Times*, the outbreaks in Luluabourg, Albertville, and Kindu, which the U.N. had been unable to eliminate, "cast doubt on whether the United Nations, assisting the Central government, can make the government work. The doubt involves the United Nations' ability to reduce tribal tensions and fears and bring the nation under the real authority of the Central government and make the nation's economy viable."[120] The United Nations certainly failed to provide a thoroughgoing solution to disorder in the Congo, as required by its mandate. But in Albertville and Luluabourg, for example, the riots could have been much worse without the restraining influence of the U.N. officers upon the troops and their commanders. The U.N. also provided protective shelter to the victims of assaults and facilitated the evacuation of those who wished to leave.[121]

Despite their differences of ideology and interregional politics, most African states were still concerned about the Katanga secession. Ethiopia, Nigeria, and the Sudan requested a meeting of the Security Council to consider it, as "caused by the lawless acts of mercenaries." Ceylon, Liberia, and the U.A.R. had a draft resolution (eventually adopted after some amendment) ready for the resultant Council session of November 13. Ethiopia's call for the U.N. to "impound, evict and deport the mercenaries by force" was echoed by Bomboko of the Congo, who told the Council that the U.N. had a duty to remove the mercenaries.[122]

Belgium was bitterly attacked by Afro-Asians then and at the next session (November 15), when, however, Paul-Henri Spaak defended the propriety of his nation's current attitude. He suggested a U.N.–Katanga agreement—modeled on that made with the Kasavubu Administration on April 17—to provide a legal and administrative instrument to facilitate the departure of Belgian and other unwelcome foreigners. He also severely criticized O'Brien's actions and anti-Belgian allegations of the previous September.[123] This represented the extreme of censure of the August–September operation delivered at the Security Council by any of those powers that had been complaining of its gross impropriety, illegality, and imprudence.

We may here notice how the Western practice usually does not require U.N. officials to answer for their actions before the Council or Assembly, but uses day-to-day diplomatic pressure in trying to restrain or remove them. Although this practice complements that of Secretariat diplomacy so highly developed by Hammarskjöld, it does not promote the *institutionalizing* of U.N. activities—a process that might help solve some of the problems of a United Nations force, which seems to need both an enlarged and more specific code of operations and a better defined chain of command and answerability.

At the session of November 16, sharp differences appeared between the American and the British attitudes to U.N. intervention in the Congo and in general. Adlai Stevenson, outspokenly against Katangan independence, tried also to implicate the Lumumbist province of Orientale in secessionism, called for action against the mercenaries, for retraining of the ANC, and for supplying Léopoldville with a small air force. (This aspect of the debate will be discussed at length below.) Sir Patrick Dean pleaded instead for "pacification and conciliation," pointing to the recent massacres in Kivu and elsewhere as somehow demonstrating the "dangers of encouraging force"—implicitly, a force employed by the U.N. and the Central Government.[124] Next day, Sir Patrick further opposed the search for a "military solution" to the Congo problem, saying: "Were the UN empowered to act in this way, we would not only be weakening the effect of the Charter, but we would be creating a very dangerous precedent indeed for the future. There would be no end to the responsibilities which this international Organization would be undertaking." It would find itself, he continued, "at the beck and call" of any state wishing to suppress a dissident minority. The Congo experience, especially the unfortunate events of August 28 and September 13, showed that there was no real "military solution," which at best could only patch up matters, leaving powerful forces of discontent to erupt after military force had been withdrawn.[125]

This was notable as one rare instance of a senior and responsible power's expressing to the U.N.'s supreme body a concern for the precedents that the Organization might be setting itself. Senior members, though usually more cautious in drafting their resolutions than are the enthusiastic and inexperienced newer members, have not throughout the Congo affair seemed to look much farther than have the Afro-Asians beyond considerations of short-run political advantage. In the event, even Great Britain's concern was not great enough to prompt it to use the veto against those clauses of the Three-Power resolution that the United States supported, even though they demanded the very kind of "military solution" that Sir Patrick Dean had deplored.

Nevertheless, in criticizing the resolution, Sir Patrick went on to object not only—as Stevenson had—to the resolution's singling out of Katanga but also to Operative Paragraph 4 of the resolution. In its final and hardly altered form, that paragraph was adopted with the United States' favoring vote and despite British and French abstention:

> 4. *Authorizes* the Secretary-General to take vigorous action, including the use of requisite measure of force, if necessary, for the immediate apprehension, detention pending legal action and/or deportation of all foreign military and para-military personnel and political advisers not under the United Nations Command, and merce-

naries as laid down in paragraph A-2 of the Security Council resolution of 21 February 1961. . . .[126]

(The paragraph's provisions answered neatly to an "Ordinance No. 83" proclaimed by President Kasavubu on November 13, explicitly to supplement that Ordinance No. 70 that licensed the U.N.'s action against mercenaries of August 28. The new ordinance declared: "All non-Congolese officers and mercenaries serving in the Katangese forces who have not entered into a contract with the Central Government of the Republic of the Congo shall also be liable to the penalties of imprisonment. . . ."[127] The terms of imprisonment were those of the Penal Code of the Congo of January 30, 1940.)

Sir Patrick complained that Paragraph 4 was "loosely and widely drafted" and predicted that it would call forth Katangan resistance. One wonders, since on both counts he was proved correct, why the United Kingdom took no more conclusive action to oppose this draft on the Security Council.[128] It is fatuous of the British Government to inhibit its representatives from using in U.N. bodies the remedies to which the Charter entitles them, and then to have its ministers denigrate the Organization—as they did for several months afterwards—because, in their view, the General Assembly has been swamped by inexperienced powers who do not know how to draft a resolution or when to stop.

Sir Patrick found himself on November 21 no less opposed to two of the amendments[129] that the United States had proposed to the Three-Power resolution. He objected in the one case because it did not remove the objectionable reference to "use of force," and in the other case because it proposed to authorize the Secretary-General to "remove or prevent the use for military purposes" of aircraft and other weapons of war—which, he thought, would also provoke the Katangese. Yet he announced that if all the U.S. amendments were adopted (in the event, some were not), he would vote for the amended resolution.[130].

In practice, then, the United Kingdom fell in behind the United States, which was very willing to see Tshombe brought to heel, provided the resolution, sufficiently "broadened and strengthened,"

would also oppose "secession" of Orientale and Kivu and, if necessary, empower action against the pro-Communist movement (as
Washington regarded it) of Lumumbists in Stanleyville. Mr.
Stevenson feared that "the Soviet threat of a veto" might paralyze
operations in the Congo.[131]

The U.S.S.R. did indeed veto the U.S. amendment that was presumably directed at Gizenga and at threatened Soviet-bloc assistance to him, and that denounced military action against the Central Government. Yet the Congolese elements that Washington
supported were—despite Mr. Stevenson's fears—so little paralyzed
that in the New Year, with U.N. connivance, they brought about
Gizenga's defeat. We contend below that the Acting Secretary-
General—by instructing U.N. forces to undertake in January, 1962,
a joint operation against the Orientale gendarmerie who were supporting Gizenga—disregarded the Security Council's having rejected at this meeting of November, 1961, the U.S. amendments
that would have mandated a U.N. action against the Orientale "secession" that Gizenga was alleged to be inspiring. Thus in 1962, U
Thant seems to have been more influenced by Washington's and
Léopoldville's mistrust of Gizenga than by the Security Council's
expressed intentions.

Similarly, in December, 1961, deferring to British, French, and
other Western opinion, he apparently decided to authorize
"limited" action against Katanga's gendarmerie and mercenaries,
without availing himself of the additional military and political
powers that the Security Council had given to UNOC by the resolution of November 24. Paragraph 4 of that resolution, as we shall
see, was not invoked to justify the successful December action of
the UNF—"the second Battle of Katanga"—though its adoption
did impassion Tshombe and the mercenaries and thus indirectly
assisted the latter's schemes for renewing warfare in Katanga. If
that paragraph was meant to provide the "teeth" for the U.N. that
Afro-Asian powers were demanding, then the Acting Secretary-
General and his officials must have come to think within a fortnight
that no new teeth were really needed; for the legal justification of
the December action was found by the Secretariat in previous resolutions of the Council and the Assembly.

The November meeting of the Security Council thus seems to

have become a bewildering tangle of cross-purposes and misjudgments. The Afro-Asians who had convened it and who furnished the resolution it finally adopted had evidently believed that UNOC's mandate to deal with mercenaries needed further strengthening; and they clearly recognized that before November, 1961, there had been at the very most a merely implicit mandate to end Katanga's secession. Britain feared the consequences both of a further empowering of UNF to use force and of UNOC's receiving a mandate to conduct a patently political intervention. The United States feared rather that the new force and the new intervention would be pointed away from the most important—i.e., the Gizengist—target. Yet in January, 1962, Gizenga was brought down with U.N. assistance furnished under pre-November mandates. And in December, 1961, the successful military action by UNF that so much reduced Tshombe's pretensions was—after the event—also justified, not by the November resolutions, but by the UNF's right of self-defense.

The Council's confused debates thus issued on November 24 in a resolution that was certainly ill-drafted and wordy, probably *ultra vires* of the Charter, and possibly superfluous for the U.N.'s actions of the following months. But against its being superfluous stands our contention that the December action in Katanga was pushed beyond the UNF's established right of self-defense and beyond the limits of non-intervention and impartiality as imposed by the resolution of August 6, 1960. Moreover, some further resolution or declaration by the Security Council does seem to have been required in order to nerve the Secretariat and UNOC to reformulate their policy toward Katanga so that diplomatic pressure, exercised in tempo with circumstances of military tension or war, might reconcile Tshombe with the Central Government.

After the three powers' amended resolution had been adopted on November 24, that kind of policy was adumbrated by the Acting Secretary-General. In this, his first statement to the Security Council, U Thant declared his resolve to implement "with determination and vigor" Paragraphs 4 and 5 (the latter requests him to take measures preventing "the entry or return of such elements"—i.e., undesirable aliens—"under whatever guise and also of arms, equipment or other material in support of such activities") and openly endorsed U.N. intervention against secession and in support of the Central Government. "Everything possible," he declared, "must be done to avert civil war, even by the employment of force, should this prove necessary as a last resort. This I believe necessarily implies a sympathetic attitude on the part of UNOC toward the efforts of the Government to suppress all armed activities against the Central government, and all secessionist activities . . . ."[132]

Thus was buried the "nonintervening" policy of Dag Hammarskjöld, and with it, perhaps, his scruples about compliance with the Charter. For though Paragraphs 4 and 5 of the resolution look much like "enforcement measures," and though Paragraphs 1 and 8[133] pronounced upon Congolese law in a manner that all varieties of international opinion had found improper during 1960 and 1961, yet the Security Council in adopting them did not invoke Articles 39, 41, and 42. U Thant's remarks were particularly significant in that they construed implementation of the anti-civil-war, use-of-force resolution of February 21 as "necessarily implying" (the most powerful of logical relations) ONUC's being sympathetic toward suppression of "all secessionist activities." Does this support establishment of a precedent for U.N. military action, under the Security Council but without invocation of the "enforcement" articles, in aid of *de jure* governments bothered by possibly peaceable secessionists? It certainly foreshadowed the U.N.'s later justification of military action to "prevent civil war." And it goes to confirm the view—much put about by the American press in December—that the Acting Secretary-General was bent upon "victory" for the UNF in the second battle of Katanga.

He now had a mandate—explicit, and thus going beyond the mere implications of previous resolutions—to help end Tshombe's secessionist activities. He had not, on the other hand, been given by the resolution of November 24 any license—let alone any mandate—to use the UNF to end Katanga's secession by military action. Paragraph 8 was certainly peremptory, "*demanding*" the cessation forthwith of secessionist activities. This Tshombe had brought on himself by a telegram that even M. Spaak, who had been pleading for a conciliatory approach to the Katangese, pronounced "bad" and apt to make negotiations with Tshombe impossible.[134] The telegram referred to Katanga as "a sovereign and independent nation," offered to negotiate "an economic, customs, monetary and military union" between it and the Central Government, and invoked the principles of the Charter. In a later telegram Tshombe asked the Council's help "to halt the invasion of Katanga."[135]

In Katanga, the situation after the September fiasco had steadily deteriorated. As we have seen, there were repeated breaches of the cease-fire. The Katangese authorities, it was said, ceased entirely to hand over mercenaries to the United Nations for evacuation.[136] The day after the Security Council had passed its resolution, Tshombe told a large crowd in Elisabethville that "The Léopoldville government . . . will ask for U.N. aid in settling the Katanga situation and, under paragraphs 7 and 8 of the resolution adopted the day before yesterday in New York, U Thant will launch a war on our territory. The text is vague enough to allow any interpretation." Tshombe then called for a war of resistance: "Not one road must remain passable, *not one U.N. mercenary must feel himself safe in any place whatever.*" The speech was frequently rebroadcast.[137]

George Ivan Smith, Officer-in-Charge of UNOC, commented by a letter of November 29, saying that such an inflammatory speech violated Article 8 of the cease-fire agreement (thus presupposing the latter to be still in force). Moreover, he interpreted the new Security Council resolution as merely confirming previous ones, so as to "make explicit some of the implications of those resolutions, particularly as regards use of force for apprehension" of mercenaries and other undesirable aliens. But the letter provides no evidence that its writers knew of any plan to make those explications the ground for a UNF military initiative against Tshombe's regime or the Katanga gendarmerie. He continued: "the resolution does not authorize an Organization whose principal purposes are the maintenance of international peace and security to start a war against anybody." But, fearing that Tshombe's alarm at the terms of the resolution might—as it did—motivate him to give way to the "Ultra" mercenaries, who were themselves threatened and spoiling for a battle, he warned Tshombe against being "so intemperate as to unleash hostilities against which ONUC would be obliged to exercise its right of self-defense"—thus foreshadowing the justification that he and Brian Urquhart (O'Brien's successor in Elisabethville) were to offer for UNF's assault on the roadblock on Decem-

ber 5.[138] (Considering that those two U.N. officials had been beaten
up by Katangese gendarmerie on the night before its dispatch,[139]
this letter maintains a remarkably moderate tone.) In fact, the
situation at Elisabethville may have already deteriorated too far
for Tshombe to do much about it. Effective control of the gendarmerie seems to have passed from Tshombe and his ministers
to Colonel Faulques and other mercenary leaders. On December 1,
after a press conference at which he claimed to have been merely
re-establishing the truth about those details of the resolution of
November 24, "which embodied a declaration of war," Tshombe
left the country for Brazzaville and later for Paris, handing over to
Kimba, the "Minister for Foreign Affairs."[140]

Several days of sporadic violence followed in Elisabethville. By
December 3, it was apparent that further numbers of gendarmerie
were returning to the city in violation of the cease-fire and were
reinforcing two strategically placed roadblocks—in the traffic tun-
nel and on the main route to the airport. On December 4, the U.N.
reported that to date there were fourteen U.N. personnel missing.[141]
By that time not only was the U.N. reduced to impotence and subject to violent attacks but its very presence in Katanga was threatened. Kimba, passionately alarmed by the story that eighteen U.N.
planes were proposing to take off from Léopoldville, was informed
by Ivan Smith that they were probably being used for the "planned
rotation of U.N. troops" that was imminent.[142] (United Nations
sources later suggested that the mercenaries were planning to strike
when the UNF was known to be weakest—i.e., at the time of that
"rotation." In the event, UNF was able to keep at Elisabethville
both the contingent about to go on leave and that replacing it.)

The Acting Secretary-General was officially reported as sending
two teletype messages of his instructions to his representatives:

> In the first conversation [of December 3], U Thant asked his repre-
> sentatives 'to act vigorously to re-establish law and order and protect
> life and property in Katanga,' in line with the resolution adopted by
> the Security Council on November 24. In the second conversation
> [of December 5], he said he must insist on complete freedom of
> movement for United Nations personnel and ordered the UN Com-
> mand to take necessary action.[143]

This would suggest no objective for the UNF operation beyond measures for "self-defense." But on December 5, Brian Urquhart told reporters that "we must now carry out the terms of the mandate," which suggests that at least the forcible expulsion of mercenaries was under consideration.[144]

On December 4, gendarmerie continued to reinforce the roadblock. Between ONUC headquarters and the airport, Kimba (who, with Munongo, was apparently trying to leave for Jadotville) undertook to have it removed. The next day, December 5, it was still there; gendarmerie were encircling the airport; a Katangese bombing plane was seen. At midday, Brigadier Raja of the UNOC forces was therefore asked to deal with the roadblock situation.

VIII

The Second Action at Elisabethville
and Its Aftermath

I F THE SEPTEMBER operation was regarded as a U.N. defeat, then with equal justification the December operation could be called a U.N. victory. But if we are to determine whether it succeeded as a peace-keeping enterprise, we must examine the operation in detail; for a military triumph may conceal changes subversive of a peace-preserving organization.

On the afternoon of December 5, 1961, the Katangese and U.N. forces clashed once again on the outskirts of Elisabethville and around military installations elsewhere in Katanga.[1] The immediate occasion, as we have seen, was the setting-up of roadblocks by the Katangese gendarmerie, meant to cut off the U.N. detachments from the airport and from each other. The cease-fire agreement had prescribed that "no movement of the troops to reinforce a garrison or position shall be allowed."[2] According to United Nations sources these moves were part of a master plan drawn up by the foreign officers to "strangle" the UNF in and around Elisabethville.[3] The United Nations obtained evidence of a plan for a full-scale attack on the U.N. forces, drawn up by the mercenaries' leader, Colonel Faulques, but divulged by a defecting associate: The plan was to create panic and uproar by killings and by the taking of U.N. hostages who would be valuable in negotiation, and then to separate and isolate the various UNF units in and around Elisabethville by erection of roadblocks that would prevent both intercommunication and reinforcement from the airport, thus enabling the mercenaries to eliminate the UNF units one by one.

This second U.N. action was in no danger of cancellation. The Acting Secretary-General had drawn up a new plan of approach to the whole Congo operation[4] and his aversion to Tshombe and the mercenaries was obvious. The fact that UNF soldiers had been placed in situations where they were being attacked and could not defend themselves had been causing concern among the states that had supplied troops to the world force, particularly India.[5] Withdrawal of their contingents would spell the end of the U.N. operation in the Congo.

The second Katanga operation was fought by the United Nations to a successful conclusion. Its first and most orthodoxly military action, the assault by Brigadier Raja's Gurkhas on the airport roadblock, was completed in half an hour with one U.N. officer killed and four men wounded, against at least forty major casualties on the other side—a result typical of the whole operation.[6] After its first few days, the UNF managed to clear its lines of communication to the airport and around Elisabethville.[7] On the tenth, the Commander-in-Chief of the United Nations Congo Force, General McKeown, appeared confident that in a matter of days the U.N. would restore law and order in Katanga and be in a position to remove the foreign officers and mercenaries.[8] Air-strikes, usually for purposes of interdiction, made an important contribution to the U.N. victory;[9] generally, these avoided the city, to preserve civilian lives; but one of them, against the post office of Elisabethville on the morning of December 9, caused international controversy though there were no casualties.[10]

Airlifting of reinforcements for the U.N. troops in Elisabethville was completed on December 14,[11] and, in the offensive action fought between December 14–18, the U.N. forces drove the Katangese authorities out of the capital and captured the main base of the Katangese troops, Camp Massart, while Tshombe, who had returned to Elisabethville late in the battle, fled to Kipushi.[12] When, on the night of December 18, the fighting was halted,[13] only the Elisabethville radio station, the Union Minière building (captured on the morning of the nineteenth), and Tshombe's residence remained to be captured.[14]

In many respects the December action in Katanga provided interesting contrasts to the September operation. Different circumstances surrounded the two engagements. In December, tensions built up by close proximity to two hostile armies, and also strategic considerations involved in protecting the U.N. from assaults on its positions, were larger determinants than they had been in September. The Katangese gendarmerie's September resistance was reported to have been an impromptu affair, set off by rumors of U.N. intervention on behalf of the Central Government and by the European officers' antagonism to the mass evacuation of non-Congolese elements from Katanga, as required by the mandate; and it is difficult to say who initiated hostilities.

For this difference there is an illuminating explanation. As in September, the outbreak of the fighting immediately provoked an outcry from some governments and newspapers of Western Europe against the use of force by the United Nations. In order to justify the operation and defend it from its critics, the Acting Secretary-General, U Thant, fell back on the one undisputed right of the U.N. troops to employ force, the right of self-defense. In Katanga, this was no mere pretext. However, U Thant went out of his way to deny that the action was intended to implement the mandate or had in view political ends of any sort. He told the world on the seventh[15] and again on the tenth of December that he had ordered the action in Katanga to attain the "limited objectives" of self-defense, freedom of movement and security of U.N. personnel, and to ensure that "we shall be able to go ahead with the implementation of the Security Council . . . resolutions . . . especially of November 24, 1961" (notice the future tense).[16] Such a declaration of aim should have quieted the opposition of the British, whose representative at the United Nations Security Council meeting had said: "There are some circumstances in which force by the United Nations is indispensable—for example, in self-defense . . ."[17] However, U Thant's interpretation, pacifying as it was to the British, carried with it certain, probably unintended, implications for future uses of the world force.

The scale of the operation in December was quite considerable. It involved at its peak, 6,000 U.N. soldiers,[18] as compared with 1,400 in September,[19] and offensive weapons such as aircraft,[20] which were banned in September. It further involved resort to offensive tactics. In December, the U.N. ground forces were no longer under orders, as in September, to shoot only in self-defense.[21] On December 14, when the arrival of reinforcements for the U.N. had been completed, it was reported that "thereafter ONUC could take a more active role in securing freedom of movement, instead of staying within its positions."[22]

The operation, unlike that in September, was intended to proceed, as explained by U Thant at the outset, to a military victory.[23] According to influential newspapers, the September defeat had diminished the prestige of the U.N. and had adversely affected its chances of implementing the mandate. It was now suggested that the reverse might follow from victory and that "such a triumph would fortify the case for an enlarged role for the U.N. as a genuine international police force."[24]

As a result, military considerations carried much more weight in the decisions of the U.N. Command than they had in September. The case of the strafing attack on Camp Massart illustrates this development: Brigadier Raja thought that the UNF should attack it, as being the stronghold of the Katangese Army in the Elisabethville area and a center for mortar fire against U.N. troops.[25] He was alleged to have been overruled by his civilian superiors on political grounds when he had proposed this in September. Now, the report ran, "the brigadier is understood to have been given a free hand to deal with Katangese troops as he sees fit from a purely military viewpoint."[26] So it was no longer the rule that all military tactics must be defensive. This had important consequences, for a defensive campaign or operation is quite a different matter from defensive tactics. Most wars are allegedly fought in self-defense. To determine whether tactics are defensive can be made to seem a relatively simple matter. One tries to fix responsibility for the firing of the first shot. That may be difficult or impossible at times but it is still a matter of discovering the facts. A definition of a defensive operation is much more difficult because it depends on the interpretation of known facts, and there is wide room for disagreement. The U.N. may thus expose itself to charges of aggression when it is claiming to be acting merely in self-defense. About the December operation, for example, Senator Dodd (Dem.) of Connecticut told a news conference on December 19 that the U.N. had engaged in "naked aggression" in Katanga.[27]

By thus committing the U.N. forces to fighting for no other avowed military object than victory in a defensive campaign, U

Thant indicated a new way in which military force might in future be used by the United Nations. The new interpretation would give the Secretary-General much wider discretion as to when to use force and would take some of the decision-making out of the hands of the Security Council, because it is impossible to define before-hand the precise circumstances under which force must be used even for self-defense. This would in turn make the consequences of U.N. intervention less predictable.

If the mandate under which an operation with United Nations troops is undertaken should cease to be the sole guide as to when force on a major scale may be used, then a series of actions *described* as defensive—but perhaps unwarranted or unnecessary—may lead to useless breaches of the peace by an organization committed to act as peace-keeper. Indeed, there may be a risk that, under the guise of self-defense, the Secretary-General or the U.N. Command may misuse force in a way not intended by the Security Council or im-plied in its mandate.

It should be remembered, however, that when U Thant said that the action in Katanga was purely defensive, he was trying to disarm opposition to the use of force by the United Nations and therefore to limit rather than widen the scope of the action. Both the Acting Secretary-General and the U.N. representatives in Elisabethville were saved by the cocksure aggression of the mercenary leaders from the desperate choice of whether and when to take a military initia-tive in order to implement Paragraph 4 of the November 24 resolu-tion.[28]

By that resolution, the Security Council clearly did not authorize the Secretary-General to use military means for solving the Congo's political problems. Paragraph 4 was the only one that explicitly dealt with the use of force, and this referred only to the removal of mercenaries. An implicit and subsidiary political aim, however, might be discerned if Paragraph 4 were to be read in conjunction with Paragraphs 1 and 8, in which the Security Council

1. *Strongly deprecates* the secessionist activities illegally carried out by the provincial administration of Katanga, with the aid of external resources and manned by foreign mercenaries. . . .

8. *Declares* that all secessionist activities against the Republic of the Congo are contrary to the *loi fondamentale* and Security Council

decisions and specifically *demands* that such activities which are now taking place in Katanga shall cease forthwith.

Apart from the fact that Britain and France did not—on the ground that it was contrary to the Charter and therefore illegal—decide to veto the resolution, several things should be noted. First of all, by making a rule on Katanga's secession, Paragraphs 1 and 8 of the November resolution had taken the U.N. some further distance since February 21 toward intruding in matters of domestic concern. In conjunction with Paragraph 4, they may be construed as having set a precedent for use of force in such matters. But an important distinction must still be made. The collapse of Tshombe's regime and the end of Katanga's secession owing to forcible removal of foreign officers were only indirect results, though—to the sponsors of the November resolution—anticipated and desired ones. Thus Mr. Loufti of the U.A.R. in the Council debate of November 15 explained that .Paragraph 4 was intended "to assist in putting an end to the secession."[29] Even so, this was not the same as application of military coercion to the Tshombe regime directly and specifically in order to end the secession. Extraction of foreign elements from a country where they are considered to constitute a threat to international peace cannot be equated, whatever the indirect consequences, with actual intervention by force between indigenous groups claiming power and authority. The substance of this argument was admitted in a London *Times* editorial that expressed British anxieties about possible consequences of the new mandate:

> The Security Council, in endorsing the Afro-Asian resolution that all secessionist activities in Katanga must cease forthwith, has not on paper widened the existing mandate to the Secretary-General to expel foreign military and political personnel. But the resolution adds a menacing note of urgency, and it points directly at President Tshombe.[30]

When the fighting started, Britain immediately expressed her reservations. Mr. Edward Heath, on December 6, said in the House of Commons on behalf of the government that Britain would oppose the U.N.'s using armed force except in self-defense and cautioned against an attempt to proceed to a political solution for Katanga.[31]

Similar objections were soon to be heard from France, Belgium, Portugal, the Rhodesian Federation, and South Africa.[32] It was said that the devotion with which this group of states applied principles of pacifism in the United Nations corresponded in some measures to their interests:

> Britain, France, Belgium, Portugal and other states which oppose action against Katanga are partly influenced by political and economic commitments in the area. The Congo's neighbor states include Britain's Rhodesian Federation, the former French Congo, Belgian Ruanda Urundi and Portuguese Angola—all of which fear a strong, united Congo. In addition, there is fear of a precedent for U.N. military intervention in colonial and former colonial areas.[33]

Whatever the truth of these allegations, it is the nature of the objections, and not the motives of the powers who advanced them against the United Nations possibly using force for political ends, that need concern us here. In general, it can safely be assumed that any police action undertaken by the United Nations would run into the vested interest of some power; and from the U.N.'s point of view the type of vested interest that it encounters is or should be irrelevant.

We shall now examine some of the consequences of U Thant's explanation that the U.N. military operations in Katanga would be limited to self-defense. In the beginning his efforts proved successful in placating the British. Although France continued adamant in her opposition, Britain at first contributed money and material to the Katanga operation.[34] Nevertheless, she retained her suspicions, and her declarations in support of the U.N. were at most lukewarm. But though the new interpretation served thus to placate opposition to the U.N. operation, its pitfalls became apparent. What the British meant by "imposing a settlement" was not always clearly defined in the various statements by members of the government, but perhaps *The Times* came close to epitomizing their views and the fears evoked by the character of the operation:

> In Katanga, it is now clear, it is impossible to disentangle expulsion of mercenaries and Congolese political issues. To expel the mercenaries means overthrowing Mr. Tshombe and it is hard not to believe that the United Nations had come to feel that the best way to expel

them was to crush Mr. Tshombe's forces by military action—however provoked in "self-defence."[35]

So it was now thought by Britain and other critics of the U.N. that U Thant might be employing the method of sovereign states: crushing the opposition first and then seeking a settlement—which was a possible but a strictly illegal way of carrying out the mandate.

One possible reason why Britain did not continue to insist upon her objections against the Katanga operation may have been her wish to maintain a common front with the United States, which supported the operation. According to the London *Times*: "The British Government are convinced that there has to be a move to a new cease-fire, but are nonplussed by the difficulty of mediating as well as by the wholehearted American backing for the United Nations military action."[36] The occasion for a shift in British policy occurred when the U.N. pressed an earlier request for twenty-four 1,000-pound bombs to be used in Katanga. The decision of the British Government to supply the bombs, announced by the Foreign Office on December 8,[37] touched off what was described as "the toughest party rebellion since the heyday of the Suez group" in the Tory ranks.[38]

Although the offer was hedged with conditions meant to ensure that the bombs were to be used against aircraft only and not against persons, thus ensuring their use for defensive purposes,[39] the government suspended the delivery on December 11[40] in order to placate the opposition of its own backbenchers.[41] In this way it averted a threatened rebellion from about fifty Conservatives—one group of whom, led by Sir Peter Agnew, tabled a motion asking for a cease-fire, to which was added an amendment, from another group composed of Suez rebels led by Lord Hinchinbrooke, turning the original motion into one of censure of the government.[42] Under this pressure the government, on December 12, tabled a motion of confidence calling for an immediate cease-fire in Katanga, thus ending the crisis as far as the British Government was concerned.[43]

On the thirteenth, Britain lodged with the U.N. a formal note requesting an immediate cease-fire.[44] U Thant rejected the British request upon consulting his Advisory Committee,[45] and the fighting went on for another five days. That Britain and her diplomats in the Congo failed to equal their success in September[46] was probably due in large measure to the military and political support given to the U.N. by the United States, whose "involvement in the Congolese events during the last two weeks has been unusually direct and unusually deep."[47] The United States and British governments were reported to disagree sharply over the U.N. operation in Katanga: Britain and France wanted an immediate cease-fire.[48] On the thirteenth—the day the United Kingdom handed in its memorandum—George Ball, the U.S. Under-Secretary of State, declared that the United States did not believe any cease-fire was feasible until the minimum U.N. objectives had been attained.[49]

The extent of U.S. support in securing for the United Nations a military success in Katanga was revealed by Mr. Ball in another statement made in Los Angeles on December 19, 1961, when he said: "The prompt action of the United Nations [was] made possible partly by our diplomatic support, our military airlift and our financial contribution."[50] However, the differences between the British and American approaches should not be exaggerated, for they did not represent utterly opposed schools of thought. The British Government did not wish to carry its opposition to the point of either destroying or leaving the United Nations.

On December 13, Mr. Turton and thirty-one other Conservatives joined Lord Hinchinbrooke and tabled an addition to the government motion, in which they called for the withdrawal of financial support for the U.N. failing a cease-fire.[51] Mr. Macmillan said on the following day that withdrawal of financial support by Britain "would be a bad decision. It might even be a tragic decision if we were to take action which made people think we were abandoning the United Nations at a critical moment merely because we disagreed with a particular operation or a method of a particular operation."[52] On December 18, Lord Home seemed to contradict this statement when he warned that the situation in the Congo could reach a point at which the government would have to withdraw its financial support for the U.N.[53] However, in a later speech, on December 28, he qualified his remarks by adding: "Whatever its faults, the aims of the U.N. are sound and its aspirations true. Britain cannot afford lightly to discard an instrument dedicated to peace which is struggling to put together the elements of peace-keeping machinery, however elementary it may appear."[54] Nor did Britain, in spite of the furore over the bombs and in spite of U Thant's rejection of the British appeal for a cease-fire, boycott the operation in its military aspect. On December 23, it became known that the British Admiralty had been supplying the U.N. with 20 mm. ammunition for Hispano cannon,[55] and on December 31, it was announced that the British had agreed to supply 750 mortar smoke bombs.[56]

Neither Britain nor the United States urged that the operation should be extended to implement the section of the mandate dealing with expulsion of the mercenaries, and both agreed that the United Nations was entitled to use force in self-defense. United States officials emphasized that they based their approval of the operation on the U.N.'s using force in Katanga for self-defense only. This was the substance of the arguments advanced by Lincoln White[57] on behalf of the State Department on December 6, 1961, and by Dean Rusk on December 8.[58] George Ball said on December 21: "The United Nations forces have stuck loyally to the limited aims set for them by Acting Secretary-General U Thant in New York."[59]

The British Government, on the other hand, found this proposition increasingly hard to believe. Mr. Macmillan told the House of Commons he feared that in Katanga the United Nations might be found slipping into a war of conquest and then having to set up an administration.[60] For the Katanga operation's success, a favorable attitude on the United States' part proved indispensable, particularly in view of British reservations.

As a measure of its support in the military field, it may be noted that after the fighting started, the United States donated to the U.N. twenty-one Globemaster transport planes, which solved a vital logistics problem by airlifting thousands of U.N. troops and large amounts of equipment into the fighting zone in Katanga from other parts of the Congo and from overseas.[61] The United States indicated that it would, if required, supply other equipment.[62] The airlift raised threefold the number of United Nations troops in Katanga. *The Observer* reported on December 17 that, by the time the airlift was completed, the 2,000-man Katangese garrison in Elisabethville was outnumbered three to one by the U.N. troops.[63] This should be compared with the 1,400 Indians who were the main attacking troops available to the U.N. in September.

As already pointed out, in the diplomatic and political sphere the U.N. operation received from Washington unswerving support and encouragement. During the fighting the United States kept in close consultation with U Thant,[64] and it assisted at the appropriate moment in bringing the hostilities to an end and in negotiating a settlement between Tshombe and Adoula.

To this end Ambassador Edmund Gullion returned to the Congo on December 7, 1961.[65] The opportunity for negotiating came when, reportedly under pressure from the State Department,[66] Tshombe addressed himself to Kennedy on December 14–15 asking the President to mediate.[67] The White House immediately took appropriate steps. Instructions were issued to Ambassador Gullion to obtain an agreement from Tshombe and Adoula for a meeting between them.[68] The State Department hinted on December 15 that such a meeting was Tshombe's best chance to induce the now victorious U.N. to suspend hostilities in Katanga: "The question of cessation of hostilities is up to the United Nations. But we would hope that once Mr. Tshombe has actually left Elisabethville for an agreed meeting place with Mr. Adoula, fighting could be suspended."[69] To this end the State Department, according to its spokesman, Mr. Lincoln White, was in close touch with U Thant,[70] from whom the United States was understood to have assurances that fighting would cease once Tshombe had left Elisabethville.[71] Thus it was not altogether surprising that when Tshombe had agreed to depart for Ndola on December 18 (he was delayed until the nineteenth), U Thant ordered the fighting to stop.

The initiative in bringing Tshombe and Adoula together seemed to have remained with the Americans. It was Ambassador Gullion, described by the U.S. Embassy in Léopoldville as a "facilitator" but not as a "mediator,"[72] who on December 17 obtained Adoula's agreement to meet Tshombe.[73] The arrangements with Tshombe for his departure to meet Adoula were worked out in Elisabethville by Lewis Hoffacker, the U.S. Consul in Katanga. When Tshombe flew to Ndola, Ambassador Gullion met him there and brought him to Kitona in a U.S. Air Force plane under formal guarantees from the United States for his personal safety.[74]

At the talks at Kitona Base, which lasted all day on December 20 and into the morning hours of the next day, there were present— as well as the entourages of Tshombe and Adoula—diplomatic teams from both the U.N. and the United States.[75] Both teams stayed at Kitona throughout the talks, and on the night of the twentieth helped with advice when negotiations threatened to break down.[76] On December 21, an eight-point declaration was signed by Tshombe, which in effect meant the end of Katanga's secession. It recognized the unity of the Congo, with President Kasavubu as head of state, and the application of the *loi fondamentale* to the whole territory of the republic.[77]

The diplomatic efforts at Kitona promised to end the secession of Katanga and thus to implement on the U.N.'s behalf part of the November 24 resolution. It was claimed that the agreement made there "achieved an important objective toward which the United Nations had been continually directed for many months."[78] Dr. Bunche, in a news conference held at the U.N. headquarters on December 22 on his return from Kitona, emphasized that the fundamental purpose of the U.N. position taken by Hammarskjöld and U Thant had been to bring about a peaceful reconciliation of the differences between the various factions in the Congo.

It is true that reconciliation of the Congolese leaders was part of the U.N. mandate, and it is equally true that the November 24 resolution ordered the "cessation of secessionist activities forthwith." But, as already pointed out, it did not authorize use of force to obtain such a political solution. In the unlikely case that the fighting in Katanga bore no relation to Tshombe's amazing change of heart when he signed the Kitona agreement, it is even less likely that the continued U.N. military pressure, backed as it was by continued American support, had no influence in overcoming his hesitation to keep the agreement.

The foregoing account should have made clear that the United States played a prominent part in the Kitona negotiations. The question is whether the U.N. was in any way compromised by the United States' active participation in U.N. business. We must note that the political settlement between Tshombe and Adoula was in accord with the wishes of the U.S. Administration. It was said that the administration hoped to justify its Congo policy before Congressional investigation through this agreement, which made possible a settlement in the Congo of at least superficial durability "in which there will be no demonstrable proof of world Communist infiltration of the Central Government at Léopoldville."[79] We may compare American "facilitation" in December with U.K. "mediation" in September, 1961: what the United States helped to achieve in the Kitona agreement clearly implemented part of the November 24 resolution; Lord Lansdowne's actions in September were taken in the conviction that the UNF operation had exceeded its mandate—and, indeed, the limits of the Charter. The White House and the State Department seemed in December to have a close understanding with U Thant; in September, Hammarskjöld seemed to need little prompting from the United Kingdom toward seeking a cease-fire and a meeting with Tshombe. In December, though the UNF was able to conduct some cleaning-up operations on the nineteenth, the hold-fire arrangements may have prevented it from implementing Paragraph 4 of the November 24 resolution by forcible apprehension and expulsion of the mercenaries; the cease-fire arranged under British auspices after Hammerskjöld's death in September was turned (during negotiations about detailed terms conducted with Irish troops as hostages) into a symbol of U.N. defeat. In September, the British consul gave succor to Tshombe; in December, the U.S. President did not reject Tshombe's appeal for intercession as of no diplomatic standing. Our question becomes whether the U.N. and its servants may ever accept the mediatory assistance of great powers in the implementing of mandates that have been laid upon the Secretary-General (rather than, as in Korea or on other possible occasions, when they have been laid upon some *national* military agent). And to that formulation of the question, the answer seems to be that there is nothing else for it. The U.N. is not as yet a sovereign power: in Congo-like situations the Secretary-General has no authority to accept a surrender, dictate a peace treaty, or take over administration of a defeated state. The UNOC might perhaps have invited the Congolese Central Government to send in troops of occupation and commissioners, such as Davidson-Bocheley in September. But that precedent was an unhappy one, and to follow it in mid-December would have cost many more lives. Nevertheless, as we shall see, UNOC went a

long way in late December and January toward acting as military
agent for the Central Government against Tshombe's regime.

Did President Kennedy's response to Tshombe's approaches, following as it did the British, French, and other expressions of mis-
giving about U.N. military action, improperly influence the decisions of the Acting Secretary-General and his subordinates? To
return, for an answer, to an earlier point in our narrative: On
December 4, *The Hindu Weekly Review* reported that its U.N.
source in the Congo said that India had agreed to delay the rotation
of her troops in the Congo in order to help implement the latest
Security Council resolution on the Congo. The paper's sources said
that normally the process of rotation would involve temporary gaps
and delays. India's decision was therefore very helpful.[80] The same
source said:

> The U.N. Command has received much-needed air reinforcements
> lately but its ground forces number only 15,000. While these may
> be enough for policing the Congo, obviously they are not enough to
> undertake a military action of the nature contemplated under the
> Security Council resolution. Secretary-General U Thant has ap-
> pealed for more troop contributions and it is to be hoped he will get
> them.[81]

Just after hostilities began, *The New York Times* reported that
U Thant was preparing a plan to implement the November resolution: "According to reliable authorities, it provides for a house-to-
house search by United Nations troops for 'mercenaries' who would
be arrested and placed in joint custody of United Nations and
Congolese forces to prevent them from re-entering Katanga service."[82] Furthermore, as we know, the Central Government had
signed an agreement with the U.N. on November 27 that, among
other provisions, enabled the UNOC to hand over for trial to the
Congolese authorities any mercenaries apprehended.[83] As one
might expect, therefore, commentators were to be found suggesting,
after the hold-fire instruction given by the Secretary-General on
December 18, that he had been persuaded against a more thoroughgoing military action. *The New York Times*, for example, suggested that

some of his [U Thant's] subordinates . . . would not have agreed to
a cease-fire until the Katanga forces were crushed and the European
mercenaries in Katanga's service had been captured.

Mr. Thant, however, stopped the fighting before it went that far.
Protests in the United States and Western Europe against the
liquidation of the Katanga Government were rising. A number of delegates feel that Mr. Thant showed a realistic understanding of the
need to reconcile conflicting tendencies within the Organization.[84]

If in fact the U.N., having resorted to force, was sacrificing lives
to achieve something less than the mandate because of the en-
thusiasm expressed by the Western powers for the "limited" character of the operation, then Security Council resolutions appear to
be less determinative and the Secretariat more responsive to pressures from powers acting outside the Council than the Charter warrants. If, on the other hand, mercenaries were by December 17 already scattering into the Katanga countryside, part of the point of
the U.N. operation was disappearing with them. On December 18,
General McKeown, its Commander, stated in Léopoldville on his
return from Elisabethville the day before:

> At this stage it is not possible to forecast accurately when actual hos-
> tilities will be brought to an end. This depends on the degree of re-
> sistance offered by the Gendarmerie and armed civilians. I do not
> envisage that this resistance will be a long one. Consistent with the
> fulfillment of the Security Council's mandates, I would hope that
> the present operation may be ended soon. Our operations in Elisa-
> bethville have been carried on with great restraint in order to pro-
> tect to the fullest extent possible the innocent civilian population.[85]

This strongly suggests that both military and humane considerations would have brought the action to a halt in any event about
the time of the hold-fire order; in which case the Acting Secretary-
General is not to be arraigned for having acceded to improper
pressures.

United States officials were reported to be persuaded that negotiations with Tshombe could be successful only if United Nations
forces maintained their pressure on him.[86] Thus when U Thant
ordered the fighting to stop, the U.N. did not sign a cease-fire
agreement but proclaimed it would hold fire, retaining the right to
retaliate when attacked or fired upon.[87] Tshombe tried to exact a

cease-fire as a condition for going to Kitona, but this was refused by ONUC.[88] When on December 21 the Congolese Information Minister, Joseph Ileo, announced the terms of the Kitona agreement, he pointedly held the U.N. responsible for enforcing Tshombe's promises. He urged the U.N. forces to hold their positions in Katanga until "every minute agreement has been carried out."[89] Two days later, echoing a statement by Adoula, a U.N. spokesman in Elisabethville said that the U.N. would give Tshombe until December 27 to endorse the Kitona agreement.[90] Although it was not made clear what action the U.N. might take if the agreement were not endorsed, *The New York Times* concluded that if "the Kitona accord is rejected the United Nations is expected to take a strong action against Mr. Tshombe and his highest ministers."[91]

It was inferred further by the same source that the U.N. was preparing for such a showdown when it accepted 1,000 Congolese soldiers into its international force[92] and that this had the desired effect on Tshombe. On his return to Elisabethville Tshombe tried to invalidate the Kitona agreement, claiming that it was subject to ratification by the Katanga Government and the Assembly and that he had been pressured into signing it.[93] But in the end he went a long way toward implementing it, and Katangese deputies were sent to the National Parliament in Léopoldville.[94] On February 15, the Katanga Assembly after six weeks' debate approved the end of secession. Some of the more stringent conditions attached to its resolution, particularly those directed against the UN, were modified the next day.[95] At the time of writing, however, the final outcome was still uncertain and there was even talk of renewed fighting.[96]

It has been argued that because the U.N. did not crush Tshombe completely and thus carry its operation to ultimate victory, the December action, in the words of the U.N. Chief Representative in Katanga, Mr. George Ivan Smith, "never was and never could have been anything but defensive."[97] Even if in this event the U.N. was within its rights, a large-scale military engagement must involve some political consequences, whether intended or incidental. There is at least some evidence that under U.N. military pressure Tshombe was induced to negotiate, which was contrary to some provisions of the mandate,[98] and to the Charter.[99] In this way the December action and its results may have indicated how in the future a UNF, while engaging in defensive or peace-keeping operations, may also become an instrument for enforcing political solutions.

About a chief item of the mandate for which the Security Council had authorized use of force by the U.N. in Katanga—the eviction of the mercenaries—the Kitona agreement was vague. In the eight-point declaration, points 7 and 8 were relevant to this problem. By them, the President of the Province of Katanga

7. Agrees to the placing of the Katanga gendarmerie under the authority of the President of the Republic.

8. Pledges himself to ensure respect for the resolutions of the General Assembly, the Security Council, and to facilitate their implementation.[100]

At the close of the Kitona talks, Dr. Bunche estimated there were still from 275 to 300 non-Congolese who could be classed as mercenaries fighting in Katanga.[101] A more conservative estimate of only about a hundred was given by *The New York Times* on January 11, 1962.[102] But the difference in the estimates seems chiefly due to difficulties of accounting—not to evacuation. Only thirty-one persons suspected of belonging to the mercenary class were apprehended by the U.N. forces during the December hostilities. The hard core of this group, the leaders of the military operations against the U.N. in December, were reported by Linner on January 9 to be still at large.[103]

The Russians, in a letter of January 25, 1962, requesting a meeting of the Security Council to consider the Katanga situation, complained:

Despite the Security Council's instructions that vigorous action, including the use of force, if necessary, should be taken to expel all foreign mercenaries, in order to prevent the secession of Katanga from the Republic of the Congo, the United Nations has completely halted military operations, regardless of the fact that the provisions of the Security Council resolution concerning the expulsion of these mercenaries and the elimination of the sources of colonial interference in the internal affairs of the Congo have not been complied with.[104]

The letter then went on to quote a report by Linner later than the one already referred to: "No positive measures have as yet been taken by the Katanga provincial authorities to facilitate the implementation of the relevant clauses in the Security Council resolutions of 21 February and 24 November 1961 . . ."[105] On February 16, *The New York Times* abruptly reported that Tshombe had said that all mercenaries had gone, and "United Nations sources say that as far as they know this is true."[106]

This was contradicted four days later when on February 20 Robert Gardiner, the new U.N. Chief of the Congo operations, reported that efforts to round up remaining mercenaries had slowed down and that Katangese authorities were very slow in providing a list of mercenaries to the two mixed Katanga-U.N. Commissions recently set up.[107]

After the hold-fire of December, 1961, the U.N. had tried to follow up by diplomatic means the advantage conferred by the recent military engagement and to ensure that Tshombe carried out the terms of the Kitona agreement. With regard to the mercenaries, U Thant told the Advisory Council on January 9, 1962, that to continue to apply force in order to carry out the mandate would be unwise both politically and militarily.

He explained that even after the Katangese resistance collapsed, the U.N. forces were tied down in Elisabethville in an effort to eliminate sniping and to restore normal life to the city and that therefore

> With the necessity of thus consolidating itself in Elizabethville which required the retention of major strength in that area, ONUC could not undertake a new operation against mercenaries in such places as Kaminaville, Jadotville, Kolwezi and Kipushi where, according to information, the remaining mercenaries in Katanga were mainly to be found.

Moreover, U Thant argued that had the U.N. persisted with military action in order to pursue the mercenaries, the Kitona talks would not have taken place; and that to resume the fighting now might cause Tshombe to abandon the Kitona declaration just as some of its points were being implemented.[108]

The problem of the mercenaries was to be resolved therefore—according to a U.N. statement in Katanga—"by peaceful means."[109] In this decision, for the time being at least, the U.N. Secretariat was supported not only by the Western powers but also by the Central Government,[110] the Monrovia group of African countries meeting at Lagos, [111] and even by the more radical African powers like Ghana and the U.A.R. Only the Soviet bloc was bent on pressing the Secretariat to use force to carry out this portion of the mandate. At the Security Council meeting called by Russia for this purpose, which convened on January 30, 1962, the motion to adjourn the Council *sine die* without reaching a decision was opposed only by Russia and her satellite, Rumania, while Ghana and the U.A.R. abstained.[112]

Meanwhile, the U.N. made an effort to establish good relations with Tshombe and to normalize life in Elisabethville. An agreement was signed between the U.N. command and the Katangese chief of police after some negotiations, and on December 29, U.N. forces and the Katangese police set out on joint patrols to stamp out the looting.[113] The U.N. reported in early January that in Katanga "the mood is good" and that the Acting Chief U.N. Representative at Elisabethville, Brian Urquhart, had made successful contacts with Tshombe in regard to practical cooperation in Elisabethville[114] and was trying "behind the scenes . . . to make the temporary reconciliation between Mr. Tshombe and Mr. Adoula a lasting one."[115]

In addition to this diplomatic effort, attempts were being made to cut off the sources of foreign political support and military supplies to Tshombe, for it was thought that his opposition could not last without foreign aid. The supplies were believed to come from Rhodesia and from the Union Minière in Katanga itself.[116] Through Rhodesia came munitions and men. From the Union Minière more than $26 million had been paid in 1960 to the Katangese Government, and in 1961 some $52 million in dividends and taxes was expected.[117] With these sums Tshombe could buy weapons and pay mercenaries; and, as we shall see, he had obtained other benefits as well.

At the November Security Council meeting, where the question of arms traffic had at last received the attention it deserved, the

Ethiopian representative, Mr. Gèbre-Egzy, had alleged that Rhodesia was the source of men and materials for the anti-U.N. forces in Katanga.[118] To stop this sort of incursion, the Security Council introduced Operative Paragraphs 5 and 6 into the November 24 resolution, which read:

> 5. *Further requests* the Secretary-General to take all necessary measures to prevent the entry or return of such elements under whatever guise and also of arms, equipment or other material in support of such activities;
> 6. *Requests* all States to refrain from the supply of arms, equipment or other material which could be used for warlike purposes, and to take the necessary measures to prevent their nationals from doing the same, and also to deny transportation and transit facilities for such supplies across their territories, except in accordance with the decisions, policies and purposes of the United Nations.

Although, at the Council meeting of November 17, Sir Patrick Dean had strenuously denied the charges against Rhodesia,[119] these were renewed by U.N. officials during the fighting in December.

On December 16, U.N. sources had claimed that recruits were coming into Katanga from Rhodesia.[120] On December 23 they charged that forty-eight jeeps carrying armed white mercenaries crossed the border into Katanga;[121] and, three days later, that the Dornier aircraft that bombed U.N. forces at Elisabethville airport on the night of December 13–14 had taken off from the airport at Ndola in Northern Rhodesia and was flown by two Rhodesian pilots. Another report said mobile heavy mortars accompanied by thirty Rhodesian experts in mortar fire and gunnery had crossed into Katanga.[122] As late as January 9, Dr. Linner was complaining of the influx of arms and personnel into Katanga and, to illustrate his point, cited the case of thirty-six suspected mercenaries brought by a French aircraft into Rhodesia from Brazzaville on their way to Katanga. Because of protests from the U.N., twenty-seven of these persons, who could not produce transit visas, were turned back to Brazzaville by the authorities of the Federation.[123]

To stop this flow of men and materials into Katanga, U Thant had suggested to the United Kingdom and Portugal, on December 29 and 30 respectively, that U.N. observers be stationed at a few selected airports and roads leading from Rhodesia and Angola into

Katanga, under the provisions of Paragraph 5 of the Security Council resolution of November 24, 1961. But both governments refused,[124] the United Kingdom maintaining that it had no authority to compel Northern Rhodesia to accept such observers.

The Secretary-General had stressed that "This proposal carries no implication at all that the authorities in Angola are giving assistance to secessionist activities in Katanga."[125] He refused, however, to accept the Rhodesian denial of similar charges.[126] He told the Advisory Committee on January 9 that the approach to the British Government had been made "because we finally had some concrete evidence of illicit assistance to Katanga from the Rhodesian side, which we immediately presented to the British Government and which Sir Roy Welensky promptly denied in phraseology that could not be described as gracious."[127] In spite of Sir Roy's indignation and refusal, it seems that diplomatic exchanges alone exercised considerable pressure against the arms traffic from Rhodesia. On January 11, it was reported that Rhodesian authorities had recently set up strict controls of flights to Kipushi[128] on the Katangan border, while on the eighteenth of that month, the British Foreign Office spokesman announced that Britain was considering revoking Rhodesia's visa agreements with certain countries in order to prevent mercenaries from passing into Katanga through the Federation.[129] So once again "quiet diplomacy" was used instead of more direct or forcible measures to implement the mandate.

Negotiations with the Union Minière were likewise conducted behind the scenes, but the mission was undertaken by the United States. Owned as it is by individuals and companies of several different nations, this big concern presents special problems to the United Nations. It was alleged by the Afro-Asians present at the November Security Council meeting that the Union Minière not only supported the Tshombe regime with taxes[130] but also manufactured equipment and provided personnel from among its employees to fight the United Nations. The U.A.R. delegate asserted that

> According to reliable reports, the personnel and the establishments of the *Union Minière* have been carrying out purely military activities. This personnel is said to have taken part in and organized hostile acts against the United Nations, and the factories of the *Union*

Minière are stated to have ensured the supply of munitions. More-over, bombs and munitions have been manufactured and armored vehicles have been constructed there. In brief, the industrial estab-lishments of Kolwezi are said to have been the center of these activi-ties and of the organization of rebellion in Katanga.[131]

Similar accusations against the company were made by Bomboko, the Congo's Foreign Minister,[132] and by Gèbre-Egzy, the Ethiopian representative, who claimed that its activities brought the Union Minière under the resolution of February 21 and that therefore the U.N. Command should "take prompt measures and bring them [the activities] to an end."[133]

At the meeting, Paul-Henri Spaak, Belgium's Foreign Minister, said that the firm denied these charges.[134] He repeated this denial during the December fighting but was violently contradicted by the Secretary-General, who claimed that the Union Minière had placed mercenary troops on its payroll and had "proudly admitted the manufacture of armored cars and of bombs which have been dropped on the airport and [U.N.] headquarters in Elizabeth-ville."[135] United Nations' reports of the fighting referred to the Union Minière installations in Elisabethville as the strongholds of Katangese resistance from which U.N. troops were attacked even after the hold-fire was announced.[136] The U.N. was obliged on the afternoon of December 17 to strafe the Union Minière buildings from which attacks were being made[137] and, as the shooting per-sisted, on the morning of the nineteenth the Ethiopian troops oc-cupied the Union Minière factory in Elisabethville and its slag heap. It was reported: "In so doing they captured a 40 mm. Bofors anti-aircraft gun and later a large quantity of small arms ammuni-tion. It was discovered that there had been two Katangese military camps in the Union Minière area."[138] On December 29, Union Minière and Katanga's "Foreign Minister," Evariste Kimba, again denied charges that the company had been involved in political or military activities against the U.N.;[139] but the U.N. claimed that from time to time even more evidence was coming to light that workshops, rolling stock, communications networks, and experts were put at the disposal of the Katangese troops by the Belgian companies in Katanga, and by Union Minière in particular.[140]

Directly to prevent such enterprises from supporting Tshombe would, of course, have exceeded the U.N.'s authority, even had some of their activities fallen under the anti-civil-war ban of Paragraph A-1 in the resolution of February 21, as suggested by Mr. Gèbre-Egzy. The UNOC did indeed insist, before allowing Union Minière to reopen its plants, upon strictly controlling its operations;[141] but the U.N. could not, for example, itself intervene in the crucial matter of the company's paying taxes only to the Katanga Administration.

The United States therefore undertook the task of persuading the Union Minière directors to change their company's policy toward the Central Government. On January 2, *The New York Times* reported that the company's officials in Brussels had been approached the previous week by (among others) Admiral Alan G. Kirk—president of a U.S. affiliate of the Union Minière—to support the Kitona agreement. Kirk went to Brussels on this mission (which was apparently inspired by the State Department but was described as unofficial) on December 28.[142] Although its outcome was judged in early January to be still uncertain,[143] some progress was registered by February 7, when it was announced that Union Minière was negotiating to shift part of its tax payments to the Central Government by channeling the exports from its mines through Léopoldville rather than through Angola and Rhodesia.[144] Withdrawal of the Union Minière support from Tshombe might have been sufficient to end the secession of Katanga. The United Nations has not been equipped (except when it has resolved upon "enforcement measures") to deal with problems created by the interests of investors from the metropolitan country in an ex-colonial area, however much they may threaten international peace or internal harmony. This issue, like that of the mercenaries and the illegal traffic in armaments, suggests that new legal provisions and general principles in line with Hammarskjöld's summary study of October, 1958, need to be formulated if the U.N. should again be required to deal with such interests, which cannot be effectively called to account by some responsible government.

Responsibility for unrest and intermittent outbreak of violence in the poverty-stricken province of Orientale was usually attributed in the American press to Antoine Gizenga, who held no office in

the provincial administration but did lead the remnant of Lumumbists in Stanleyville. One of two vice-premiers in Adoula's
Government, Gizenga had spent most of the time since his election
in Stanleyville, ignoring frequent summonses from the Central
Government to return to his post.[145] It was feared in the West that
he was planning a secession or attempting a left-wing takeover of
the Central Government, possibly with Soviet assistance, and using
the Katanga issue as a lever.[146]

For the moment, however, Gizenga had very little to further his
alleged aims—a militia of 300 men and the support he could rally in
Stanleyville by anti-government propaganda and agitation.[147] He
was, however, a nuisance; so on January 8 the Chamber of Representatives of the National Parliament voted a resolution requesting
the government to order the Vice-Premier to return to Léopoldville within forty-eight hours, to answer charges of secessionism and
of maintaining a private militia. Gizenga in turn issued an order to
arrest General Lundula, ANC commander in Orientale, and members of the mixed U.N.-Central Government Commission established to investigate the Kindu murders of November 11–12 in
which pro-Gizenga troops were implicated. Officers commanding
the provincial gendarmerie (which had previously ignored both the
ANC and provincial authorities and given its entire allegiance to
Gizenga) refused to enforce the order.[148] The refusal was ascribed
to the U.N.'s alerting its troops in Stanleyville.[149]

When it became obvious that Gizenga would not return within
the specified time limit, the Parliament introduced on January 12
a motion of censure which, if passed, would have lifted Gizenga's
ministerial mandate. Mr. Losala, the President of the Provincial
Government, declared on January 13 his support of the Central
Government and his wish that Mr. Gizenga leave Stanleyville. On
the same day fighting broke out between Gizenga's gendarmes and
the Central Government troops commanded by General Lundula.[150]
The latter had commanded the section of the ANC loyal to Gi-
zenga, but on November 11 he had sworn allegiance to the Central
Government.[151] The General now asked for U.N. assistance against
Gizenga's gendarmes, and his request was endorsed by the Prime
Minister.[152]

The day before the fighting started, a *New York Times* columnist, Arthur Krock, had speculated that "a U.N. refusal to discipline Gizenga for renewed defiance of Léopoldville and his attempted arrest of the U.N. Commission would be consonant with the history of the U.N. resolution of November 24, 1961, that affirmatively excluded Gizenga's secessionist activities from policing."[153] However, the Secretary-General ruled that the U.N. would assist the Central Government under the mandate directing the United Nations to maintain law and order, and under Paragraph A-1 of the February 21 resolution empowering the U.N. to use force to prevent civil war in the Congo. These instructions were conveyed to the U.N. commander in Stanleyville on the evening of January 13.[154]

This ruling broke new ground, although the U.N.'s participation in the Central Government action against Gizenga's forces in Stanleyville may not have had a very startling effect on the future of the Congo. It seems that in the event only one platoon of U.N. forces took part and did not fire a single shot throughout the operation. United Nations activity was confined to assisting with the disarming of the gendarmes, in helping the Central Government troops to maintain law and order in the city, in guard duty over prisoners, and notably (at his own request[155]) in guarding the person of Mr. Gizenga.[156]

The importance of the Secretary-General's ruling resided in its involving the U.N. for the first time in a joint operation with the government against rebels. As U Thant had given the disturbance a political twist by labeling it civil war, the UNOC was not merely cooperating with the government in a police action to maintain law and order.

United Nations policy concerning civil war in the Congo, along with its correlative attitude toward political and other Congolese factions, had been changed by two events: the passing of the February 21 resolution and the expression of views by U Thant at the Security Council meeting on November 24. To recapitulate the three stages: In his report on the implementation of the Council resolution of July 14, 1960, Hammarskjöld had stated that "the United Nations units must not become parties in internal conflicts, that they cannot be used to enforce any specific political solution of pending problems or to influence the political balance decisive to such a solution."[157] It was on the basis of that report that the Se-

curity Council adopted its resolution of August 9, 1960, requiring
that the U.N. in the Congo should not become "a party to or in any
way intervene in or be used to influence the outcome of any internal conflict, constitutional or otherwise."[158] Now, Operative Paragraph A-1 of the February resolution did not directly contradict or
abrogate that restriction upon intervention. But neither did it define *how* the U.N. should apply force to prevent civil war. Whereas
Hammarskjöld seems to have maintained to the end that the use of
force by the U.N. could and should be restricted to prevention of
conflict and not allowed to tilt the balance against any particular
faction, U Thant contended on November 24 (as we have seen
above, p. 128) that the U.N.'s mandate to "avert civil war," by
force if necessary, entailed a "sympathetic attitude" toward the
Central Government's efforts at suppression of secessionist activity.

Evidently, the Acting Secretary-General decided that he could
use the anti-civil-war mandate of February 21 against dissidence in
Orientale. On the other hand, he did not have in reserve against Gizenga the kind of mandate to end secession that the November 24
resolution had given him, should he have needed to invoke it
specifically against Tshombe.

Thus, U Thant's interpretation of UNF's mandate to prevent
civil war was not (at least when he applied it against the Gizengist
gendarmerie in January) indubitably compatible with the provisions of Paragraph 4 of the Security Council resolution of August
9. His ruling in ordering the action in Orientale can be further
called in question by the fact that the U.S. attempt to authorize
U.N. action against Gizenga had been defeated by the Security
Council. On November 16, Mr. Stevenson had outlined to the
Council a three-point program that he wanted incorporated in the
Afro-Asian draft resolution. The program called for the retraining
of the Congolese Army by the United Nations so that it could of
its own accord deal with any rebel movements;[159] the empowering
of the Secretary-General to neutralize weapons coming into the
Congo;[160] and the extension of his powers to deal with Gizenga's
secessionist activities in Orientale.[161] The United States failed to
persuade the Afro-Asian sponsors to incorporate these proposals in
their motion,[162] except for an amendment to Paragraph 8, which it

managed to get adopted. This paragraph in its original form referred only to Katanga, but as finally adopted it reads:

> 8. *Declares* that all secessionist activities against the Republic of the Congo are contrary to the *loi fondamentale* and Security Council decisions and specifically *demands* that such activities which are now taking place in Katanga shall cease forthwith. . . .

(The wording of this paragraph strongly suggests that no action was to be taken by the Acting Secretary-General to end any "secession" —except Katanga's, which was openly proclaimed—until the Security Council had designated it as such. The Congo's spokesman on the Security Council, Mr. Bomboko, had during the November meetings specifically denied that there were in the Congo any other secessions than Katanga's.) So on November 21 the United States presented its proposals as amendments to the draft resolution. The amendment dealing with retraining of the Congolese Army received nine votes but was vetoed by Russia.[163] Likewise the amendment was vetoed[164] that was to make Operative Paragraph 2 of the resolution deprecate "all armed action against United Nations forces and personnel and against the Government of the Republic of the Congo."[165] The amendment that would authorize "the Secretary-General, in consultation with the Government of the Republic of the Congo to neutralize and where necessary to prevent their use for military purposes against the United Nations, the Republic of the Congo, or the civilian population, aircraft and other weapons of war which have entered the Congo contrary to its laws and U.N. resolutions,"[166] failed to gain the necessary seven votes.[167] Although in moving these amendments Stevenson no longer referred to Gizenga as their object, their purpose was obvious from his statements on November 16 and was commented on in the press.[168]

During January 14, 15, and 16, the U.N. troops assisted those of General Lundula in disarming the gendarmerie.[169] This was not the first time that the U.N. had disarmed troops in the Congo: for instance, in Katanga on December 2 and 3, Indian troops at the Elisabethville airport had disarmed Katangese gendarmerie because of their drunken behavior.[170] But this was the first time that *all* military forces on one side were disarmed in a situation construed as civil war.

The U.N. operation in Orientale provided an interesting contrast with the case in Katanga. It is worth noting that in November the request from the Congolese for U.N. assistance in their war against Katanga had been rejected.[171]

The personal fate of Mr. Gizenga, who on January 15, 1962, was deposed from his vice-premiership by a motion of censure adopted in the Congolese Parliament,[172] was a matter of concern to the U.N. In general, by its Charter, the U.N. is committed to uphold human rights. In particular, the recent publication of a U.N. report on the fate of Lumumba[173] gave grounds for fearing repetition of such a crime, with all the material that would provide for Soviet propaganda. As it was, on January 27, the Russians printed a half-page article in *Pravda*, claiming that Lumumba's fate was now plotted for Gizenga.[174]

When U Thant ordered the United Nations troops into action in Orientale, U.N. sources in New York were asked whether the U.N. would help the Congolese troops to arrest Mr. Gizenga. In reply, the U.N. spokesman pointed out that

> even in the action in Katanga, where the Secretary-General's instructions from the Security Council were much more precise, no attempt had been made to arrest the Katangese leader, Moise Tshombe.
>
> In response to a question, a spokesman here emphasized that Mr. Thant's instructions were directed to a peace-keeping function and "not against any individual."[175]

It was Gizenga himself who requested that United Nations troops replace the ANC guard outside his residence.[176] However, it seems possible that in guarding Gizenga the U.N. went beyond the arrangements necessary for his safety. At the request of the president of Orientale Province and of General Lundula, and endorsed by the Congolese Prime Minister, he was flown on a U.N. plane into Léopoldville,[177] where he was put under U.N. protection,[178] officially as a "guest" but actually under heavy guard.[179] When Gizenga requested on January 22 that this U.N. protection be lifted, he did not become a free agent, but, in the words of the U.N. report, the protection "was now left to the Central Government."[180] *The Observer* described the situation thus: "Mr. Gizenga has formally been given U.N. protection at his own request and with the agreement of Mr. Adoula, the Congolese Premier, though 'protective custody' would perhaps be an apter term."[181] It is not clear by what right, if any, the U.N. could have extended "protective custody" on behalf of and with the consent of the host government. It certainly has no right—except when taking the "enforcement measures" never employed in the Congo—to imprison on its own behalf the dissident political leaders of a member state.

There can be little doubt as to what Gizenga's real status had become. His confinement continued, although the Central Government maintained that it was purely for his own safety.[182] He was shifted about from one place to another five times, until on February 8 it became known that he had been transferred to an island on the Congo River.[183]

In justification of its keeping Gizenga under guard, the U.N. could plead Gizenga's own request and its evident duty to protect the inhabitants of the Congo. But having committed itself in Stanleyville to taking charge of him, its understanding with the Central Government and the now-amenable Orientale Government seemed to compel it to transfer him (as it had never done with Lumumba) to the capital, Léopoldville, where he was likely to be charged with offenses and to become the prisoner of the central authorities. A UNF action against the pro-Gizengist gendarmerie could also be justified as a measure preserving law and order, since the gendarmes were beyond the control of their proper administrative authority—the provincial administration—and had thrown out their officers. But the UNF action was made to look suspect as a piece of political intervention by being taken in such close collaboration with the legitimate but "anti-Gizengist" authorities. Although the Acting Secretary-General could cite his mandate in support of assisting the Central Government to restore law and order, the assistance that he rendered in January, 1962, contrasted with the U.N.'s apparently more distant and formal relationships during the Katanga operation of December, 1961, and during earlier actions of Hammarskjöld's regime.

IX

U.N. Forces: Their Limitations and Possibilities

THE LAST UNF OPERATION in Stanleyville brought ONUC full-circle, for it was certainly "providing the Government with . . . military assistance" so that the "national security forces might be able, in the opinion of the Government, to meet fully their tasks"—i.e., implementing its very first mandate of July 14, 1960, though without Hammarskjöld's noninterventionist qualifications.

Eighteen months of U.N. military presence had evidently been insufficient to enable the national security forces to meet their tasks. Part of the reason was that they had not yet been retrained or even brought completely under discipline. During the hiatus in constitutional government between September, 1960, and August, 1961, there had been no real opportunity for UNOC to assist in retraining the ANC. But a more important cause of delay had prevented the integration of Congolese military units as a *national* armed force. This was the political, regional, and tribal conflict, which, after all, had become acute only *after* the first Security Council resolution of July 14, 1960. Now, the meaning of "technical assistance" can be stretched—as that first resolution had stretched it—to cover the "military assistance" of a UNF presence; but it cannot possibly be made to include internal political reconciliation, settlement, and unification. Nor is any such purpose explicit in the U.N. Charter. Indeed, help in promoting internal law and order is the more readily to be regarded as technical assistance, the more one thinks of "law and order" as apolitical.

Secession, when it exceeds the limits of legal protest, is necessarily a violation of constitutional law as well as a political act. Hammarskjöld held that it was probably not proper for the U.N. to seek to

maintain constitutional law; the new Acting Secretary-General has
evidently taken a different view. With it, he also maintains a different attitude toward all secessionist movements in the Congo,
considering them, apparently, to be deplorable as such. Hammarskjöld, in contrast, assumed that the wish to secede was by itself no
crime—though in the case of the Congo and Katanga certainly in-
advisable. He was most anxious to reconcile Tshombe with the
Léopoldville authorities, but by Secretariat diplomacy and not by
any formally mandated action—certainly not by force.

There can be no denying, all the same, that under either secretary-general the whole U.N. enterprise in the Congo depended
upon the success of an act of political therapy: Until the Republic
of the Congo was made politically viable, there could not be the
slightest assurance that foreign intervention—whether by states, by
international movements such as Communism or white extremism,
by business organizations, or by individuals—would not irrupt again
and again. Hammarskjöld's launching of ONUC in July, 1960, was
therefore in the direct line of his duty under Article 99 (to bring to
the Security Council's notice all threats to international security).
But difficulties about the scope of U.N. authority immediately
arose at every turn, since its Charter so narrowly restricts its right
to practice the healing of internal political ills. Afro-Asian powers in
particular have tried throughout the Congo crisis to make the
Charter's concern for "political independence and territorial integrity" serve not only against any kind of foreign intervention but
even more against Katanga's secession. In November, they evidently abandoned that attempt in favor of obtaining a direct disap-
probation by the Security Council, though not to the extent of enjoining the use of force to subdue Tshombe. Was that a violation of
domestic jurisdiction?

Before we attempt to explore that question, we may as well recognize that if the Security Council had indeed adopted a resolution
violating the Charter, possible injured powers or interests would
have had no means of redress—none, at least, that are not available
to any power wishing to resist *valid* enactments of U.N. bodies. The
Security Council cannot itself be made to answer for anything it
can get away with, nor has the possibility of veto by permanent
members made Security Council resolutions evince respect for the

principles of the Charter or of international law. On the contrary, as our account of the Congo operation has shown, the prospect of a Soviet veto of Western-sponsored resolutions has induced the United States and the United Kingdom to leave formulation of Security Council resolutions to the nonpermanent Afro-Asian powers; while fear of seeming to part company with the United States has made the United Kingdom refrain from using its own veto or its own right of proposing amendments in order to avoid, for instance, the more imprudent and legally questionable aspects of the November 24 resolution.

To answer our question whether that resolution violated the "domestic jurisdiction" provisions of Article 2 (para. 7), let us first decide whether the resolution was an "enforcement measure" under Articles 41 and 42, which would therefore override 2 (para. 7). Though the preamble to the resolution specifically referred to all previous Council and Assembly resolutions anent the Congo, and though it reaffirmed under five headings the "policies and purposes of the United Nations with respect to the Congo," none of these referred in any way to Article 41 or 42 or to any measures that might have been taken thereunder. Nor did any of these clauses in the preamble involve Article 39 by "determining the existence of any threat to the peace, breach of the peace, or act of aggression" (where "peace" and "aggression" refer exclusively to relations *between* states). Therefore, there was no "enforcement measure."

Secondly, we must ask whether the parts of the resolution (i.e., Operative Paragraphs 1, 3, and 8) that variously "deprecate," "declare . . . contrary to the *loi fondamentale* and Security Council decisions," and "demand the cessation" of secessionist activities in Katanga, amounted to "intervention in matters which are essentially within the domestic jurisdiction of any state." Clearly, a central government's *counter*-secessionist action, by whatever means, *would* be a matter of domestic jurisdiction. It is also clear that a central government might well be willing to have the U.N. assist it peaceably or forcibly in suppressing secession. Is it proper for the U.N., and in particular for the Security Council, to take any formal cognizance of secessionist activity?

It would be proper if the secession were being supported by the intervention of a foreign *state*—not on account of the secession *per se* but on account of the intervention. In such a case, the Security Council could make a determination under Article 39 that intervention by another state was actually occurring, and then either take enforcement measures under Article 41 or 42 against the intervening state; or, if it preferred those other procedures, alternative to enforcement measures, that are provided for in Article 39, it could take "provisional measures." But the objects of any such U.N. action should be to prevent the foreign intervention and not to suppress secession *per se*.

Now, since no aggression had been determined, or any enforcement measures adopted in this case, the frequent allegations of foreign intervention in support of Katanga's secession could not justify the U.N.'s proceeding against it. (As a matter of fact, no foreign *state* could be said to be "intervening" in Katanga by November, even though a Belgian *company* was assisting Tshombe, and *individual* foreign mercenaries were fighting for him, and arms and men allegedly passing to him through Rhodesia.) We may now consider whether the anti-secession clauses in the November 24 resolution were implicit in the anti-civil-war paragraph of the resolution of February 21 and, if so, whether it would be proper for the U.N., in implementing a mandate for suppression of civil war between secessionist and anti-secessionist forces, to suppress the secessionist party.

No doubt the occurence of civil war can be prevented or at least made less likely by a third party's threatening to intervene with such preponderance of force upon one side that the other side is deterred from offering battle. No doubt, either, that both the Soviet bloc and some of the Afro-Asians wished all along that the U.N. would thus threaten Katanga. But, short of its adopting enforcement measures, the U.N seems to be allowed no such procedures by the Charter. Nor did Paragraph A-1 of the February 21 resolution (see p. 80) enjoin or suggest such a procedure. Yet the December, 1961, operation in Katanga, which was no mere threat but an actual initiation of battle, was justified, without mention of any mandate for the use of force, by the quite different, apposite, and altogether legitimate right of the UNF to defend itself. And the January, 1962, action at Stanleyville, justified principally as an anti-civil-war measure, was, as noticed above, a joint operation with Central Government forces. (We shall not labor the point with reference to the Katanga operation of September, 1961, since it seems to have been a result of a mistake or misappropriation of authority.) In practice then, as well as by the Security Council resolution of November 24, a prime lesson of the Congo operation is that the U.N. has become willing to conduct extremely partisan military operations not so much to prevent as to terminate civil wars. And since the source of war was a secessionist movement, the U.N. almost inevitably chose to intervene on the Central Government's side.

Secession characteristically differs from "popular" revolutionary movements, on whose behalf the U.N., at least since 1961, could be imagined as intervening *against* a central government, especially if that government were white, or "multi-racial," or rightist, and the popular revolution were that of a colored colonial people. Popular revolution aims at taking control of an entire state: Secession is often the resort of a cultural, linguistic, traditionalist, or locally patriotic minority that has no chance or has never wished to dominate or has abandoned hope of dominating the whole nation. Of all forms of "nationalist" insurrection, it should be, therefore, the least aggressive and the most defensible. In fact, the new ex-colonial states consider secessionism the gravest of political dangers: They interpret it as a manifestation of neo-colonialism, and as a threat to their territorial integrity no less acute than foreign invasion. Several of them have been remarkably successful in preventing formal recognition of secessionist movements by other states (compare the cases of the Sumatran and Celebes rebels in Indonesia, the Nagas in India, and, of course, Katanga). In Africa and Southeast Asia, the U.N. may well find itself committed to military measures similar to those of ONUC, in which the issue of secession could again arise. Will the Organization content itself with purely *ad hoc* measures, or will the major powers or the Acting Secretary-General follow Dag Hammarskjöld's lead in trying to devise from precedent, UNF experience, and the philosophy of the Charter a set of principles and policy that could be embodied in agreements with the host states?

The former is much the likelier alternative: even Hammarskjöld failed to persuade either the Security Council or the General Assembly to espouse the principles of his summary study. The most he could do was to arrange that some of its more important provisions were enunciated in the various resolutions, in his own administrative instructions, and in the agreements made between ONUC and the Léopoldville Government. After the later stages of the Congo affair and the much more "interventionist" resolution of November 24, it will be much harder to get consensus upon any principles for operation of a United Nations force. Those of the summary study have been more and more openly repudiated by the Soviet bloc. On the other hand, any new principles enshrining the anti-secessionism of late 1961 would surely displease France and the United Kingdom.

Let us then distinguish two possible new types of principle and two corresponding policies for use of a U.N. paramilitary force in circumstances where no "enforcement measures" have been adopted by the Security Council. The first kind would allow the U.N. to follow a positive *political line,* favoring the government of the host state or perhaps the dominant popular faction in a country that has not yet a satisfactorily established government. These principles might well, for example, include anti-secessionist objectives. They would entail a formal act of recognition by the U.N. that such-and-such a group was to be regarded as the "legitimate government"—perhaps until it was succeeded by another one constitutionally elected. The UNF would then provide "technical assistance" in the establishment of internal security, somewhat after Hammarskjöld's intention, but with the substantial difference that the UNF could be used to further the political objectives of the established government and to suppress all but permitted political opposition to it. (This was what Lumumba wanted and what the Soviet bloc and many of the Afro-Asians thought he should have had.) Even as technical assistance, it would subordinate U.N. instrumentalities much more to the will of a national government than has any former nonmilitary assistance.

A second type of governing principle would give the UNF *internal policing powers.* Something of this sort might have come about in the Congo if in the first few weeks of the operation UNOC had managed to disarm the Force Publique and the provincial gendarmeries or had persuaded them to disarm themselves. An agreement would be required between the U.N. and the host state, by which all armed forces—both what are known as the "armed services" in British and other Western states, and all internal security services—would come for some fixed period (say, a year) under a United Nations Command. No other body within the country would be allowed to bear arms during that period. Some of the force thus constituted would be drawn from the former national forces, while other contingents would be supplied, as in UNOC, by member states. The U.N. Command would have authority to check all incomings and outgoings of persons and goods. It would have an ordinary police force's powers of arrest and detention and would be permitted to serve writs of habeas corpus and obliged to enforce them. If the local judiciary were inadequate in numbers or training, it would be supplemented under a U.N. program independent of the organization of the United Nations force. Open and peaceable political opposition, including secessionist movements, would have legally enforceable rights. In order to avoid constitutional breakdowns like the mutual dismissals of Kasavubu and Lumumba, resort should be available to a court of constitutional appeal, possibly the World Court. The national constitution's procedures for change of government and of parliament would be ensurable by the UNF.

This type of U.N. approach has never of course incurred direct comment. Hammarskjöld would presumably have believed, on the basis of the Suez, Lebanon, and Jordan experiences, that no host state could accept such complete, even though temporary, abrogation of sovereignty—certainly, Lumumba and Kasavubu would have objected, though not perhaps finally. The Soviet bloc, which has habitually supported the maintenance of national sovereignty against supranational attempts to overrule it, might nevertheless assent to the making of a "policing" agreement, provided this suited Soviet policy, and provided it were clearly a treaty arrangement between the U.N. and the host state. (The other, "political" type of arrangement between the U.N. and the host would be of course also a kind of treaty—this surely must be the case where no enforcement measures have been adopted.) France has of recent years approached all such issues with a certain detach-

ment: One can imagine her representatives finding wry amusement
in the prospect of a "policing" agreement between, say, the FLN
and the U.N. The traditions of the United Kingdom, both at
home and in its colonial administration, are very much in the
"policing" spirit, but its Security Council representatives have apparently considered that the U.N. would be ill advised to take on
administrative responsibilities. The United States has not on the
whole expressed such doubts but, as the power likely to bear most
of the financial burden of a policing operation, it may consider that
"negative" kind of approach less satisfactory than one in which a
positive "political" agreement is reached with a reliable central government. This impression is somewhat borne out by the United
States' tentative support of the "strong man" Mobutu and its unequivocal adherence to Adoula.

We are at present considering the merits of two different types
of predetermined or codified principles for UNF action. (Later we
shall consider the merits of more or less *ad hoc* U.N. *action* on
either of these bases, taken without prior codification.) Policing
principles lend themselves much more readily to codification, since
the political kind could be codified only after development of
much more elaborate methods for identifying "legitimate" governments. A "political line" of any sort is necessarily particular and is
oriented to the interests of some power or powers. A policing procedure, being more general, is not necessarily tied to the interests of
specific powers, though it may produce political results that incidentally affect some nations and not others. If, therefore, the U.N.
is to undertake several further policing operations in post-colonial
and other societies from which the forces of law and order have
been withdrawn, some prearranged code of operations—as Hammarskjöld foresaw—would be helpful; and a "nonpolitical" policing
code would be the better variety. There are plenty of likely prospects for policing action—e.g., not only in Africa but also in Southeast Asia, New Guinea (both East and West), and possibly
Arabia and the Indian subcontinent. Even Europe may someday
provide instances. In the Congo itself, as we have seen, the re-
establishment of central and parliamentary government by no
means obviated the need for policing assistance to deal with tribal
and criminal disturbances, let alone political and constitutional

conflict. The new Congolese-U.N. Agreement of August, 1961, seemed designed to transform UNF assistance from a holding of the political ring into a more orthodox police operation. But if that trend is to continue and any sort of codification is to be attempted, the initiative for it will have to come from the Secretariat, which of recent months has seemed to favor a positive political line in the Congo.

The outlook for any codification of the U.N's approach in law and principle to cases calling for major interventionist action is thus rather dim. (This does not apply to codification and improvement of UNF operational directives, with which U.N. officials appear at present to be engaged.) We shall now consider the merits of various uses of a U.N. force without prior codification.

Though the U.N. will very likely have again to provide intranational assistance, the preservation of peace between nations will remain its more important duty—even when the international danger arises, as in the Congo, from a breakdown of internal order. The most acute international dangers in Africa are likely to be intervention escalating into racial war, or racial war between indigenes and white colonists evoking intervention by other "white supremacists" of Africa. As long as these are possible dangers, the Communist powers may try to champion a promising faction among the indigenous anti-colonialists; either directly, as the U.S.S.R. tried to help Lumumba's regime and its successors; or, perhaps at the same time, through Communist parties recruited from the indigenous people or from Africans of neighboring states, and, quite as readily, from the former "imperialists"—for instance, Belgian Communists in the Congo. Only direct intervention by Communist China or by states of the Soviet bloc would constitute, of course, the unquestionable business of the U.N.

The cosmopolitan partisans of white supremacy or autonomy (even the mercenaries of Faulques' stamp) were not, in the Congo, either as ideology-ridden or as well organized as the rightist "International" of Fascists and Nazis of the 1930's; nor, despite Afro-Asian and Soviet allegations, could the non-Belgians in Katanga be proved agents of any Western or white African power. Yet Northern Rhodesian and South African, as well as much Belgian, sympathy was patently with Katanga and might have been more actively so, given different internal circumstances. In future situations, when some kind of racial conflict divides an ex-colonial state, the white-dominated nations of Africa might very well intervene. If so, the Communist powers would almost certainly intervene in opposition. From what neutrals, then, could a United Nations force capable of separating and repelling such interventionists be recruited?

In the Congo, ONUC was got under way quickly enough to cut off at least Russian intervention before it could go far. The re-entry of Belgian forces in July, 1960, moreover, prevented Belgian civilians from resorting at that stage to self-defense on their own account. The first lesson of the Congo is that the Belgians, having prepared so one-sidedly for independence, should have been dissuaded from withdrawing so precipitately and with so little "hand-over" in June, 1960. We say that their preparation was "one-sided" since, though they left a prosperous economy and an educated proletariat (both judged by African standards), they also left a far too large Force Publique with too many weapons and no trained Congolese officers, and a constitution that neglected living traditional distinctions and instead established artificial provinces. Above all, they had failed to create a civil administration staffed by Congolese with tertiary or at least advanced secondary education—a failure that could not have been remedied in less than several years. If, however, Belgium had braved the demands of Lumumba and others for immediate evacuation and had lent authority to her own pre-independence policy of opposing secessions such as Tshombe's and Kalonji's, and above all had left the Force Publique smaller and better-disciplined and effectively officered, there might have been no call for UNF intervention (though, paradoxically, the Communist cause might have done rather better). In other African countries where European settlers seem readier to stay put, it is highly unlikely that 15,000 or 20,000 U.N. troops could deal effectively with them, should they take up arms against an ex-colonial indigenous government.

Former imperial powers, on the other hand, are sometimes able to combat armed insurgence by their European colonists. Against their disadvantages (in Algeria, the partiality of many French servicemen to the *colon* and his cause), we can set the great advantage of their tendency to break up the common front of white-dominated African governments. The latter might secretly encourage mercenaries and volunteers to assist the settlers against a combination of imperial European troops and an indigenous government: They could hardly make open war against the combination—and if they did, the imperial power might then refuse to veto Security Council sanctions against them under Article 41 of the Charter. The bloodiest upheavals in Africa are likely to be racial wars, which a UNF alone would find almost impossible to stop. Responsible hand-over arrangements by a vacating imperialist administration, with guarantees of security to the incoming indigenous administration, seem more likely to avoid bloodshed. A further consideration is that a U.N. intervention is likely to be more effective in breaking a stalemate between ex-imperial and white-colonist forces than in dealing from the start with an ex-imperial power concerned solely, as Belgium seems to have been in the Congo, with liquidating its former position as easily and safely for its white colonists as it can.

This suggests the somewhat unexpected conclusion that a U.N. force may not be, at least in the first instance, the best agent to intervene and preserve peace in an ex-colonial situation: It may be that the former imperial power can sometimes initiate more easily than the U.N. itself the peace-preserving action that is a major part of the U.N.'s *raison d'être*. In the kind of circumstance contemplated, it probably would not be wise to have the imperial power act on behalf of the U.N., as the United States and other powers did in Korea.

Again, the Soviet bloc and some of the Afro-Asians are even less likely to refrain from pressures within the U.N. to exclude former imperial powers from ex-colonial situations than they are to entrust such a situation once more to a noninterventionist UNF action like that which Hammarskjöld initiated in the Congo. But the policies of the United States, France, and the United Kingdom could perhaps be directed to bringing imperial powers to the recognition that their obligations to maintain order end neither with "Independence Day" nor with that on which the U.N. also acknowledges its own responsibilities for an ex-colonial situation.

Of the two types of intranational action conducted directly by the U.N., we have noticed that the positively "political" kind is likely to be opposed as a matter of principle only by Britain and France among the permanent members of the Security Council, and then to no very great effect. As for the United States, its close collaboration from November, 1961, to February, 1962, with positively political actions of the Acting Secretary-General is a sign that in future it may favor such a policy from the beginning of any U.N. operation. If, furthermore, the new line in the Congo produces a modicum of success (say, the adoption of a new federal constitution, a sharing of Union Minière revenues by the Central Government, a major financial settlement between the Congo and Belgium, some retraining of the ANC), American opinion is likely to consider the positive policy, which also has the approval of many Afro-Asians, as vindicated and serviceable as a precedent. Against this acceptability among important U.N. members should be set the considerable difficulties of implementing a mandate based from the beginning on a firm political preference but without invocation of enforcement measures.*

* Since Security Council authorization was not to be sought for U Thant's phased program of "economic sanctions," a second version of which was promulgated by the United Nations on November 29, 1962 (see *The Times* [London], November 30, 1962, p. 9), no enforcement measures could be invoked for its implementation. Indeed, reference to the Security Council might have caused a French veto, and would have seriously embarrassed the United Kingdom, whose doubts (see *The Times*, December 1, 1962, p. 7) were overcome, along with Belgium's, for the less official program of "sanctions." Whether this precedent could be followed in future cases would seem to depend upon the degree of support the United States may manage to rally on behalf of Secretariat diplomacy.

At the present time (early December, 1962), the United States strongly supports U Thant, though not all the conditions mentioned in the text above as constituting a "modicum of success" have been met. The ANC is being trained and disciplined under Generals Mobutu and Lundula with U.N. assistance (*The Times*, November 21, 1962, p. 13). But the proposed federal constitution (also published on November 29) has not yet been endorsed by Katanga, whose position still impedes a Belgian-Congolese financial settlement; nor has a division of Union Minière revenues between Léopoldville and Elisabethville yet been agreed on.

Nevertheless, the employment of UNF against Katangese troops is still regarded as a last resort. In August, 1962, while presenting an early version of his plan for imposing economic sanctions against Katanga, U Thant ruled out the use of force as means of ending Katanga's secession (see *UN Review*, IX, No. 9 [September, 1962], 51), but in November he suggested that other means be used if economic sanctions failed to persuade Katanga to join the rest of the Congo. (*The Times*, November 30, 1962, p. 9.)

Here the Congo experience may mislead us, if not considered chronologically. While it showed that deployment of the UNF throughout the Congo, followed by substantial evacuation of Belgian national forces, was not a sufficient condition either for reestablishment of internal order or even—without supplementary pressure in the Council and Assembly—for the deterring of overt Russian intervention in the Congo, it did not of course demonstrate that a U.N. policy of supporting the unstable government of Kasavubu and Lumumba against both Tshombe and Kalonji could have been guaranteed military success. Even in December, 1961, when the new Central Government was so much stronger, when experienced Belgian advisers had been withdrawn from Katanga, when Kalonji was quiescent and, above all, when the ANC under control of Léopoldville was for the time being so much more orderly, it was no simple matter to reduce Elisabethville's resistance. Fifteen months earlier, as Dr. Bunche suggested at the time, the UNF might have courted military disaster in attempting a military and political solution. For a year from September, 1960, when there was no clearly constitutional government to be supported by a political line, the candidate for "strong man" proved most ineffectual, while the President—who most nearly enjoyed U.N. support—was at odds with UNOC in March, 1961. Only Soviet-sponsored resolutions indicated the direction of a distinct political line, and that, had it been followed, would almost certainly have been bloodier than the course that the U.N. extemporized.

The Acting Secretary-General's regime, new as it is, has shown, on the other hand, that Security Council resolutions may be neither necessary nor sufficient for the U.N.'s adopting a political line (see our discussions above of the November 24 resolution, the Katanga operation of December, 1961, and the Orientale operation of January, 1962). Just as Hammarskjöld's "impartial" attitude was bound to find expression in the gaps of unspecified policy left blank by the U.N. bodies' quite sketchy resolutions, so U Thant's anti-colonial and anti-secession convictions enabled him to find a not-indefensible course of positive political action. In any new ex-colonial situation, a political line may be taken, not by the Council or Assembly, nor thus in open violation of the Charter, but in a quite administrative way by the Secretariat. Some political analysts favor the view that this kind of thing is bound to happen, the Security Council being neutralized by the possibility of veto, and the General Assembly by a near-majority of Afro-Asians. In fact, the Congo experience seems to show that when the initiative so completely falls to the Secretary-General, he is also most likely to come under intense day-by-day pressure from interested powers. This may make him less free than one who has a more specific mandate and is more evidently the servant of the Council and the Assembly. For example, a Secretary-General who has been given initiative but is under political pressure may find it *harder* to retain control over his subordinates in the Organization. Moreover, if the political line is not mandated by a Council or Assembly resolution, and therefore suitable for embodiment in an agreement with the host state, the Secretary-General's relations with the government of that state (and, less importantly, with its neighbors) will have to be the subject of constant diplomatic management. In many ways, he would have the greatest freedom of action under the mandate of a resolution that enjoined on him the policing type of action and that enabled him to obtain a corresponding agreement.

In the first month of the Congo operation, Hammarskjöld had resolutions largely of his own choosing adopted, but stopped short of asking for an agreement of the policing kind—which both Kasavubu and Lumumba might in any case have refused to sign, except perhaps under the threat that otherwise they would get no U.N. assistance at all, or under the promise of a U.N. policy of subduing Katanga. Since it seems highly likely that white minorities in ex-colonial Africa will in the future attempt secession from indigene-dominated states, the best hope of avoiding racial war on the Algerian pattern in such states would be for the Security Council to resolve upon a policing mandate for the UNF and at the same time to insist that there should be peaceable negotiations on the issue of secession. With the latter, a European colonist minority's best hope would be at the conference table; without it, they would be likely to attempt a generalization of their own racial war, involving other multi-racial states. "Secession or not" is an issue for the Council and the Assembly—it is evidently beyond the authority of the Secretary-General, and the mere presence of a UNF would not be an effective measure against it.

We shall now turn to the question of organizing and managing a United Nations force, and shall first consider its command, beginning with the Secretary-General and the Advisory Committee that he may appoint of his own initiative or that may be selected for him by the U.N. body that has instituted the operation. Unless the operation were so purely a policing activity that no questions of international politics arose, the Secretary-General's position as supreme commander would have to be maintained.

The Congo affair has shown that an Advisory Committee is needed to assist the Secretary-General in day-to-day management of the operation for which no mandate could be sufficiently explicit. An Advisory Committee can share his responsibilities for implementation of a Security Council mandate or a policy resolution from the General Assembly; it can shield him from the pressures exercised by interested powers; and, from the point of view of U.N. bodies, it can represent their interests in his carrying out their intentions.

Considering for the moment only intranational operations that are not enforcement measures, we believe that the committee's power should be advisory and confidential, not executive. If appointed by the Council or the Assembly, it should presumably report at some stage to the relevant body, but a detailed minuting of its proceedings is probably not desirable. If it consists of national delegates, as we should expect of Council or Assembly appointees, their ability to inform their national governments confidentially would be a measure of insurance against the Secretariat's seriously exceeding or neglecting the relevant mandate. An Advisory Committee, however, should not have access to the lower echelons of U.N. staff, who must remain servants of the Secretary-General, but should deal only with the Secretary-General or, at most, with any assistants formally appointed to work with him as representatives of geographic regions.

The selection of an Advisory Committee presents difficulties. So far as its function is to represent the Council or the Assembly, it might best be recruited from the actual interested powers who authorize the operation. So far as a principal problem is to find national contingents for a United Nations force and to ensure that no contributing nation misuses its contribution to gain control of the operation, the practice of selecting an Advisory Committee from the contributors has much to recommend it. But the regional neighbors of the host state provide a distinguishable group of candidates for an Advisory Committee. The Charter takes note of the regional principle, and in some parts of the world, notably the Americas, an insistence on this principle may be a way of preventing more general intervention in an internal dispute. On the other hand, not all areas possess the clearly defined boundaries of the American or even the African regions; and in Africa itself where nationhood and national boundaries are not yet established, restriction of an Advisory Committee or of a United Nations force itself to members of the region may play into the hands of the more ambitious and unscrupulous among them. Perhaps the best arrangement is to combine the three classes of delegates, to include all nations contributing contingents to the force, a balanced selection of the regional neighbors (in Africa, for instance, both the Casablanca and Monrovia groups should be represented), and representatives from the permanent members of the Security Council. It would be prudent to include this third group even if the operation has been initiated entirely from the General Assembly, since the experience of all the U.N. military operations has shown that at some stage the permanent members of the Council involve themselves in discussion of any operation.

An incidental benefit resulting from care in recruiting the Advisory Committee may be a reduction in the public debate and open intervention of Council and Assembly members. While Hammarskjöld was at first much helped by the intervention of middle powers—e.g., Tunisia—the later overfrequent participation of all sorts of nonpermanent members in the Security Council debates seemed to have cluttered the agenda and induced an obsession with producing draft resolutions that were not always suitable to the Republic of the Congo or to UNOC. The more valuable aspect of interested parties' contributions might find expression in an Advisory Committee rather than in the Security Council itself. The agreement with the host state—necessary whether the operation is to be a policing action, a mere U.N. presence or act of observation, or the following of an overt political line—should be initially discussed by the Advisory Committee, though as a form of treaty it could be finally authorized only by the Security Council itself.

Here we may notice a peculiar difficulty of using a United Nations force for a specific political objective. When the force is used as a "presence," an Observer Group, or a substitute for internal police, or for any other "limited" objective, the problem of *terminating* the operation, though difficult, is not insuperable. But if the agreement is in effect a treaty of coalition between the United Nations and the host government, in which the United Nations agrees to put its forces at the disposal of that government for the purposes of repression of internal opposition, it is hard to see how the Secretariat or any U.N. body short of the Security Council itself could provide the machinery to effect completion of its part of the contract. Suppose, for example, the Security Council—without adopting enforcement measures—had authorized the Secretary-General to end Katanga's secession, if necessary by force: Presumably, it would have had to authorize the U.N.'s commander in the field to accept submission of the Katangese forces at a point in the conflict to be jointly determined by the Secretary-General and the Prime Minister and Chief of State of the Congo; it would have had to instruct the United Nations Force to set up a military administration of the conquered province and to put down by force any remaining pockets of Katangese resistance.

These and many unforeseeable consequent measures would have had to be taken under the shadow of possible disagreements and even Security Council vetoes by the members of the United Nations, which would have made the concerting of the whole operation even more difficult and less calculable than it was. While the threat of enforcement measures might have deterred official intervention by other nations, it would not necessarily have prevented a much larger reinforcement of Katanga by irregulars, and almost certainly have resulted in much more bloodshed. The already obvious inadequacies of the UNF code of operations would probably have led to its abandonment and possible replacement by the ordinary laws of war. Likely enough the affair would have ended, after a stalemate on the Security Council, with a resolution of the General Assembly uniting for peace, and the United States leading a coalition of Afro-Asians with Soviet support and against the

opposition of many other Western powers. Certainly, the character of an operation to restore law and order would have been lost
in an unpredictable sequence of political exigencies. If the United
Nations ever intends to take this sort of political line, it would be
best advised to seek Security Council agreement upon enforcement
measures from the outset. When Hammarskjöld in August, 1961,
pleaded for a "dynamic" view of the role of the United Nations he
was right to envisage technical assistance and quiet diplomacy, not
military force, as the instruments of that dynamism. By the same
token, there is little point in resolutions to "put might behind" the
United Nations unless a political line is being taken: for "policing
operations," new powers are indeed required, but they are characteristically those of the right of search, arrest, and control of
weapons and security forces.

No U.N. military or paramilitary operation is practicable unless
the secretary-generalship retains most of its present shape and
authority. Even the kind of internal policing that we have sketched,
governed though it would be by a set of lawlike principles and a
predetermined code of operations, could not be conducted except
with the oversight of a supreme executive officer. The necessary
political negotiations alone seem to rule out anything like a troika
of Secretary-Generals. An essential of the role is that there be one
international figure who can keep in his mind the confidential views
of all national leaders. We shall not here go far into the question
of the secretary-generalship, which is much larger than that of the
United Nations force. Yet they are connected: Whether the sole
task of the U.N. is to keep peace between nations or whether it also
has a responsibility for helping ex-colonial peoples establish themselves in statehood, someone who does not represent a particular
nation must take the initiative so that meetings of national representatives may come to collective decisions and have them implemented in a degree of detail they simply could not supervise
directly.

It is a silly notion that no one can do this kind of job; but that is
what Khrushchev's "No neutral men!" amounts to. Hammarskjöld
believed that the chief danger arising from the Congo situation was
a second interventionist "Spanish Civil War" between Communist
partisans and Rightist supporters of white supremacy, and he did

something to prevent Soviet intervention in the Congo. U Thant evidently believes that secessionist movements in new states, especially when encouraged by *colon* regimes like that of Northern Rhodesia, are a more present threat to international peace and order. Each one's emphasis is perhaps natural to his social context; but each is in itself a quite arguable view of world affairs. Though each may tend to sway its proponents toward action favorable, from time to time, rather more to one nation than to another, these are incidental results that cancel out in the long run. The U.S.S.R., of course, may not want a stabilizing international organization, nor a peaceable transition from the old imperialist order in Africa; and if it does not, an attack on the possibility of a one-man secretary-generalship may be the best way to achieve its ends. But that is no reason why the rest of the world should allow Khrushchev's epigram to befuddle its consideration of the structure of the Secretariat.

A more important issue concerns the limitations of what may be reasonably expected from a single Secretary-General. This would become acute if the U.N. ever had to mount two or more Congo-type operations at the same time—a less manageable situation than a nation-state's having to fight a war on two fronts, since the U.N. Secretariat is so much tied up with organizational and legal restrictions and has so small a potential of resources and staff to draw upon. Intrastate operations are in marked contrast here to frontier-patrol procedures (such as the UNEF operation) or to deployment of an Observer Corps. The last two can be routinized without loss of efficiency. Our suggestion that intrastate operations might be organized along policing lines has been in part intended as a way of routinizing them, by elimination as far as possible of the need for political decisions. But, in any case, the current requirement that a Secretary-General shall be finally responsible to the U.N. bodies for all UNF operations restricts not only the number but also the types that may reasonably be ventured upon.

There is one possible way of widening this particular limitation, but it would take time. The "international civil service" of the Secretariat could be much further developed, both by recruitment and training, and by the creation of new departments or cadres. The famous "Congo Club" might be a prototype of the latter.

While the Secretary-General himself is more like a roving prime minister than the permanent head of a government department, there is no reason why his staff should not be permanent and organized by departments and by projects. The Congo experience has several lessons for us about pressures on the Secretary-General's immediate subordinates, and on the courses for their recruitment.

Even Hammarskjöld could not completely protect all of his closest helpers in the Congo—Bunche, Dayal, O'Brien, and Linner were all criticized (and sometimes eulogized) by the press and the delegates of various nations, and the first three at least were subject to severe pressure during the course of their work. Such men are in so exposed a position because the immediate management of a U.N. operation is theirs, and it is they whose actions impinge upon national interests. Dr. Bunche, as an American citizen, was quite unfairly accused of national partiality, and there seems for that reason to have been a tendency to appoint "neutrals"— Swedish, Indian, Irish, Moroccan—to the leading positions in ONUC. Perhaps a more effective form of protection would be to recruit career staff in larger numbers so that criticism of them would have to be criticism of the organization to which they owed a permanent allegiance. Ten or fifteen years' experience, furthermore, would not be superfluous for someone who has to extemporize details of the policy for employing an international armed force. National or political agents could of course be planted in this kind of civil service, though in such public positions the harm that they could do would be limited.

A more subtle problem arises with the growth of a corporate ethos and loyalty among the U.N. staff members themselves. Quite properly they become ambitious on behalf of the Organization, wishing to extend its scope and function. Hammarskjöld's initial response to the Congo's troubles in July, 1960, and his evident intention three months later to keep ONUC going as a big nonmilitary enterprise after the imminent departure of the last Belgian national troops exemplify this U.N. entrepreneurship. An institution so dependent upon the decisions of major powers could not of course expand by such methods into a world government, nor could the Secretary-General and his staff gain, by its misuse, anything like dictatorial powers. The danger, if there is one, lies rather in the staff's assessing the merits of a course of action for the U.N. not simply as a contribution to international order or to national well-being but as a stroke of policy that might bring credit to the Organization—a temptation most serious and most acute, as we have seen, when a United Nations force is involved and especially insofar as its employment, deliberately or incidentally, is apt to have major political consequences.

There is no trick of social engineering that could eliminate such temptations; the danger of them is necessarily involved in the existence of any international organization that is more than a mere conference. But the major powers could do something by shaping their policies for action in the U.N. on the assumption that it will remain a leading institution in international life with its own peculiar history, problems, and achievements—instead of treating it as an instrument to be exploited for short-term objectives. The permanent U.N. civil service needs more cultivation than any other part of the Organization. It is not enough to rely upon the Secretary-General's gathering a group personally loyal to himself, since it appears that his office, being elective, is likely to change its incumbent each decade or so.

During the Congo operation the chain of command that deployed the UNF seems to have been most tangled between the first and second links of civilian control and between national headquarters in Léopoldville and provincial headquarters. Considering the operation as a whole, one cannot but be impressed—despite the various debacles—with the Organization's efficiency and power of recovery from setbacks and confusions, particularly in comparison with the performances of nation-states in wartime. The most serious of the confusions arose, as we have seen, in Katanga during September, 1961, when the UNF appeared to make its first departure from the noninterventionist policy of not taking a military initiative. We shall now consider chain-of-command problems and the bearing of their likely occurrence upon three different ways of employing a United Nations force—the noninterventionist, the policing, and the political.

If the UNF is confined to a strictly nonmilitary function (at most, that of a "presence") and is armed only for self-protection, breaks in the chain of command or possibilities of its misappropriation by interested or overzealous officers are perhaps not very serious. In such circumstances, the practice of restricting the *political* tasks of the Secretary-General and his officials to conciliation and "quiet diplomacy," segregated from the day-to-day functioning of the military force, simplifies the command and control of the latter, since it is not being used as an active political instrument. (In their discussions of mid-January, 1962, British representatives are alleged to have favored a return to this type of operation.) Nevertheless, the O'Brien-Khiari affair occurred while the leadership of the Secretariat was still formally committed to noninterference in Congolese political issues.

Confusion in the chain of command is more likely, and apt to be more serious in its consequences, if the UNF operation is a policing action, as discussed above. The force would be in constant contact with the citizens of the host country in their political and social activities, so that there would be greater scope and need for management and manipulation by the Secretariat. The UNF itself would have to be larger than in the nonpolicing, nonpolitical case. It would need more provisioning and supply, more accurate and readier disposition, a more intricate communication network, and better intelligence. Its commanders, and the U.N. civilians who directed its operations, would be responsible for its strict observation of the rule of abstention from political action; such a guardianship entails a precise and continuous *political* appreciation of the situation. But, like the operations of a civil police, those of a policing UNF would be subjected to formal regulations. (For example, some of the instructions that Mr. Khiari is alleged to have given to Dr. O'Brien would have been *ultra vires* for a police force.)

Difficulties of command and control are quite the most acute problem for UNF operations that have specific political aims. These difficulties set in at the level of the Security Council's and the General Assembly's resolutions. Each body may well contradict both itself and the other—indeed, the Congo provides examples of considerable changes in trend: The resolution of February 21, 1961, was more "interventionist" than that of July, 1960, and that of November 24, 1961, more interventionist again. Whenever the Council or the Assembly happened to be in session, the UNF and its officers in the field might be seriously inhibited for fear of a

Security Council veto or a change in the policy of the General Assembly's majority.

Secondly, if the Secretary-General and his assistants were responsible for overseeing a military campaign with political objectives and probably for the tenure of the officers commanding the UNF, they would have to be assigned some of the powers of a national prime minister and his cabinet. The difficulties discussed above of terminating the military operation would be acute for them. Political aims, furthermore, evoke political opposition—we should expect that countries opposed to the aim would not be overscrupulous in the methods they use to hinder or to subvert it. (Britain, for example, was alleged, truly or falsely, to have prevented four badly needed Ethiopian jets from landing at a British colonial airport en route to the Congo.) As well as all the functions required for the purely policing alternative discussed above, the U.N. might well have to acquire a counter-intelligence and a counterespionage staff. In the event of any really serious national or irregular opposition, there could be attacks upon U.N. transport and lines of communication outside the host country.

Finally, precautions of a most elaborate kind would need to be taken against the sort of misunderstanding that occurred between Mr. Khiari and Dr. O'Brien. It is doubtful whether the U.N. has the means to maintain a control over its civilian staff adequate for such purposes—a nation-state at war uses the most stringent of its powers to do so. Enforcement measures produce a quite different operation: If taken as far as military action, they transform the U.N. membership or the participants among it into a wartime coalition whose members then exercise their own sovereign authority to control the operation on behalf of the U.N. The relevant experience then becomes that of Korea, not that of the Congo. The December action in Katanga and the January action in Orientale were ostensibly without political objectives, and no resolution went so far as to mandate the employment of force to unify the country; though the inconclusive political result of the militarily successful Katanga operation somewhat favors the view that military force cannot be guaranteed to yield political results otherwise required by the Security Council.

The disagreement in August, 1960, between Dr. Bunche and

General Alexander about the degree of force that the UNF might use, in particular toward the ANC, appears at first sight to have been just a contingent failure of liaison between civilian and military officers. On closer examination, however, it seems to have occurred only for want of an adequate operational code for the UNF. The model code which Hammarskjöld in his summary study derived from UNEF experience proved inadequate for the intranational Congo operation. In future cases, even without going as far as the adoption of the policing principles that we have suggested, the United Nations should certainly reformulate the instructions that it issues to its soldiers.

United Nations officials have already digested the Congo experience as far as concerns the strictly military organization of the force and have referred to the following notable problems. Firstly, a multinational force has, as well as the expected language difficulties, the problem of combining national contingents of quite varied military training and tradition. When, as in the Congo case, the great powers were precluded from supplying contingents, these discrepancies in training and organization were exaggerated by the fact that many of the contributing nations had armies of brigade-size organization. India, almost alone, could supply both the required logistics and also a sufficient number of experienced staff officers. The consequence was that staff work had to be conducted upon an Indian (in origin, a British) model, while many of the contingents thus managed came from small neutral countries and had no experience of working with such a staff.

Among contingents available for any similar intranational action, a variety of traditions is unlikely to be avoidable; but much could be done and something is being contemplated to create and train a U.N. military staff for these operations. It is unlikely that this will be done through the U.N.'s own Military Staffs' Committee; rather, as Alastair Buchan has recently suggested:

> What is clearly needed is a small staff under the Secretary-General, chosen from the most militarily efficient neutral countries, which can do some forward planning and can study logistics and other problems involved in situations that require U.N. action, as well as keeping close track of what forces, both fighting and support units, the countries that are politically likely to be called upon can in fact

provide. . . . It was no accident . . . that the speed with which UNEF was brought into being after Suez was the result of brilliant staff work by Indian and Canadian officers who could co-operate smoothly because they had been trained at British schools and staff colleges.[1]

Secondly, logistics were necessarily inadequate quite apart from staffing. Armies with formations no higher than a brigade also lacked the transport, supply organization and, above all, the signals needed for a Congo-type operation. (Fortunately, the Canadian unit was bilingual.) Air transport *to* the Congo was supplied by some great powers, and future operations will probably continue to depend upon this, but it should be investigated whether the U.N. should not have at its disposal a small transport air force and air staff, a pool of signals equipment, independent of the U.N. civilian communications that Hammarskjöld in his summary study had considered adequate for any U.N. military operation he could then envisage. As we noticed, the success of the December operation in Katanga compared with that of September was partly attributable to the UNF's having a fighting air force on the later occasion. If a case were to be made for this also being a permanent U.N. establishment, it would have to be argued in the context of something larger and altogether more ambitious than the United Nations force which we have been considering.

Thirdly, U.N. officials have singled out for commendation the work of the trained riot police of Ghana and Nigeria. It has been said that for most of the policing work in the Congo they were worth twenty times their number of the best fighting infantry; and that the U.N. could help itself by encouraging neutral nations to train riot police whom it could make available for international operations. They could also help by supplying other antiriot specialists such as detectives and antiriot intelligence workers.

The Congo operation itself could, in many of these aspects, be turned to good effect by the U.N. since it has provided the national contingents with the experience that some of them had previously lacked. For example, India was the only contributor that before the Congo could supply staff officers and troops who had been through big enough wars to give them any useful training. If the UNF has to remain in the Congo for much longer, an effort might be made to give other neutral countries some experience in international policing work.

A fourth problem is that United Nations force commanders have disciplinary authority only over their own nationals in their contingents—the donor nation being the ultimate disciplinary authority, as pointed out in Hammarskjöld's summary study. One is at a loss to see how this state of affairs could be changed short of the establishment of a permanent United Nations force; and even in that event it is not clear by which authority discipline would be exercised. Rhodesian sources have alleged that in the December operation U.N. discipline in some contingents was so bad as to permit atrocities. Official U.N. reports on this matter are not yet available; a U.N. spokesman, replying on March 28, 1962, to allegations by Professor Van Den Haag for an American pro-Katanga organization, said that the "charge of deliberate atrocities has no basis." It is clear that during the earlier stages of the Congo operation discipline was excellent, several African contingents being warmly praised in this regard.

Fifthly, as we noticed during the narrative, it was found necessary to deploy the UNF in at least battalion strength in provincial areas, since in smaller units they were liable to attack by irregulars and criminals. Imperialist forces have not always been driven to this extremity, since they can also deter attack by threatening punitive expeditions against districts in which their troops have been interfered with. Even the most forcible proponents of military and political action in the Congo did not recommend that the U.N. should go as far as this. The consequence of the limitation is that United Nations forces taking over from imperial powers may find that they have to replace these in more than a one-to-one proportion. It will be noticed that this applies to the deployment of United Nations forces for any purpose, whether showing the flag, policing, or pursuing a political objective.

The last of the difficulties encountered in the Congo derived from the sources that supplied contingents. It is known that some, especially the Africans, were subjected to political pressure from their own nations. Some nations sent contingents under geographic or political limitations. Most serious of all, contingents could be withdrawn at any time, so that some states threatened to do so and others actually carried out the threat—as a political protest, for instance, especially after the death of Lumumba. Once again, the absence of enforcement measures made this possible. It also suggests the question whether recruitment of contingents should be upon a regional basis.

Contingents from regional neighbors are more likely than others to be politically involved in, with, or against the host country, and against each other. (Quincy Wright in *A Study of War* and Lewis F. Richardson in *Statistics of Deadly Quarrels* have shown that the incidence of conflict is highest among neighboring countries.) Hammarskjöld's motives in insisting upon a major African contribution—though he resisted the proposal to make it merely African —seem to have been less out of regard for the Charter's penchant for regionalism than in order to rid the UNF of the appearance of neocolonialism. If Africa could organize its own regional association in which all the African national groupings participated, it might by itself provide enough "universality." Meanwhile, the danger of asking for an All-African United Nations force is that it could give an international disguise to one or another of the intra-African factions. In other regions such as Southeast Asia, the objections are even more obvious.

Similar considerations also tell against the frequently canvassed proposal for a permanent United Nations force, as distinct from a United Nations military staff and logistics organization. For each new crisis a new mixture of contingents selected on military and political considerations will have to be made up. A permanent force would have to be maintained idle in time of peace and yet enlarged with national contributions in major crises. The sole advantage of permanency is that the Secretary-General can be sure that some force will be available and will be ready. The above objections apply only to a United Nations force for emergencies: a permanent body required, say, to police a nuclear test ban would consist of full-time specialists who could not be detached to deal with emergencies.

We have concentrated attention upon the use of a United Nations force in intranational operations because the Congo affair was the first of these and because the status of the whole class is doubtful. The UNEF in the Suez crisis has shown that the United Nations can patrol and maintain peace upon a border. The

UNOGIL and the Jordanian affair have shown that it can deploy an Observer Corps effectively. Korea has revealed the unavoidable partisan features of operations conducted as a military enforcement measure. The tendency of our narrative was to emphasize the shortcomings of the United Nations operation in the Congo. To redress the balance, it must now be stated that ONUC did enable the withdrawal of official Belgian forces in about three months—a record that can bear comparison with the withdrawal of French, British, and Israeli forces after Suez.

Secondly, a combination of United Nations presence, protest from the Secretary-General, and firm but polite opposition from Afro-Asians on the Security Council and in the General Assembly brought to an end official intervention by countries of the Soviet bloc, which they had represented as independent assistance to the sovereign government of the Congo. Though the UNF was unable to prevent a number of tribal massacres and some civil war in the Congo, and though in the end it had to take military initiative itself, the number of lives lost in the course of establishing a new independent nation of 14 million people does not compare too badly with lives lost in other ex-colonial situations (compare India and Pakistan). And, as an incidental effect, the whole operation seems to have brought to the Congolese people in at least a majority of provinces a sense of national unity that they had hardly acquired from the previous Belgian occupation.

These positive achievements fulfill many of the hopes that Hammarskjöld professed at the outset of the operation. That is, they confirm in some measure the feasibility of a nonpolitical and noninterventionist intranational operation. Our suggestion that, in similar future cases, the United Nations force and its command should be endowed with certain legal authorities to enable it to take over policing functions is intended as a method of improving the performance of a noninterventionist operation. Policing would still fall within the field of what are called "limited" objectives for U.N. action in contrast with unlimited or political ones.

If the U.N. should set about using force to achieve political objectives—say, the elimination of colonialism or foreign domination —it would implicitly be promising more than it could perform. The preponderant might of the great powers would forbid it to conduct such a campaign universally, so that it would be acting as an international policeman only against the minor international "criminals." The policy would also be overambitious insofar as the U.N. seems unlikely for the next decade or so to be able to cope with more than a very few Congo-type situations. These objections, added to those already referred to, suggest that the Organization should confine itself to "limited" objectives.

How much innovation would be involved in the U.N.'s authorizing the policing powers that we have suggested? Firstly, no change in the Charter seems to be required; nor need enforcement measures be adopted, given the following caveat: If, as in the Congo, there is civil war or secessionism in the host country, members of the Organization must agree to channel all military relevant assistance, even to the sovereign host government, through the United Nations. Though the Security Council, and even to some extent the Assembly, can bind members by an instruction to that effect, the Council may find it necessary to *threaten* the introduction of enforcement measures against any nation that refuses to comply. It would be irresponsible to confer powers of enquiry, search, and arrest upon a United Nations force, or to enjoin it to patrol the borders against the influx of arms and men, and then allow some outside nation to have free access through a treaty with the host.

The troubles of ONUC with mercenaries and with unauthorized foreign political advisers not under the authority or instructions from their states of origin suggest that a way must be found to legalize the exclusions of such *individuals* during the tenure of a United Nations occupation. A direct authorization to this effect by the Security Council is a serious measure and could be open to abuse. The best way past this difficulty seems to be the making of a treaty or agreement with the host government, which would then enact something like President Kasavubu's Ordinance 70 of August, 1961, and authorize the United Nations Command to enforce it against the influx of both men and materials. Powers of arrest and enforcement of writs of habeas corpus could be conferred in the same way. (As we have seen above, pp. 84, 88, UNOC did upon occasion before November 24, 1961, both arrest a number of foreign military and political aides and impound a plane.) None of the measures that we have been able to suggest, however, would enable the United Nations to control financial transactions within the host country or between its citizens and economic organizations in other countries. Nor can it prevent partisan economic pressure.

Our policing suggestions are not a panacea for all internal conflicts. There are still some territories—e.g., New Guinea—which, though divided by internationally recognized boundaries, do not comprise nations except in a putative sense. Yet they could become centers of conflict between other nations. Apart from the present or former colonial governments, they lack even a *de facto* authority with whom the United Nations might make an agreement.

A related question concerns the propensity of the U.N. to recognize and designate a nation-state with specific boundaries and a discernible government. The matter of attempted secession, which will also be a potent source of international disagreement, arises in this case. Though the General Assembly's accreditation in December, 1960, of the Kasavubu delegation was considered not to prejudge the matters in dispute between the Léopoldville Administration, Lumumba's party, and the Katangese, it did in practice assist the establishment of the Kasavubu party as the government of the Congo. In November, 1961, the Security Council took it upon itself to refuse recognition and deny the existence of Katanga as a sovereign independent state. Since recognition by other states is one of the marks of sovereignty and nationhood, a determined secessionist movement denied that recognition could achieve its objectives only by acquiring other and equally important marks—such as the ability to exercise authority by force over its own territory and to exclude others. In this way, the Security Council's recognition of the national unity and its corollary, rejection of a secession, can easily provoke the internal conflict that it is endeavoring to prevent. The making of a policing agreement with a central government under these circumstances is both a legitimist disguise and an arbitrary enforcement of what is in fact a political decision. It may be the only way to prevent civil war and international intervention, but it will have the best hope of succeeding if the United Nations by its agreement insists on enforcing the political liberties of secessionist and unitarian alike.

Here, we are not only pleading for justice, and apparent justice, in the operations of the U.N.: We are also contending that such an appearance of justice, whether to individuals, to sub-national groups, or to nations, is a necessary condition for the Organization's being effective in the preservation of peace. The foregoing analysis should have made it clear that the U.N. cannot hope to exercise so much military force of its own that it comes, in effect, to hold the balance of power among its members. (In a generally disarmed world, this might be possible; but the present study can be no more than part of the prolegomena to an examination of that problem.) Nor, as the Congo experience pre-eminently revealed, does the Charter by itself provide a body of precepts sufficiently general or explicit to afford a rule for action by the U.N. "in accord with the Charter" in the many kinds of crises that can arise affecting international order. Thus a U.N. executive or its military forces cannot, as can a civilian police force, dispense with all questions of "justice" upon the ground of their being a sufficient guide in "legality," i.e., in the prescriptions of some legal corpus. (In civilian life, we do not usually question the justice of a police action, though we may question the justice of the legal enactment under which it has been taken.) In short, the U.N. cannot in itself be an effective balancing power, nor will its Charter serve adequately as the constitution and law of a world government or of a world police force.

Nevertheless, the Organization, at least before its involvement in some of the more questionable aspects of the Congo operation, derived much of its effectiveness from the moral authority attributed to it. We may suppose an unexpressed belief that for every crisis of world politics there are certain adequate principles of just action, not yet formulated but discoverable; and that the U.N. is the agent which, by its nature and constitution, seeks to discover and to act upon those principles. If it should lose the authority bestowed by that kind of belief, the U.N. can hardly hope to wield more power or to be able to enlist more support than could the executive of any rather flimsy alliance for collective security—which, admittedly, members may decide to submit to even in courses that temporarily discommode them, on the assumption that "next time" the executive's action will further and not obstruct their interests. Only by the "myth," if you will, of an ideal law among nations can the

U.N. hope to retain more than such calculated and ephemeral support.

A doctrinaire realist might here interpolate that the Congo experience has exposed the myth of transcendent justice among states and has shown up the U.N. as merely the machinery of a collective security alliance. We would rejoin that, so far as in the Congo operation UNOC departed from strict impartiality, it did so through contingent frailty and not from logical necessity. And we would add, on the other hand, that on numerous and difficult occasions the U.N. and its Secretariat acted with scrupulous objectivity. The future effectiveness of the Organization and of its forces as instruments for the preservation of peace is likely to depend much upon which policy is remembered. If, as suggested at the beginning of this study, there is an international community of persons self-chosen as political and thereby ethical critics of international relations, the criticism from this group presupposes the subsistence and relevance of principles of world political justice.

POSTSCRIPT

Operations of the U.N. Force:
December, 1962–February, 1963

The Breakdown of Negotiations. On December 28, 1962, in reply
to fire from Katangese gendarmerie in Elisabethville, the United
Nations Force took a third military initiative. There were at least
four weighty considerations that might have induced the Secretariat
to take such action at any time between November, 1962, and
January, 1963. Finances for the UNOC were in a parlous state. The
Katangese were building up their forces,[1] and had been accused of
perpetrating a series of incidents hostile to the U.N.[2] The Secretary-General had not yet succeeded in persuading all the interested
powers to implement his plan. Above all, the U.N. authority to
maintain military forces and political missions in the Congo was to
expire on December 31;[3] and meanwhile the Chinese threat had
made it likely that the Indian troops, the most seasoned in the
UNF, would be withdrawn.[4]

There are reasons to suppose that the U.N. had for some time
contemplated use of force as a last resort if the U Thant plan were
not successfully applied and if the policy of economic pressures
envisaged by the plan were to fail. Throughout the summer and
autumn of 1962, the U.S. was lobbying among the countries most
concerned with Katanga to obtain their agreement for participation
in the economic boycott. In October and November, moreover, a
military plan, to be used against Katanga should the U.S. fail in its
efforts, was said to be in preparation.

On October 11, the American Committee for Aid to Katanga
Freedom Fighters produced a "secret *aide-mémoire*" attributed to a
U.N. delegation. It claimed to disclose three alternative military
plans, in which, it alleged, Indian U.N. troops had been ordered

to be ready for action on November 12.[5] Whether by coincidence or not, this was close to the date subsequently imposed as a deadline by the Secretary-General upon Tshombe and Adoula. Nevertheless U Thant, on October 12, in his statement to his Advisory Committee denied that the U.N. planned to take military action in Katanga "or elsewhere in the Congo," and that the *"aide-mémoire"* was authentic.[6]

More, however, was going on than had been disclosed in reports of the Advisory Committee. On October 14, Adlai Stevenson was summoned to New York by the President of the United States for a conference on the Congo situation. Mr. Stevenson indicated that the Secretary-General might soon make an announcement concerning "new developments based on events in the Congo and not on the recent meeting of the Advisory Committee."[7] This would suggest that an understanding had been reached, at the highest U.S.–U.N. levels, on the need to take a "tough line" in the Katanga situation, which in the event was postponed as a result of the Cuba crisis.

In any case, Dr. Bunche left for the Congo on October 21, to "undertake broad consultations about the political and military aspects of the United Nations operation in the Congo."[8] The trip had been planned for some weeks.[9] Its purpose was nothing less than to prepare for a third operation in Katanga if such measures as the boycott failed to end secession. Dr. Bunche disclosed this fact in reporting on January 10, 1963, on quite a different matter:

> A plan of operations to achieve freedom of movement for ONUC throughout Katanga in the event of a continued denial of this freedom by Katangese authorities, which would also ensure the elimination of mercenaries and assist national unity, was devised in the course of consultations involving Mr. Gardiner, the Force Commander, General Prem Chand and myself during my visit to Leopoldville in October of last year. That plan was subsequently approved by you for ultimate execution, if all non-military efforts finally failed.
>
> The first phase of that plan had unexpectedly been activated on 28 December. . ."[10]

This U.N. military project had been by no means unprovoked. On October 8, a U.N. report was published, giving evidence of a Katangese military build-up[11] and leading *The New York Times* to predict on October 10 that the Secretary-General would recommend the initiation of a boycott to his Advisory Committee meeting of October 12.[12] In the event, it apears that "several strongly anti-Tshombe members of the Committee" had demanded an immediate meeting of the Security-Council," but that the Secretary-General feared that this might give Tshombe, in his negotiations with Gardiner, a pretext to attack the U.N. "He also expressed today his opposition to any move now to have the Security Council authorize the use of force to compel Katanga to accept the plan."[13] Nevertheless, he asked whether the Committee would favor a Security Council resolution "calling on United Nations members not to buy Katangese exports."[14] (Such a resolution, unlike the boycott measures for which the Secretary-General actually sought to get unofficial Government agreement, would, of course, have constituted an enforcement measure.) It was also reported that Mr. Thant had outlined two contingencies—(1) a threat to Union Minière installations; (2) a Union Minière decision to resist the Secretary-General's demand that it pay its foreign-exchange earnings to the Central Government instead of the Katangese Government—in which the U.N. might take a military initiative. While the same sources hinted that U.S. opinion was hopeful of Tshombe's readiness to end Katanga's secession even without recourse to boycott or U.N. military intervention, they also stated that Mr. Thant was asking for increased Sudanese troops for the U.N.[15] The Advisory Committee meeting scheduled for October 23 was postponed by the Secretary-General until after Dr. Bunche's return. The latter reported to the Committee on November 6, which also heard demands from Mr. Bomboko for the ending of secession, and a statement from the Secretary-General that time for implementation of the Thant plan was "rapidly running out." Meanwhile, diplomatic sources were reported as saying that he had given Mr. Tshombe until November 15 to end his secession.[16] About this date (November 6), Mr. Thant had "privately and separately" asked the Philippines, Greece, Italy, Pakistan, and Sweden for jet fighters. On November 14, a U.N. spokesman confirmed that the Philippines had agreed to send some.[17] A few days later Sweden also agreed. However, the November 15 deadline passed and nothing happened.[18]

To explain this delay in implementing of the Thant plan and

also the hastened UNF build-up of December, we must refer both to the course of events in the Congo and to the successive stages of the State Department's policy.

In the Congo, so U.N. sources maintain, it became eminently clear by the end of November that the President of Katanga would not carry out his part of the Thant plan.[19] The attitude of the Adoula Government had also stiffened. Adoula was under growing pressure to adopt more drastic policies against Tshombe and in increasing danger of being overthrown by the pro-Gizengist opposition.[20]

What of the U.S.? Evidently the State Department had the same end in view as the U.N. Secretariat and the Adoula Government—ending Katanga's secession—yet its attitude to the question not only diverged but at times conflicted with theirs. Even within the State Department itself there were two approaches to the Katanga problem. During the summer of 1962, the U.S. had encouraged if not indeed conceived the Thant plan, "and, in order to make Tshombe give way," the U.S. with Mr. Thant's "complete support," thought up the idea of boycotting Katanga's exports of copper and cobalt.[21] This tough approach to Tshombe's regime was associated with Edward A. Gullion, the U.S. Ambassador to Léopoldville, and Mennen Williams.[22]

The difficulty in implementing the coercive part of the Thant plan at once became apparent. The three Western Allies—Britain, France and Belgium—served notice that they would not take part in the boycott, but the U.S. managed to win over West Germany.[23] Early in autumn, Belgium agreed to join the U.S. and West Germany on two conditions: if it could be established that the deadlock was due to Tshombe, and if there was reason to believe that this economic pressure would do the job despite the nonparticipation of Britain and France.[24]

The U.S. continued its efforts to rally the countries concerned; but in order not to offend them, and in view of the difficulty of obtaining their cooperation, a shift in Washington's policy became evident around October and November of 1962 in favor of the more moderate policy associated with the name of Mr. McGhee, the Under-Secretary of State for Political Affairs.

He had returned from the Congo on October 19, allegedly hopeful for a peaceful end to the secession of Katanga. This first mission, apparently taken on Kennedy's initiative, partly to show Tshombe that the U.S. stood firmly behind the Thant plan and partly to make a reappraisal of the plan's prospects. Mr. McGhee was expected to report to the President that application of sanctions would be premature, that negotiations should continue, and that the Administration should press for various agreements of a practical nature, e.g., "resumption of commercial air traffic between Léopoldville and Elisabethville."[25] On October 22, authoritative sources in Léopoldville claimed that the United States no longer required Katanga to meet the Thant plan's deadline for the ending of secession. The sources also claimed that U.N. policy was following this new U.S. line.[26]

Mr. McGhee visited London and Brussels November 12–16, but he could not persuade Britain to join the boycott or Belgium to alter her conditions.[27]

Mr. Spaak had been consulting in New York on the Congo problem, and there were reports of a McGhee-Spaak plan, which was believed to allow Katanga somewhat better than the fifty-fifty division of Union Minière revenue formerly proposed and greater autonomy than that offered in the projected constitution.[28] On November 28, Mr. McGhee presented to Mr. Thant a proposal that the Thant plan be modified and that a mission under U.N. auspices be sent to the Congo.[29]

Officially, the U.S. position was that it still supported Thant's plan, with sanctions to compel Katanga to yield. However, diplomatic sources reported that Washington considered such measures unwise at this time.[30] In view of this U.S. attitude, Thant was reported to have told his Advisory Committee meeting between November 22–23 that for the time being, his threat to seek a boycott of Katanga's copper and cobalt production had been dropped.[31]

The U.S. could not have been entirely comfortable about this change of line, which carried with it a risk of seriously undermining the Adoula Government. In October, reports had circulated that the Russian Embassy had been offering Congolese politicians transport planes and fighter support should they decide that U.N. operation in the Congo had failed. The pro-Gizengist opposition, if in power, would not have been averse to accepting such offers.[32]

Therefore the new U.S. line of compromise was somewhat disguised; on November 27, Kennedy and Spaak authorized a statement handed to Tshombe on December 1, reaffirming their countries' support of the Thant plan and threatening severe economic measures if there were no substantial progress in negotiations.[33] Consequently, another attempt was made to bring together the Congolese leaders in conference under the patronage of the Secretary-General. But it was rumored in Washington that if the conference failed to take place, a "hard" American approach would replace the "soft" McGhee line.[34] And the two leaders did refuse to meet.[35] The McGhee plan collapsed as much because of their attitude as because of its rejection by the U.N.

A *New York Times* correspondent wrote that McGhee's views and thus the recent views of the State Department were "getting small visible acceptance in the Secretariat of the U.N. and the Congo advisory group," which believed in the policy of sanctions and ultimatums.[36] The Secretary-General consequently asked for reports on the Congo situation from Gardiner and Rikhye. Both left for the Congo on November 30—Gardiner, it was said, to sound out Adoula on the suggested concessions to Tshombe and to review the position of his Government in the light of the nonconfidence vote in the Congolese Parliament on November 28; and Rikhye to assess the strength of the UNF in the event of full-scale fighting in Katanga.[37]

On December 1, a U.N. spokesman in New York announced that the McGhee plan was no longer under consideration, but would give no reasons why this was so or whether it had been rejected by U Thant or the Congolese leaders[38] but another source quoted U Thant as having said: *"Il ne faut pas donner l'impression qu'on a conçu un nouveau plan Thant apres l'échec du premier."* (This no doubt was the meaning of the declaration made on December 13 by Thant *"Il n'y a pas de plan Spaak, pas de plan Thant . . ."*) The Secretary-General was also, as we shall see later, opposed to the idea of a mission to the Congo under U.N. auspices.[39] The reasons that had inclined U Thant to reject McGhee's plan were probably also convincing to the U.S.; for on December 3, the U.S. began assisting the U.N. military build-up.

Probably, then, the State Department gave up its conciliatory policy toward Katanga on account of the critical position of the Adoula Government and partly because there were now better prospects for organizing a boycott against Katanga. It was reported that early in November an agreement had been reached between Belgium, the United States, and West Germany to impose a boycott on Katanga if the McGhee plan should fail.[40]

On December 3, the U.S. resumed its airlift, carrying both equipment and personnel from abroad into the Congo and from Léopoldville into Elisabethville. According to the U.S. Embassy reports, more planes would then be provided to transport 4 Swedish jet fighters, and nearly 3,800 Indonesian troops en route by sea, from Tanganyika into Katanga.[41] Further, it was rumored in Brussels that December 10 was the date set by the U.N. to implement a program of economic pressure combined with joint military action by the UNF and the ANC against Katanga.[42]

On December 10, in fact, the U.N.'s intention to apply economic pressure on Katanga was announced by Robert Gardiner. In a letter to Tshombe, he complained that Katanga had made no serious effort to carry out the plan and that Tshombe had not given up his secessionist designs: consequently, phases II–IV of the plan would be applied. Gardiner then demanded the cessation of hostile acts perpetrated by Katanga, such as bombing and demolitions in North Katanga and the blockade of U.N. supplies at Sakania. He required that Tunisian soldiers detailed by the Katangese should be released and the gendarmerie road blocks in Elisabethville area be promptly dismantled. The UNF was a "peace force which was at war with no one and would take no offensive military action"; but, he warned, it would vigorously use its weapons if attacked, and would henceforth take such protective measures as it might deem necessary to prevent recurrence of attacks."[43]

On December 11 and 12, U Thant invited various governments to apply economic pressure against Katanga. On December 11, U Thant asked the Belgian Government to persuade the Union Minière to stop paying its revenues to the Katangese Government[44] and on the following day he asked the governments of Portugal, South Africa, and the United Kingdom to prohibit the shipment of Katangese copper ore through the territories under their jurisdiction.[45] On December 14,[46] he supported Adoula's approach

made three days earlier to seventeen interested governments requesting them to forbid copper and cobalt imports from Katanga
not authorized by the Central Government.[47]

Although by the end of November the United States had secured Belgian and British support for sanctions,[48] yet in December
both allies were still anxious to avoid their application and any U.N.
resort to force. In an attempt to persuade Tshombe to divide his
Union Minière revenue with the Central Government, the Belgians
on December 10 sent a mission led by Marcel Dubuisson to Katanga,[49] and the British Foreign Office instructed Derek Dodson,
their Consul in Elisabethville, to urge Tshombe to come to terms
with Adoula.[50]

In response to these persuasions, and no doubt in order to avert
the boycott, Tshombe offered to carry out part of the Plan of National Reconciliation.[51] His Government, so he informed the Secretary-General on December 12, would authorize the Union Minière to transfer to the Monetary Council all foreign exchange
from Katangese exports. This sum, less the expenses of the Union
Minière, was to be divided equally between the Central Government and Katanga, provided that Katanga received not less than
250 million Belgian francs monthly.[52]

Thus Tshombe underlined his claim to "authority" over the financial arrangements between the Union Minière and the Congolese Government. Moreover, the stipulation that Katanga was to
receive a minimum sum could mean that at times the Central
Government would receive less than the Province.

For these reasons, and because of Tshombe's record of promise-
breaking, the ONUC received his offer with some reserve. In a letter of December 17, Gardiner informed Tshombe that Thant ap-
preciated his offer, but that the proposals raised questions that
could best be clarified by the Central Government and the Union
Minière.[53] U Thant told the meeting of the Advisory Committee
on December 13 that he did not propose to alter his policy in
any way:

> we are now in a phase in which all of the pressures available to us
> will be exerted . . . with every effort made to avoid armed conflict.
> If, however, Mr. Tshombe should elect to order his gendarmerie to
> attack us, we will defend ourselves fully and hit back to the fullest

extent of our capacity. The United Nations troops are alerted and are being prepared for such eventuality.[54]

The difficult negotiations persevered in by the United States for British and Belgian support of sanctions were now frustrated by Tshombe's *démarche*. Many U.N. delegates were reported to have deplored U Thant's letter of December 14 to the interested governments on the ground that it did not take into account Tshombe's conciliatory gesture.[55] The British delegation told U Thant on December 12 that in view of Tshombe's promise they opposed sanctions against Katanga.[56] On December 13, a Conservative backbenchers' motion in the House of Commons called on the Government to prevent coercion of Katanga by taking an initiative in the Security Council.[57] Belgium advised U Thant on December 19 that as a result of Tshombe's offer they now considered the boycott to be premature.[58] France of course opposed sanctions throughout. Reliable sources also said that Portugal, Britain, and South Africa had not replied to Thant's letters requesting them to deny transit for Katanga's exports, but that refusals, except perhaps from the U.K., were expected.[59]

Why had the Security Council not scrutinized the Thant plan, with its provision for economic coercion of Katanga, accompanied as it was by the U.N. military build-up? There was little hope that the seven votes required for a majority could have been obtained from the Council for the sanctions.[60] U Thant, however, argued that

no question of "sanctions" is involved here. Despite Mr. Tshombe's ambitions and declarations, Katanga is just a province and not a state. In over two years of striving, Mr. Tshombe has won recognition for his attempted secession from no state and there is no prospect that this situation will change. Mr. Tshombe's declarations have not achieved independence or statehood for Katanga. Indeed, even Mr. Tshombe, on several occasions, as in the declaration he signed at Kitona last December and in his formal acceptance of my Plan, has renounced secession by accepting in principle integration in the Congo as a whole. What I ask you, therefore, is only to respect the laws of the Republic of the Congo, which forbid the export of mineral ores on which the legal duties and taxes have not been paid, and the spirit of the resolutions of the Security Council.[61]

Tshombe's offer did not mature into a negotiated settlement. He himself did not follow it up. Adoula, on the other hand, saw in it a new delaying maneuver[62] and on December 18 ruled out any further negotiations with Tshombe.[63] It is hard to see how the U.N., with the best will in the world, could have brought the two leaders to the negotiating table.

Tshombe told U Thant on December 18 that the contacts with the Monetary Council would have to be effected not by the Union Minière, but by officials whom Tshombe would appoint, accompanied by a Union Minière expert.[64] Thus he would evidently relinquish none of his authority. On December 19, Spaak and McGhee, joined by Gardiner in Brussels on December 22, made a last attempt to convince the Union Minière, but the company said it would not pay anything to the Central Government until authorized by Tshombe.[65] And on December 21, Union Minière denied press reports that its representatives were proceeding to Léopoldville to discuss the matter. Nor was Mr. Van Roey, director of the "National Bank of Katanga," prepared to go to Léopoldville, since Tshombe would not authorize him to do so.[66]

At the Nassau conference, held between December 19 and 21, Kennedy and Macmillan "discussed the current state of affairs in the Congo, and agreed to continue their efforts for an equitable integration of this troubled country. They expressed support for Mr. Spaak's proposal for a fair division of revenues and noted with concern the dangers of further discord in the Congo."[67]

This communiqué probably reflected the views of the British, who hoped for realization of Tshombe's promise so that the sanctions would not be necessary. The U.S. was willing to give compromise proposals a chance, but if necessary was prepared for more direct action.[68] Thus Tshombe's refusal to negotiate, and the U.N. failure to secure cooperation for the boycott of Katanga must have inclined the U.S. to support, if not indeed to initiate, the second U.N. military build-up in mid-December, 1962.

It was now reliably reported that U Thant, with all-out U.S. assistance, was building up the UNF for a test of strength with Katanga.[69] On December 18, the President ordered a U.S. military team—the Truman mission—to fly to the Congo that week. On the same day, a U.N. spokesman announced that the U.S. had agreed to supply additional equipment to the U.N. U Thant, he said, had requested such help from several nations, but not from the Soviet Union.[70] However, on the next day, *The New York Times* reported that it was the U.S. that had taken the initiative in offering the equipment to Thant.

On December 19 and 20, U Thant outlined his preliminary requirements to the head of the mission, Lieutenant General Louis Truman, who then left for the Congo accompanied by Stevenson, to examine these requirements on the spot. U.N. Headquarters was reported to have emphasized the need for transport aircraft, helicopters, jeeps, and light pontoon bridges. More than twenty fighter planes provided by Sweden, the Philippines and Italy, and about a thousand Indonesian troops and a Norwegian anti-aircraft battery were to join the U.N. force in a few days.[71]

The wisdom of sending the Truman mission was immediately questioned. We are particularly concerned with the impact of such a national undertaking in the U.N. presence. It was rumored that when McGhee returned to the U.S. from his European tour in November, he had suggested sending a mission to the Congo, but under U.N. auspices. At that time U Thant sarcastically rejected the idea: "*Si vous voulez une mission au Congo, organisez-la vous-mêmes.*" In the opinion of *Le Soir* this was an impossible suggestion, since the Western countries could not afford to give the impression of interfering in the internal affairs of the Congo.[72] Yet Washington went ahead in this highhanded fashion. *Le Soir* later reported that U Thant had not been consulted or advised by the U.S. concerning the projected mission until two days before the public announcement was made.[73]

The Secretariat did not officially criticize the U.S. decision; but the press reported that they did not seem to favor the mission, even though it had gone to the Congo to consider U.N. military needs.[74] Although Britain gave her support,[75] some U.N. delegates said they could see no necessity for an American check of U.N. effectiveness.[76]

Nor were all the objectives of the mission clear. Reports from Washington let it be known that the primary purpose was to counter Soviet intrigues in the Congo, including alleged maneuvers to oust the Adoula regime and to replace it by a left-wing government presumably headed by Gizenga.[77] There was little evidence of Soviet intervention at that time,[78] so the U.S. was *actually* intervening in order to forestall merely *possible* intervention by the Soviet Union.

The Russian bloc delegates accused the U.S. of trying to interfere in the Congo in violation of Security Council resolutions[79] barring the Great Powers from providing troops for the UNF.[80] In the Congolese Parliament, the opposition saw in the sending of the mission an attempt at setting up a U.S. base in the Congo that would rapidly become active outside the U.N.[81] Another report had it that the Truman mission was intended to build up the ANC.[82] It was claimed that an American Embassy official, Mr. Green, had in early 1962 drawn up a plan for reinforcing the ANC[83] and that Adoula had been demanding such assistance unsuccessfully for about a year.[84] Although during his stay in Léopoldville Truman indicated that he had no intention of leaving any officers behind or of establishing a military mission to train the Congolese Army,[85] he conferred not only with U.N. officials, but also with Adoula and the Congolese Defense Minister and several top Congolese military leaders; and on departure, he indicated that the question of supplies for the Congolese army, although not within the scope of his mission, had been discussed by the U.S. and Congolese officials. The U.S. Embassy insisted however that any training or supply of the ANC would have to be done through the U.N.[86] It had earlier issued a statement that the mission "reflects no change in United States policy regarding the support of the United Nations and channeling of United States aid to the Central Government through the United Nations," and that American officials were "astonished at reports that the mission meant the United States was contemplating unilateral intervention and dispatch of troops."[87]

If the United States in fact contemplated training of the ANC themselves, despite the U.N. presence, such a sharp reversal of American policy would have impaired U.N. authority. Moreover, the Soviet charge of unilateral intervention in violation of the Security Council resolutions would have been justified. Otherwise, the most that can be said in criticism of the mission is that checking of U.N. requirements on the spot implied a distrust of the

U.N.'s capacity to assess these needs for themselves, which gave rise to rumors bound to impair U.N. prestige. The gesture was tactless.

Truman, who left the Congo on December 26, refused to discuss his recommendations at the press conference at the U.S. Embassy. But informed sources said that the U.N. request for trucks, jeeps, and communications equipment would be fulfilled and that transport planes, pontoon bridges, and possibly some small arms might also be included. He said he would present his recommendations to the Joint Chiefs of Staff "very soon."[88]

Returning to Léopoldville on December 23 from his futile negotiations with the Union Minière in Brussels, Gardiner indicated that a showdown was rapidly approaching with Katanga. He said, "We don't have much time to waste." However, when asked if any new decisions had been made during his consultations with U.N. officials in New York, he added: "There is no need for new steps," and that the U.N. planned to continue the pressures on Katanga outlined in its plan for national reconciliation.[89]

The first round of fighting began the next day, before the Truman mission was out of the Congo. But even earlier, a U.N. report had underlined that reintegration of Katanga with the rest of the Congo was far removed from the minds of the secessionist leaders, notably Mr. Kimba, in a speech of December 20, 1962. The Katangese often referred to the possibility of joining Katanga with Northern Rhodesia and perhaps with other neighboring territories. Moreover, they often adverted to the theme of the Tananarive Conference recommendations and privately made it clear that, although negotiations over the plan might continue, action was not contemplated. A settlement not fully acceptable to them, they said, might collapse after the withdrawal of the ONUC military presence.[90]

How should we judge the United Nations' posture on the eve of the final military conflict in Katanga? In building up the UNF and even in adopting Dr. Bunche's contingency plan of late October for a U.N. military action, the Secretary-General had not violated the Charter or infringed the UNOC mandate—at least not in a technical sense. The Bunche plan itself could be regarded as simply a wise precaution in the event of Katangese hostilities. But the spirit of the mandate, at any rate as formerly understood by Hammarskjöld and by others who shared his scruples concerning the standards of conduct to be expected of the Executive and the armed forces of the United Nations, was not compatible with the declared objectives of the October plan of operations.

One declared objective was to achieve "freedom of movement for UNOC throughout Katanga."[91] Though Hammarskjöld's report of July 18, 1960, mentions "freedom of movement" as a necessary requirement for the deployment of a UNF, U Thant and his staff were obviously giving the phrase an even wider connotation than the extended sense in which it had been invoked during the second round of December, 1961. Secondly, the plan of operations "would also ensure the elimination of mercenaries and assist national unity . . . if all non-military efforts finally failed."[92] The Security Council resolution of February 21, 1961, enjoined the use of force as a last resort to prevent civil war and demanded the elimination of mercenaries, though not by force. The resolution of November 24, 1961, authorized "the use of requisite measure of force, if necessary" against mercenaries, and deprecated Katangese secessionist activities and armed action against the U.N. in support of them.[93] But even it did not authorize the use of force for ending secession—i.e., for the establishment of what Dr. Bunche called "national unity."

There are three items of evidence—(1) the U.N. military build-up during December; (2) the apparent anxiety of both the Secretary-General and the United States to see an end to Katanga's secession, before financial stringency and the withdrawal of Indian and other troops should compel a termination of the military phase of UNOC; and (3) the Bunche plan of military operations formulated October, 1962, and not made public until January 11, 1963. These together, and especially the third point, make the reiterated claims of the Secretariat that no military or political intervention was intended seem quite disingenuous. Though we cannot demonstrate the fact, we consider it likely that the U.N. would have attempted to achieve "freedom of movement" by about mid-January, 1963, had there been no Katangese outbreak in December.

The Secretary-General, then, cannot be acquitted of some responsibility for the outbreak of fighting in December, 1963, even though he made the U.N. forces hold their fire for several days until December 28. He worked consistently for the ending of Katanga's secession from the day he succeeded Hammarskjöld, when, indeed, he already foreshadowed a willingness to use force for this purpose. As we pointed out in a former context, certain aspects of the operations in December, 1961, and January, 1962, when the UNF was employed with some disregard of the mandate, set a precedent that a determined Secretary-General could extend much further.

On the other hand, the Secretary-General is subordinate to the Security Council and can employ no U.N. forces without at least its tacit consent, unless under the General Assembly's assumed "Uniting for Peace" authority. It follows that each member of the Security Council, since he is entitled to convoke the Council, must share responsibility for policies inaugurated by the Secretary-General, especially when he has foreshadowed them. Neither Britain nor France seems to have approved U Thant's extensions of the mandate; but neither convoked the Council: It is likely that Britain was dissuaded from doing so by the United States. General de Gaulle's deprecations of *"le machin"* would not incline him to take the trouble. The Soviet Union was in a cleft stick. On the one hand, it had declared its opposition to the Tshombe regime, and in 1960 had urged that "freedom of movement" permitted the kind of positive military action that the UNF undertook in December, 1962, and January, 1963. On the other hand, the Kremlin cannot have been pleased at the recent collusive relationship between the Secretariat and the U.S. Administration.

Because of its positive support of U Thant's firm policy of ending secession, Washington bears more responsibility than the other Security Council powers. Mr. Stevenson, as early as the Security Council debates of November, 1961, had supported a U.N. political commitment against secession, though not by military initiative, which infringed the "objectivity" that Hammarskjöld had been so anxious to establish as a guiding principle of all U.N. operations. In December, 1961, moreover, Washington's diplomatic initiative in bringing Adoula and Tshombe together at Kitona also assumed the kind of role for a great power in the councils and activities of the

U.N. that Hammarskjöld had tried to avoid. By August, 1962, Washington had gone even further in helping an admittedly willing U Thant to formulate a plan of economic and diplomatic pressures, followed by a residual threat of other unnamed measures, which both gave the U.N. a positive political commitment in Katanga and made apparent the dependence of UNOC on the diplomatic and logistic support of the U.S.

The McGee episode may be interpreted as a brief deviation from a continuing U.S. trend in favor of political intervention by the U.N., to forestall Soviet intervention, to please the Afro-Asians, and to rescue the U.N. from an involvement that seemed certain to lose its reputation either for effectiveness or for impartiality. In the upshot, both U Thant and the U.S. were ready to sacrifice impartiality for effectiveness.

Admittedly, one can hardly think of a cause less deserving of Hammarskjöld's magisterial objectivity than Katangese independence. Moreover, the final outcome in January, 1963, may seem to have produced a state of affairs more or less satisfactory to everyone except the Katangese. Nevertheless, the U.N., in thus demonstrating a certain effectiveness as preserver of peace in postcolonial situations, has certainly lost its name for impartial arbitration and scrupulous adherence to the principles of its own Charter. No government would be wise to call in the United Nations, as Lumumba and Kasavubu did in July, 1960, without firm assurances that some great power such as the U.S. will work to keep the U.N. close to its mandate. The U.S. Administration may not have been wise in thus devaluing the reputation of the United Nations in order to win a round in the Cold War.

Fighting in Katanga: December, 1963. The U.N.'s own account of the Christmas Eve outbreak implicates the Katangese forces alone:

> The state of tension deliberately fostered by the Katangese authorities came to a head at 1000 hours on 24 December 1962, when gendarmes facing United Nations positions in the Lubumbashi [sic] and Avenue Tombeur area engaged in sustained small arms fire at ONUC Ethiopian troops there. Some 500 rounds were fired, wounding one ONUC soldier. Shooting continued sporadically for about five hours. The Ethiopians maintained self-restraint and did not return the fire.[94]

An Associated Press correspondent, on the other hand, reported having seen the U.N. troops under Katangese machine-gun fire emplacing recoilless cannon, and a "volley of projectiles" discharging in the direction of the Katangese position. He also believed he heard U.N. officers giving an order resembling "Open fire!"[95] It is regrettable that the U.N. report, which must have been composed in the knowledge of the AP correspondent's dispatch, makes no attempt to explain such a flat contradiction.

Undoubtedly the Katangese were highly nervous, ill-disciplined, and apt to shoot at this time. A *New York Times* account of January 8 explains that the firing began from a misunderstanding by the Ethiopian troops, who had replaced a contingent of Tunisians. The former U.N. garrison had been almost on visiting terms with the Katangese, but when some of the latter approached the new contingent of Ethiopians, these fired a warning burst into the air, which the Katangese took as an occasion to open fire.[96]

General U.N. discipline, nevertheless, seems to have been excellent at this time and during the following four days of tension. At 11 A.M. on December 24, the unarmed ONUC helicopter was shot down behind Katangese lines near the golf course. The ONUC officers detailed to recover the helicopter and crew, "by force if necessary," in fact managed to recover the personnel (of whom one died of his wounds) without having to attack. The helicopter crew had been grossly maltreated while in Katangese hands, but both then and on the following day U.N. forces made no reply.[97] On Christmas Day, firing was merely intermittent. Mr. Kimba promised the U.N. representatives that it would cease. December 26 also seems to have been quiet. On the next day, however, "sporadic firing by the gendarmerie in and around Elisabethville" began again, and "by nightfall ONUC troops were under fire in the Jadotville Road and golf course areas from gendarmerie roadblock positions."[98] Meanwhile Tshombe, in a letter of the same day to the U.N. representative, Mr. Mathu, accused the U.N. of implementing "a general plan" of military operations in "predetermined episodes," having prohibited "the passage of Katangese Ministers" at U.N. roadblocks in Elisabethville on December 24. He referred to his Government as "an important moderating element" whose disappearance "would plunge the country into a full-scale war."[99]

Mr. Mathu immediately replied with countercharges, which however did not deny the U.N.'s restrictions on Katangese Ministers'
movements, but said he had imposed them to be sure that some
authorities would be there to give orders for cessation of fire and
return of the helicopter and crew.[100]

In response to renewed firing on December 27, Mr. Mathu
shrewdly "invited Mr. Tshombe by telephone to come to his house
and proceed with him and with Major-General Prem Chand,
ONUC Commander of the Katanga area, and Brigadier R. No-
ronha, on a tour of the scenes of firing. There the Katangese official
could see with his own eyes that all the firing was being done by
the gendarmes and that all ONUC troops were withholding their
fire." After a visit to the scene of conflict, apparently effective in
convincing Tshombe, the Katangese President returned to his
quarters where "he professed peaceful intentions, but then went
to another room and was heard making a telephone call to Kolwezi.
Speaking in Kiswahili, he demanded that the Katangese Air Force
should immediately carry out raids on United Nations positions."[101]
Important U.N. initiatives were taken immediately. ONUC fighter
aircraft were readied: "The plan was to destroy Katangese aircraft
found in the air or at Kolwezi-Kengere military airfield and other
airfields in South Katanga which were likely to be used for Katangese air activity in the Elisabethville area. However, to avoid unnecessary damage and casualties, Katangese private aircraft flying
in the air or taxiing on the ground, as well as Kolwezi Town airfield, located in a populated area, were not to be targets. The two
airfields at Kipushi adjacent to the Rhodesian border were also
excluded from any such action."[102] The last sentence is an answer
to the charges concerning a prearranged U.N. plan for air attack
made by the American Committee for Aid to Katanga Freedom
Fighters. The U.N. aircraft made strikes— on December 29 against
the Kolwezi-Kengere airfield, and on the thirtieth against the
Kamatanda airfield, close to Jadotville. When the action ceased on
December 31, the attacks (by cannon and rocket, not by bomb)
had virtually eliminated the Katangese airforce. From December
31 to January 4, the force was used only for reconnaissance missions
and patrolling in cooperation with ONUC ground forces.[103]

Considered as an offensive military operation, this use of U.N.

aircraft was a much more striking and important example than the ground action of December, 1962, in and around Elisabethville and than the subsequent capture of Jadotville. Moreover, the latter would have hardly been possible without it. The requirement for effective use of aircraft in any general operation is to take and keep the initiative, preferably eliminating the enemy airforce before it can be used. It follows that the U.N. inhibition, characteristic of Hammarskjöld's regime, against the taking of military initiative or firing before being fired upon, is feasible only in the case of ground forces, and not of the U.N. airforce, even though its primary purpose is to prevent air attacks upon the U.N. air and ground troops.

The other U.N. response to continuing Katangese fire was a last attempt to extract from the Elisabethville authorities an agreement to stop the firing and to remove the roadblocks from which the attacks had been in part directed. At 11:30 on the morning of December 28, Messrs. Tshombe and Nyembo were confronted at Mr. Mathu's residence with a document, to be signed by Tshombe, ordering the removal of roadblocks and cessation of fire.[104]

Tshombe maintained that he could not sign the document without the prior approval of his ministers and left the U.N. residence while Katangese attacks were intensifying. At this point, the U.N. announced that its troops would take direct action to remove the roadblocks.[105] On the following day, Tshombe replied with a call for full-scale Katangese resistance and a threat to blow up bridges, dams, and other installations if the ONUC offensive did not cease withing twenty-four hours.[106]

We shall not describe in detail the fighting around Elisabethville.[107] It was over, with few casualties, by the evening of December 29. Elsewhere in Katanga, fighting stopped by New Year's Eve, except on the road to Jadotville.[108]

The action of U.N. ground forces from December 28–30 seems to have been unexceptionable; they had been under heavy and provocative attack and their reply could be regarded as a mandated action in self-defense. Only the accompanying air strike may be criticized as having taken the U.N. beyond strict requirements of self-defense.

Difficulties of UNF communications in the capture of Jadotville.
Indian troops of the UNF entered Jadotville at noon Léopoldville

time, meeting no resistance and cheered by the population. Their commander was received by the mayor and the local general manager of Union Minière.[109] At 8:40 P.M. New York time on the same day, Dr. Bunche left New York for Léopoldville, his instructions including an investigation of the "serious breakdown in effective communication between United Nations Headquarters and the Léopoldville office."[110] It is not immediately evident why "a brilliantly executed action," which led the Secretary-General to commend the troops participating "for their professional competence and soldierly courage,"[111] should have been treated by U.N. Headquarters as a major crisis. Dr. Bunche's report of January 10, 1963, to the Secretary-General, however, "exposed glaringly" certain deficiencies in coordination and communication" between each link in the chain connecting New York through Léopoldville and then Elisabethville with the forces in the field.[112] Since this continuing problem was forced on our attention in this volume's earlier pages (completed in April, 1962), we find it remarkable that remedies for it were not devised in the interval after the last serious breakdown in September, 1961.

A chief source of the Jadotville confusion was the near contradiction between two instructions, both telegraphed from U.N. Headquarters on December 30, 1962. The first evidently specified that "any further military action in Katanga other than that required in self-defense would be undertaken after Headquarters' clearance." The second, "a cable of encouragement," sent because it had been recognized that the first was "too restrictive, in that it would unduly restrict and handicap the patrol, probing, and perimeter expanding actions normal and necessary in military field practice," seems to have "advised the military to exploit their roadblock action success, to extend their Elisabethville perimeter, and to keep the gendarmerie and mercenaries off balance and on the run." Dr. Bunche states that this advice was given on two assumptions: "That there would be little or no firing from the gendarmerie in that area" (i.e., Elisabethville's environs); and "that there was an automatic limit on how far the United Nations troops might proceed along the Jadotville road because the required reinforcements in troops, air support, and material, particularly bridging, had not yet arrived."[113] Apparently, the U.N. office at Elisabethville, or at least the UNF command in the field, interpreted this "cable of encouragement" as an authorization to press on with the second phase of that plan of operations, which Dr. Bunche himself had, with Mr. Gardiner and the UNF Commander General Prem Chund, devised at Elisabethville in late October, 1962, and which U Thant had subsequently approved.[114] General Prem Chund, it will be remembered, had had "unexpectedly" to activate the first phase (removing roadblocks and clearing gendarmerie from the Elisabethville-Kipushi area) on December 28, 1962.[115] The planned second phase had included a "move to Jadotville, followed by an ultimate move to Kolwezi."[116] The GOC, Katanga, subsequently assured Dr. Bunche that on the evening of December 31, 1962 (when a second infantry company of the Rajputana Rifles pushing along the Jadotville Road 3 miles beyond their comrades at Lukuni, near Elisabethville, had engaged entrenched gendarmerie and mercenaries until 3 A.M. on New Year's morning, losing four dead and nineteen wounded), "there was no intention that it should go to the Lufira River or do more than probe along the road."[117] On December 28, however, the Secretary-General had instructed Mr. Gardiner to inform President Tshombe, *inter alia,* that "ONUC personnel must have full freedom of movement throughout Katanga, which would necessarily mean freeing the Jadotville road and establishing ONUC presences in Jadotville, Kolwezi, and Kipushi."[118] The officer commanding the 4th Madras Battalion can therefore hardly be blamed for taking his unopposed troops across the Lufira River, by the single remaining girder of the nearly demolished railway bridge, on the afternoon of New Year's Day. (They had already, in the morning, fought their way across the Lukutwe River and improvised a "bypass" at the broken Lukutwe bridge, to bring their heavy equipment after them.[119]) The order *not* to cross the Lufira reached them only on the other side. Nor does Dr. Bunche reproach the GOC, Katanga, nor the officers in the field, who, having ferried mortars and recoilless cannon across the Lufira on January 2, moved on into Jadotville on January 3, so as not to remain exposed to Katangese attack on the dangerous side of the unbridged river.[120]

Indeed, our survey of the U.N. reports suggests that much of the immediate responsibility for the Jadotville confusion must be ascribed to U.N. Headquarters and to the Secretary-General himself. The second, countermanding telegram of December 30 could hardly have been interpreted by the military as anything but a general indication to proceed with the second phase of the October plan of operations. Though they had *strategic* reasons for not crossing the Lufira until they could take their heavy equipment with them, they could not have been expected to anticipate the U.N. Headquarters' emerging *political* reasons for deciding, apparently on New Year's Day, to hold back from occupation of Jadotville.

The first telegram of December 30 from U.N. Headquarters is to be understood as an attempt to hold the U.N. forces within the environs of Elisabethville until the heavy equipment promised from the U.S.A. should arrive.[121] But the order of January 1, which Indian forces received too late to prevent their crossing the Lufira River, requires a different and more immediate explanation. Had the order been a mere reminder of prearranged tactics, there need not have followed so thorough an investigation of failure in field communications, of which this delayed order was the most important instance.

Part of the explanation is undoubtedly discernible in the Secretary-General's statement of December 31, issued from U.N. Headquarters, New York. In this seven-page document, he had been at pains to report that by December 30, "the ONUC operation which had begun on the afternoon of December to remove all the roadblocks of the Katangese gendarmerie in the Elisabethville area had been completed. Thus, all firing and fighting had ceased on that date."[122] The U.N. forces had acted "in self-defense . . . to protect their security and their freedom of movement."[123] He was grieved that

Some may loosely say that there was a "third round" in Katanga. . . . In view of the results of the ONUC operation, there may be some who would be inclined to refer to a United Nations "military victory." I would not like this to be said. . . . We have never initiated force in Katanga or elsewhere in the Congo and we do not intend to do so. We do not use the force we have for political ends and we do not intend to intervene in the political affairs of the Congo, of the province of Katanga, or of any other province.

On the other hand . . . we do not and will not . . . recognize any claim to secession or to independence of the province of Katanga, or deal with Mr. Tshombe or any other official of Katanga in any status other than that of provincial officials.[124]

The capture of Jadotville, though marred only by the killing of two Belgian women, must have seemed to give the lie to this declaration of only three days before.

Another aspect of the U.N.'s later anxiety about the capture of Jadotville is concerned with certain understandings, which U.N. Headquarters apparently gave to particular powers concerning Tshombe. On January 1, Tshombe had returned from Rhodesia,[125] where he unsuccessfully tried to enlist Sir Roy Welensky's support. He then joined his ministers in Jadotville, where there was a large European population and some of the most important of the Union Minière installations. The British Government, which had failed to obtain any assurances of cease-fire, was now endeavoring to have Tshombe and his Government return under safe conduct to Elisabethville. The U.N., while refusing to consider any resumption of negotiations with Tshombe regarding Katanga's secession, was nevertheless in daily contact with the U.K.'s representative to the U.N., Sir Patrick Dean, who was pressing for guarantees of Tshombe's safe conduct to Elisabethville.[126] The Belgian Government had adopted a similar position.[127] Tshombe himself was using the Union Minière organization as a channel of communication to both Belgian and British authorities in order to establish that he was willing to proceed to Elisabethville under guarantees; that the consular representatives of the U.S.A., Belgium, and the U.K. should join him at the Lufira River crossing to escort him to Elisabethville; and that Mr. Van Roey, director of the National Bank of Katanga should visit Elisabethville to formulate modalities for the division of Katanga foreign exchange.[128] He sent two messages to this effect through the Union Minière network. The second of these suggests that some organization, probably the United Nations itself, had agreed with Belgian and British authorities to offer Tshombe some of the guarantees he was asking for. This message read:

President says okay. Indicates his complete agreement with text of message and asks in consequence immediate cease-fire on Jadotville

Road and that three consuls of United States, Britain, and France can come to take him under protection at Lufira bridge.[129]

Obviously, this message would have made nonsense if at the same time U.N. troops were storming across the Lufira River and up the road to Jadotville—which in fact they were! In these circumstances, especially as Tshombe did not immediately return to Elisabethville, U.N. Headquarters' subsequent anxieties about its chain of command during the Jadotville confusion are quite understandable.

Dr. Bunche, in his report to the Secretary-General of January 10, 1963, recommends a "thorough review and overhauling of the ONUC's system of coordination and communication." His specific proposals include (1) improved directives concerning the kind of military action requiring prior clearance from U.N. civilian officers; (2) improved methods of reporting from the field (apparently, the practice of situation reports twice daily, usual in national military forces, is inadequate for United Nations forces); (3) even more importantly, the assignment of "a mature reporting officer detached from ONUC headquarters whose sole responsibility it would be to report fully and speedily to the Force Commander on the progress of the action" with every unit of ONUC troops likely to see fighting (Bunche proposes this in recognition of the futility of attempts at fingertip political control of military forces while in action); (4) assignment of senior officers at Force headquarters to expedite all military reporting back to U.N. Headquarters, New York; (5) a high-level liaison officer assigned to assist the civilian U.N. Officer-in-Charge.[130]

These would be undoubted improvements, and some of them are sufficiently obvious to have been anticipated in the present volume. But if we were right to contend that much of the Jadotville confusion can be traced to political difficulties and contradictory instructions emanating from U.N. Headquarters itself, improved military communications are hardly the complete answer. Dr. Bunche's first recommendation, for improved operational directives, would be much more easily acquired in a United Nations force that, by agreement with the host country, had been given sole policing authority in the affected area. The directives could then have the much more specific character of a police code. The chain-of-command problem thus raises the whole question of the proper limits of the United Nations' employment of force.

The ending of Katanga's secession. After the capture of Jadotville, nearly three-quarters of the Union Minière's resources were in areas occupied by the U.N. force. Tshombe was reported in Kolwezi. On January 7, the Secretary-General denounced Tshombe's threats to adopt a scorched-earth policy, criticized him for having left Elisabethville, and at the same time refused to conduct any further negotiations with him.[131]

Tshombe returned to Elisabethville on January 8, still threatening sabotage in Kolwezi. Dr. Bunche and Mr. Gardiner had left just in time to avoid meeting him, their mission to Elisabethville having been misinterpreted as an attempt to secure Tshombe's return, when in fact its purpose had been a post-mortem on Jadotville. At the same time, withdrawal of U.N. forces for use in Katanga had allowed tribal fighting to break out in Kasai.[132] This conflict persisted for weeks and was reported to have killed far more people, even in its first few days, than the whole of the third Katanga operation (between December 28 and January 4, U.N. forces lost nine dead and seventy-two wounded; gendarmerie casualties are thought not to have been more than two or three times larger, and civilian casualties, though heavy for "a peace-preserving action," were only about fifty).[133]

The build-up of U.N. equipment continued from U.S. sources in the first week of January. Amphibious troop carriers were included in case the U.N. should need them for an advance on Kolwezi, which was at this time referred to as the Katangese emergency headquarters.[134] Munongo, who was thought to be the most intransigent of the Katangese ministers, was reported in various centers of resistance, including Mokambo, Mufulira, and eventually Kolwezi.[135]

Even the powers comparatively sympathetic to Katanga, such as Belgium and Britain, were working in various ways for an assurance from the Katangese Government that the scorched-earth policy would be abandoned and Katanga peacefully integrated into the Congo. This change however came too late to salvage their Congo policies, for on January 10, Bomboko gave their consuls at Elisabethville twenty-four hours to leave the country. The U.K. took this particularly hard, since its Consul, Mr. Dodson, had just been complimented for his efforts in dissuading Tshombe from devastating installations in Kolwezi.[136]

Above all, Union Minière on January 8 took fright, reporting at U.N. Headquarters and in Brussels that Katangan police had prepared extensive sabotage at Kolwezi. They appealed to all responsible parties "to cooperate in measures to prevent further damage."[137] With this collapse of his support, Tshombe quickly began to change his mind. On the night of January 9, in response to his threat at a press conference to blow up the Kolwezi installations, there were reports that the U.N. Secretariat had confined Tshombe to his residence to stop further incitements to violence. It seems that the U.N. order was reversed after an hour or so. Tshombe then gave an undertaking to respect U.N. freedom of movement, and he was then allowed to leave for Sakania.[138]

In fact on January 10, Tshombe drove to Mokambo, pausing twelve times on the 105-mile journey "to tell ragged groups of gendarmes not to resist a United Nations armored column that followed." It was reported that Mr. Dodson, the British Consul due to be expelled from Elisabethville, had persuaded Tshombe to do this.[139]

This event marked the real end of Katanga's secession. The only remaining question was whether Tshombe could carry the more intransigent of his ministers with him, and whether the gendarmes and mercenaries were sufficiently under Katangese Government control to be prevented from implementing the prepared sabotage action in remaining centers such as Kolwezi, where there was a dam supplying hydroelectric power for most of Katanga and for more than half her yearly mineral output.[140]

Tshombe joined his ministers in Kolwezi on January 13.[141] Two days later, in letters to Adoula and U Thant, he announced, "I am ready to proclaim immediately before the world that Katanga's secession is ended, to grant the United Nations troops liberty of movement throughout Katanga, and to return to Elisabethville to direct the means of applying the U Thant plan."[142] But he made this conditional on the Central Government's granting an amnesty for himself, his ministers and "all persons who have worked under their authority."[143]

President Kennedy welcomed Tshombe's declaration and urged the Central Government to make it a "decisive turning point in Congo developments"—i.e., to give Tshombe the amnesty he was asking for.[144]

Tshombe returned to Elisabethville on January 17 and agreed that the U.N. should occupy Kolwezi.[145] The U.N. did so, peacefully and in Tshombe's presence, on January 21.[146]

This was the last stronghold of the gendarmerie and the mercenaries in Katanga. Their officers were instructed to take oaths of allegiance to the Central Government. At first, the Katangese Commander in Chief refused to do so, but later submitted and used his influence to enforce the submission of other Katangese soldiers. Fears were widely expressed that the Katangese forces, which had seemed to melt away before the U.N. advance, were simply disappearing into the bush and taking their weapons with them.[147]

By January 29, Mr. Ileo, representative of the Central Government, had met in a cordial atmosphere with the Katangese Cabinet and had arranged to take over those functions of government in Katanga that the Central Administration had exacted in return for their agreement to the U.N. settlement with Katanga.[148]

Lessons of the final Katanga operation: 1962–63. In judging Mr. Thant's military initiative at the end of 1962, one should remember that he had inherited from Hammarskjöld a commitment to maintain the U.N. operation in the Congo, even though Belgian troops had withdrawn; and that by Dr. O'Brien's initiative in September, 1961, there had been established a precedent for employing U.N. forces in effect to end Katanga's secession. Until that was accomplished, the U.N. forces were so committed that they could not withdraw. Thus ONUC, which had set out to prevent foreign intervention in the Congo's internal conflicts, ended by itself forcibly intervening in them.

It may be that any intranational operation by the U.N. will have some propensity to follow the same course. Unless U.N. forces can seal the national borders, they must act against the intervening foreigner at that point within the nation where his intervention is taking effect, i.e., against the movement he is supporting. But once the U.N. has become involved in struggle against internal forces, it may have to see the internal conflict through, even though external intervention is no longer a threat. When this tendency is coupled with the fact that the U.N. seems unable to carry out any operations with forces unless it has the support of at least one of the Security Council powers as well as of many members of the General Assembly, one is less surprised that the U.N.'s third action in Katanga should have involved something much like collateral intervention by the United States. Could a mechanism be devised to counter this tendency for a U.N. action against foreign intervention turning into intervention by the U.N. and powers supporting it? In our section on lessons of the Congo operation, we outlined a type of agreement in which the host country would temporarily authorize the U.N. to take responsibility for the host's entire security, both internal and external, while abstaining from even diplomatic participation in its nonviolent political conflicts.

In that section we also expressed doubts about the effectiveness of any U.N. military initiative having an overt *political* objective. The events of December, 1962–January, 1963, suggest that those doubts were misplaced: It would seem that military action can be effective if the U.N. has predominance of force. This impression is correct only in part. While it is certain that the U.N.'s victory was much hastened by the determined air strike which eliminated the Katangese airforce, the ground operations of the U.N. were not particularly overwhelming in terms of troops employed. What seems to have been decisive was the influx of first-class means of military transport, which made it evident that U.N. forces could actually achieve the province-wide "freedom of movement" they were seeking. This kind of equipment would be indispensable also in a purely U.N. policing action.

Further, we argued that the U.N. would have difficulty in terminating operations conducted for political ends. In fact, it has now successfully terminated such action. It did however encounter certain difficulties, notably in the Jadotville confusion. There the local U.N. commander accepted the town's surrender as though he had been the officer of a national military force operating under the laws of war. But the U.N. seems to have made no prior arrangements anywhere in Katanga, despite its phased plan for the occupation of towns, either for the legal surrender of towns or for the taking of prisoners, except in the case of mercenaries. In the earlier diplomatic phase of the Thant plan, however, the absence of a termination procedure for UNOC as a whole enabled Tshombe to temporize.

Lastly, we pointed out that the Western powers in the Security Council had acquired the habit of leaving formulation of resolutions on the Congo to the nonpermanent (usually Afro-Asian) members of the Council. This, of course, has not been the case since November, 1961, when the United States delegate himself took the initiative in formulating amendments, thereby foreshadowing the United States' much more positive leadership in U.N. policy. From then on, the United States and the Western powers seem to have acquiesced in U Thant's avoidance of any further recourse to the Security Council. This development has much affected the control of U.N. forces, which have been entirely at the disposal of the Secretary-General. This is to be contrasted with Hammarskjöld's deference to the authority and consensus of the Security Council, even while he was enlarging the scope and responsibilities of the Secretary-Generalship. U Thant's change of attitude in this respect was assisted by the accident that the issue concerning national contributions to the expenses of the Congo operation happened to be a matter proper to the General Assembly and the Court, and not to the Security Council.

Along with this increasing freedom from Security Council restraints, the Secretariat has acted in increasing freedom from the mandates. In September, 1961, much trouble was taken after the event to make the action appear to accord with Security Council and General Assembly resolutions. In December, 1961, it was thought sufficient to invoke the right of self-defense. But in December, 1962, no mandate or resolution was specifically invoked. This kind of tendency may be unavoidable in the later stages of the United Nations operation, whose presiding officer, the Secretary-General, cannot readily be called to account by U.N. members.

In the Thant plan, a requirement was included that the Congolese Parliament should ratify, and the provincial administration should accept, a "Federal Constitution" promulgated by U.N. legal experts assisting the Central Government. During the December fighting, U.N. spokesmen insisted that Tshombe should agree to accept the Constitution, though at the time Mr. Adoula, who had demurred at some of the Constitution's provisions, was on the point of proroguing the Parliament for three months from the beginning of January. A precedent of considerable importance was thus established, the U.N. having concerned itself with those matters of internal constitutional law that Hammarskjöld had explicitly declared to be beyond its competence. If this precedent were to prove applicable in future situations, the U.N. would have moved appreciably closer to acquiring the prerogatives of a world government.

Withdrawal of U.N. forces from the Congo is expected to begin in March, 1963. It now remains to be seen whether, as the resolution of July 13, 1960, envisaged, "through the efforts of the Congolese Government with the technical assistance of the United Nations, the national security forces may be able, in the opinion of the Government, to meet fully their tasks." Their "tasks" at that time included a guarantee of protection for Belgian civilians sufficient to induce the Belgian government to recall its national forces from the Congo. They now seem to be understood much more exclusively as the continued suppression of Katangese and other movements for provincial independence. In Kasai, this is already difficult for the Central Government forces. In Katanga, the Central Government may have to face a resurgent Katangese gendarmerie made up of the indigenous troops who so quickly melted away in December and January last.

The significance of the gendarmerie's speedy dissolution is as yet difficult to interpret. It could mean that Katangese nationalism was never more than a façade maintained by interested Europeans such as the management of Union Minière, and that the Katangese were kept in the gendarmerie simply by good pay and discipline. Instead, it could be taken to evince a design to prevent some part of the Katangese forces, with their weapons, from being incorporated into the ANC, thereby retaining the nucleus of the revolutionary army to re-establish the secession after UNOC's withdrawal.

If the Katangese should appear to be succeeding in this, foreign powers—notably the U.S., from fear of Soviet intervention—would be very likely to intervene. Unless this could be represented as a threat to international peace and security, the U.N. would not be justified in renewing its own intervention. Successful secession by Katanga or other provinces would frustrate the policy of the Secretary-General and, since November, 1961, of the Security Council. In that circumstance, the strongest supporters of vigorous military action by the U.N. would be bound to acknowledge that in practice military initiatives have turned out a failure, despite the Secretary-General's readiness to trade the U.N.'s established reputation for impartiality and objectivity in exchange for the mere prospect of military effectiveness.

But should the Central Government, without further outside assistance, succeed in maintaining the unity of the Congo, the proponents of forceful U.N. action may be able to salvage a victory of prestige for the organization: It may appear to be an ideal instrument for transforming postcolonial situations to the shape desired by the Afro-Asian powers—and therefore an invaluable tool from the U.S. viewpoint for weaning the Afro-Asians away from their habit of looking to Moscow in such cases.

This approximates *one* of Hammarskjöld's objectives—a vindication of the U.N. as the peculiar guardian and servant of the newer and smaller nations. But Hammarskjöld would not allow it to be merely an instrument of power politics for any group of nations, nor to contravene the Charter's provisions or the principles and the precedents he had worked to establish. By his Congo venture of July–September, 1960, he had attempted a consistent *extension* of those precedents to intranational situations, but the logic of events in the Congo has meanwhile rendered the extension inconsistent at least with the principles laid down in Hammarskjöld's "Summary study" of the Suez, Lebanese, and Jordanian affairs.

In our view, something like a new Summary study is called for, by which the Secretariat should demonstrate how U.N. forces could be used effectively in future intranational operations while maintaining Hammarskjöld's standards of impartiality and objectivity. Above all, it will be essential for the Secretariat to insist that members party to such agreements as those concerning West New

Guinea and Cuba adhere strictly to the commitments they make under United Nations aegis. Permanent members of the Security Council also would be well advised to help restore the organization's reputation for consistency, and resist temptations to exploit it for short-term national advantage. In other respects, we can find nothing in the December–January operation in Katanga that would require us to alter our previous conclusions about the lessons to be derived from the Congo operation.

A. L. B.
N. H.

Canberra
March, 1963

Notes

CHAPTER II
United Nations Forces in Suez, Lebanon, and Jordan
(pp. 6–22)

1. E.g., Lincoln P. Bloomfield, *The United Nations and U.S. Foreign Policy* (Boston: Little, Brown and Company, 1960); David Ennals, *A United Nations Force?* ("Fabian Research Series," No. 210 [London: Fabian International Bureau, 1959]); William R. Frye, *A United Nations Peace Force* (New York: Oceana Publications, 1957); Thomas Hovet, *Bloc Politics in the United Nations* (Cambridge, Mass.: Harvard University Press, 1960).

2. Sources for Suez episode: *Keesing's Contemporary Archives*, 1956, pp. 15173–34, 15177–78, 15182–23, 151825, 15219; and *Encyclopedia Americana*, XXVII, 301.

3. *Keesing's Contemporary Archives*, 1958, p. 16182.

4. S/4007.

5. SCOR 823, para. 5.

6. *Ibid.*, paras. 11–12.

7. *Ibid.*, paras, 24–32; and SCOR 824, paras. 2–13.

8. S/4022; later S/2043.

9. SCOR 824, para. 111.

10. SCOR 825, para. 82.

11. *Ibid.*, para. 90.

12. *Keesing's Contemporary Archives*, 1958, p. 16295.

13. S/4051 (interim report of UNOGIL, reported to the Security Council by the Secretary-General on July 16, 1958, SCOR 829, para. 1).

14. S/4043.

15. SCOR 827, para. 76.

16. *Keesing's Contemporary Archives*, 1958, p. 16307.

17. SCOR 827, para. 35.

18. *Ibid.*, para. 36.

19. *Ibid.*, para. 64.

20. S/4047 and Corr. 1.

21. For Article 2 (para. 7), see Appendix A of this study.

22. SCOR 827, para. 123.

23. S/4050 and Corr. 1.

24. SCOR 829, para. 4.

25. S/4054.

26. For Article 51, see Appendix A of this study.

27. SCOR 830, para. 48.

28. SCOR 831, para. 88; and S/4047, Rev. 1.

29. SCOR 831, para. 36; and S/4050, Rev. 1.

30. SCOR 831, paras. 66, 68, and 69.

31. S/4055.

32. SCOR 834, para. 87.

33. *Ibid.*, para. 97.
34. *Ibid.*, para. 72.
35. SCOR 835, paras. 7–8.
36. S/4055, Rev. 1; and SCOR 835, para. 34.
37. SCOR 837, para. 9.
38. *Ibid.*, paras. 10–17.
39. S/4078; and SCOR 838, para. 10.
40. *Ibid.*, paras. 11 and 37.
41. *Ibid.*, paras. 215–16.
42. *Ibid.*, para. 225.
43. *Keesing's Contemporary Archives*, 1958, p. 16365.
44. GAOR 732, August 8, 1958, para. 36.
45. GAOR 733, August 13, 1958, para. 7.
46. S/4050, Rev. 1; S/4055, Rev. 1; and GAOR 733, para. 9.
47. GAOR 733, paras. 45–46.
48. *Ibid.*, para. 69.
49. *Ibid.*, para. 76.
50. *Ibid.*, para. 119; and A/3870 and Corr. 1.
51. A/3876 and A/3877; GAOR, 3rd Emergency Special Session, Annexes, Agenda item 5.
52. A/3893, Rev. 1; Resn. 1237 (ES-III); GAOR 746, para. 161.
53. *Keesing's Contemporary Archives*, 1958, p. 16439A.
54. S/4120, para. 37.
55. SCOR 831, para. 15.
56. S/4061, para. 40.
57. SCOR 831, paras. 19–20.
58. *Ibid.*, para. 21.
59. *Ibid.*, para. 23.
60. *Ibid.*, paras. 24–25.
61. *Ibid.*, para. 30.
62. *Ibid.*, paras. 101–2.
63. SCOR 835, para. 17.
64. SCOR 838, para. 80.
65. GAOR 735, paras. 31–33.
66. *Ibid.*, para. 37.
67. *Ibid.*, paras. 37–39.
68. *Ibid.*, para. 44.
69. *Ibid.*, para. 50.
70. *Ibid.*, para. 51.
71. GAOR 746, para. 161; Resn. 1237 (ES-III).
72. A/3934, Rev. 1, para. 29.
73. *Ibid.*, paras. 30–31.
74. *Ibid.*, para. 31.
75. *Ibid.*, paras. 34–35.
76. *Ibid.*, para. 41.
77. *Ibid.*, para. 38.
78. S/3986.
79. GAOR, 13th Session, 1958–59, Annexes, Agenda item 65, para. 149.
80. *Ibid.*, para. 151.
81. *Ibid.*, para. 161.

82. *Ibid.*, para. 155.
83. *Ibid.*, para. 156.
84. *Ibid.*, paras. 157 and 162.
85. *Ibid.*, para. 160.
86. *Ibid.*, para. 164.
87. *Ibid.*, paras. 165–67.
88. *Ibid.*, paras. 169–70.
89. *Ibid.*, para. 175.
90. *Ibid.*, para. 176.
91. A/1237 (ES-III).
92. A/3943, para. 177.
93. *Ibid.*, para. 179.
94. *Ibid.*, para. 181.
95. *Ibid.*, para. 189.

CHAPTER III
The First Phase of the Congo Operation: Deployment
(pp. 23–35)

1. For Articles 39 and 99, see Appendix A of this study.
2. S/4382, 1.
3. *Ibid.*, 11.
4. SCOR 873, paras. 1–14.
5. For Articles 41 and 42, see Appendix A of this study.
6. SCOR 873, para. 18.
7. *Ibid.*, para. 27.
8. *Ibid.*, para. 28.
9. Determination under Article 39 of "the existence of any threat to the peace, breach of the peace, or act of aggression" can lead to measures under Articles 41 (e.g., the imposition of sanctions against an aggressor) and 42 ("demonstrations, blockade, and other operations by air, sea, or land forces"). These are "enforcement measures," and they alone can override the fundamental limitation imposed on intervention by Article 2 (para. 7).
   Notice further that U.N. precedents were also against involvement in internal conflict: "It is virtually an axiom of the United Nations that internal political or factional disputes are outside the purview of the Organization. This is not merely a consequence of the 'domestic jurisdiction' clause [i.e., Article 2 (para. 7)], since that clause, after all, only goes so far to prohibit 'intervention' and not mere discussion, and since, on occasion, other admittedly 'essentially' domestic matters have been discussed in the organs of the United Nations." See E. M. Miller, "Legal Aspects of the United Nations Action in the Congo," *American Journal of International Law*, LV, No. 1 (January, 1961), 23.
10. S/4386.
11. A/1474, Rev. 1 (ES-IV). For Article 49, see Appendix A of this study.
12. See Miller, *op. cit.*, pp. 4–5. For Article 40, see Appendix A of this study.
13. Available in GAOR, 13th Session, 1958–59, Annexes, Agenda item 65.
14. Nor had it been by the General Assembly of 1958, to which Hammarskjöld had had to submit it. India had foreshadowed at a meeting of the UNEF Advisory Committee that it would vote in the Assembly against adoption; and the U.S.S.R. had threatened "withdrawal of confidence" if the sum-

mary study were not shelved. See Joseph P. Lash, *Dag Hammarskjöld: Custodian of the Brushfire Peace* (New York: Doubleday and Company, 1961), p. 181.

15. S/4405. For the text of this resolution, see Appendix A of this study.
16. S/4389, para. 12.
17. A/3943, October 9, 1958, para. 151.
18. *Ibid.*, para. 179.
19. *Ibid.*, para. 157.
20. S/4389, Add. 5, July 29, 1960, para. 1.
21. See p. 250 of this study, ref. to S/4389, para. 12.
22. SCOR 827, July 13–14, 1960, paras. 195–96.
23. S/4387 (before adoption, S/4383). For the full text, see Appendix B of this study.
24. Introduction to the Annual Report of the Secretary-General on the Work of the Organization, June 16, 1960–June 15, 1961, GAOR, 16th Session, Supplement IA, *passim*.
25. *Hansard* 496 (July 8–14, 1960), p. 982, cited in SCOR 873, para. 127.
26. SCOR 873, paras. 184–90.
27. S/4389 and Adds. 1–6, paras. 3–5.
28. GAOR, 16th Session, Supplement 1A, p. 8.
29. S/4405, operative para. 3.
30. S/4389, para. 7; (cf. A/3943, paras. 172, 175, 178, 181).
31. *Ibid.*, paras. 10 and 17; (cf. A/3943, paras. 160–61).
32. *Ibid.*, paras. 12–13; (cf. A/3943, para. 12).
33. *Ibid.*, para. 15; (cf. A/3943, para. 179).
34. See CO/20, July 22, 1960; and SCOR 873, para. 21.
35. S/4389, para. 32.
36. *Ibid.*, para. 33.
37. *Ibid.*, para. 29.
38. *Ibid.*, para. 37.
39. *Ibid.*, paras. 29 and 37.
40. *Ibid.*, Adds. 4 and 6.
41. *Ibid.*, para. 45.
42. SCOR 877, paras. 53 and 57.
43. *Ibid.*, paras. 191–93.
44. SCOR 879, paras. 93–97.
45. S/4405, operative para. 1. (For the text of this resolution, see Appendix B of this study.) The Secretary-General had suggested this authorization (SCOR 877, para. 18).
46. *Ibid.*, operative para. 2.
47. SCOR 879, July 21-22, paras. 119–21.

CHAPTER IV
The Second Phase: Katangese Resistance and Lumumba's Dissatisfactions
(pp. 36–47)

1. CO/25.
2. CO/21.
3. SCOR 885, para. 91.
4. *Ibid.*, paras. 10 and 124.
5. SCOR 884–86, *passim*.
6. S/4414—letter of July 31, 1960, to the President of the Security Council.

7. S/4417, para. 4.
8. *Ibid.*, para. 6.
9. *Ibid.*, para. 7.
10. *Ibid.*, para. 8.
11. *Ibid.*, para. 10.
12. SCOR 884, paras. 13–26.
13. SCOR 885, paras. 106–14.
14. S/4426, operative para. 4. For the full text of this resolution, see Appendix B of this study.
15. S/4417, Annex.
16. CO/20, Add. 4.
17. S/4417, Add. 6.
18. *Ibid.*, Add. 7.
19. CO/20, Adds. 4 and 5.
20. S/4445, Annexes I and II.
21. S/4451, August 21, 1960, *passim*, for the whole of the paragraph.
22. S/4475, Adds. 1–3, *passim*.
23. S/4482, Adds. 3 and 4.
24. *Ibid.*, Adds. 1 and 2.
25. S/4531, para. 9.
26. *Ibid.*, para. 12.
27. *Ibid.*, para. 27.
28. SCOR 896, September 9–10, 1960, para. 100.
29. S/4503, September 11, 1960.
30. S/4531, para. 18.
31. SCOR 887, August 21, 1960, para. 32.
32. S/4531, para. 20.

CHAPTER V
The Third Phase: Internal Stagnation and External Partisanship
(pp. 48–84)

1. S/4531, paras. 20–28; S/4800, pp. 10–13.
2. SCOR 913, December 7, 1960, para. 39.
3. A/4711, para. 67.
4. S/4417, Add. 3, Annex.
5. S/4531, para. 20.
6. A/1474 (ES-IV), September 19, 1960. For the text of this resolution, as adopted, see Appendix B of this study.
7. A/4711, Add. 1, from Kasongo, containing (pp. 25–26) a particularly inflammatory "ultimatum" of September 16, and (p. 27) a letter of the following day from Lumumba to Kasongo declaring the ultimatum a forgery; and Add. 2 from Kasavubu containing similar inflammatory documents attributed to Lumumba, along with apparently unrepudiated letters (dated September 12) to him from Nkrumah.
8. S/4531, paras. 32–40, and Annexes I–III.
9. S/4557, paras. 15–21.
10. *Ibid.*, para. 23.
11. *Ibid.*, paras. 22–24.
12. *Ibid.*, paras. 25–32.
13. SCOR 905, September 16, 1960, paras. 73 and 69.

14. *Ibid.*, paras. 88–144 and 168–89.
15. SCOR 906, September 17, 1960, *passim.*
16. *Ibid.*, para. 91; and S/4523.
17. SCOR 906, para. 109.
18. *Ibid.*, paras. 124–26; and S/4524.
19. SCOR 906, paras. 130–57.
20. *Ibid.*, paras. 173–98; and S/4525.
21. SCOR 906, para. 158 *et seq.*
22. A/1474 (ES-IV), operative para. 2.
23. GAOR 863, paras. 132–34.
24. *Ibid.*, paras. 260 and 264.
25. GAOR 858, para. 131.
26. *Ibid.*, para. 168.
27. *Ibid.*, paras. 134–35.
28. S/4557, B–3, para. 1.
29. GAOR 913, paras. 46–61.
30. A/4578.
31. A/C5, SR. 775.
32. A/4800, p. 20; and S/4557, paras. 39–54.
33. S/4557, para. 66.
34. *Ibid.*, paras. 70–74.
35. *Ibid.*, paras. 75–79.
36. *U.N. Review*, VIII, No. 2 (February, 1961), 38, col. 1.
37. *Ibid.*, pp. 38–39, cols. 3 and 1; and S/4580.
38. S/4571, paras. 1–17 and Annex III.
39. *Ibid.*, Annexes I and II.
40. A/3943.
41. A/4800, sec. 12, p. 27.
42. *The Times* (London), December 13, 1960, p. 9.
43. *Ibid.*
44. *Ibid.*, December 21, 1960, p. 6.
45. *Ibid.*, January 27, 1961, p. 12.
46. SCOR 913, December 7, 1961, para. 27.
47. *Ibid.*, para. 33.
48. A/4800, pp. 26–27.
49. S/4557, para. 54.
50. *Ibid.*, B–3.
51. SCOR 920, December 13–14, 1960, para. 71.
52. *Ibid.*, para. 37.
53. *Ibid.*, para. 82.
54. *Ibid.*, para. 97.
55. *Ibid.*, paras. 72–75; see also paras. 76–77.
56. S/4578 and Rev. 1; S/4579; S/4598; S/4597; SCOR 920.
57. S/4599 and S/4475.
58. A/4661.
59. A/4669.
60. A/L331, Rev. 1.
61. A/L332.
62. *The Times*, December 8, 1960, p. 14.
63. *Ibid.*, December 14, 1960, p. 9.

64. A/4800, p. 31.
65. S/4626 and Corr. 1.
66. S/4640, Annexes I and II.
67. S/4606, Annex IV.
68. *Ibid.*, Annex 2.
69. *Ibid.*, Annex 4; and *The Times*, January 3, 1961, p. 8.
70. S/4606, Annex 6; and *The Times*, January 3, 1961, p. 8.
71. *The Times*, January 3, p. 7.
72. *Ibid.*, January 7, 1961, p. 5.
73. *Ibid.*, January 9, 1961, p. 10; S/4616 and S/4622.
74. *The Times*, January 16, 1961, p. 10; and S/4625.
75. *The Times*, January 20, 1961, p. 11.
76. S/4629 and S/4630.
77. S/4637.
78. *Ibid.*, Add. 1.
79. S/4639.
80. S/4643 A.
81. SCOR 928, February 1, 1961, para. 70.
82. *Ibid.*, paras. 71–79.
83. *Ibid.*, paras. 86–88.
84. *Ibid.*, para. 77.
85. SCOR 935, February 15, 1961, para. 26: "It may be said to be on the outer margin of what the Security Council can decide, but the Council can point to at least one important precedent established by the General Assembly."
86. *Ibid.*, para. 27: "Again . . . on the outer margin of the mandate. . . ."
87. *Ibid.*, paras. 28, 29, and 30.
88. *Ibid.*, para. 35.
89. *Ibid.*, para. 34.
90. *Ibid.*, para. 33.
91. *Ibid.*, para. 32.
92. *Ibid.*, para. 35.
93. *Ibid.*, para. 28.
94. S/4722.
95. SCOR 935, para. 28.
96. SCOR 928, February 1, 1961, para. 91.
97. SCOR 935, February 15, 1961, para. 28, the Secretary-General speaking.
98. SCOR 941, February 20, 1961, paras. 118, 119, and 122.
99. SCOR 935, February 15, 1961, para. 14.
100. SCOR 934, para. 92, Mr. Zorin speaking.
101. SCOR 873, July 13–14, 1960, para. 28.
102. S/4387, July 13, 1960.
103. SCOR 935, February 15, 1961, para. 23.
104. *U.N. Review*, VIII, No. 5 (May, 1961), 39.
105. S/4725.
106. It is significant that the February 21 resolution made no mention of "the legitimate Government of the Republic of the Congo," nor of the releasing to it of "airports, radio stations, etc.," which had figured prominently in the original declaration of the Casablanca Conference (q.v., S/4626 and Corr. 1).
107. S/4389, para. 17.
108. See SCOR's 936–41, *passim*.

109. S/4741; in draft, S/4722.
110. S/4691, Adds. 1 and 2.
111. Letter of February 7, 1961, referred to in *U.N. Review*, VIII, No. 5 (May, 1961), 38.
112. S/4691, Annex.
113. S/5053.
114. S/4691.
115. See Article 2 (para. 7) in Appendix A of this study.
116. S/4741; S/4722, A-5.
117. S/4706.
118. *Ibid.*, para. 4. The fifth paragraph called for the Secretary-General's dismissal.
119. See SCOR 942, February 20–21, 1961, paras. 186–210, for Mr. Zorin's explanation of his abstention.
120. S/4741; S/4722, B, the fifth prefatory paragraph. For the full text of this resolution, see Appendix B of this study.
121. *The New York Times*, March 12, 1961, sec. I, p. 32, cols. 1–2.
122. SCOR 942, February 20–21, 1961, paras. 19 and 21.
123. Cf. S/4722 (quoted on pp. 253–54 of this study).
124. S/4733, Rev. 1.
125. SCOR 942, February 20–21, 1961, paras. 229 and 230.
126. S/4940, Annex 1.
127. SCOR 935, paras. 32–36.

CHAPTER VI
The Re-creation of Constitutional Government, March–August, 1961
(pp. 85–99)

1. *The Times*, February 23, 1961, p. 12.
2. *Ibid.*
3. *Ibid.*, February 22, 1961, p. 10.
4. S/4743.
5. Quoted in *U.N. Review*, VIII, No. 5 (May, 1961), 39–40 (from A/4711).
6. S/4752, Annex II.
7. *Ibid.*, Add. 1, March 3, 1961.
8. S/4750, February 25, 1961.
9. *Ibid.*, Adds. 1–7, *passim.*
10. S/4753, February 27, 1961.
11. *The Times*, February 27, 1961, p. 12.
12. *U.N. Review*, VIII, No. 6 (June, 1961), 32, col. 21.
13. A/4703; and *The Times*, March 1, 1961, p. 12.
14. S/4757 and Add. 1.
15. *U.N. Review*, VIII, No. 6 (June, 1961), 31, col. 3.
16. S/4758, A.
17. *Ibid.*
18. *Ibid.*, Adds. 5 and 6; and S/4761, Annex I.
19. S/4775, F (Bomboko to Secretary-General, March 25, 1961); and A/4800, pp. 28, 43.
20. For details of the Banana and Matadi incidents, see S/4758, Adds. 1 to 6, *passim*; S/4761 and Corr. 1, *passim*; S/4775, *passim*. The Secretary-General

himself provided a useful summary in his Annual Report for 1960–61 to the
General Assembly (A/4800, 16a, pp. 37–39).

21. *The Times*, March 8, 1961, p. 9.
22. *Ibid.*, March 11, 1961, p. 8.
23. *Ibid.*, March 1, 1961, p. 12; *ibid.*, March 21, p. 11.
24. *Ibid.*, March 7, 1961, p. 12.
25. A/4707.
26. *The Times*, March 16, 1961, p. 12; and A/PV972, p. 26, March 30, 1961.
27. A/PV 970.
28. A/PV 972.
29. A/PV 965.
30. A/PV 969.
31. See A 4800, sec. 17, pp. 43–47.
32. *Ibid.*, p. 42.
33. S/4807, Annex I; and *The New York Times*, April 23, 1961, sec. IV, p. 5, col. 5.
34. S/4752, Add. 3.
35. S/4807, Annex I; operative para. 3.
36. *The New York Times*, April 30, 1961, sec. IV, p. 5, col. 4 (Henry Tanner).
37. Lash, *Dag Hammarskjold*, p. 259.
38. A/4800, 16h, p. 43; and *The New York Times*, May 28, 1961, sec. IV, p. 9, col. 8.
39. *The New York Times*, May 14, 1961, sec. IV, p. 2, col. 2; and S/4841, Annex III.
40. *Ibid.*, April 30, 1961, sec. IV, p. 2, col. 6.
41. *Ibid.*, May 13, 1961, p. 1, col. 5, and p. 4, col. 6.
42. *Ibid.*, April 30, 1961, sec. IV, p. 5, col. 4.
43. *Ibid.*, p. 2, col. 6.
44. *Ibid.*, May 8, 1961, p. 1, col. 6; p. 11, col. 3 (Henry Tanner).
45. *Ibid.*, April 29, 1961, p. 1, col. 6 (Henry Tanner).
46. *Ibid.*, May 7, 1961, p. 27, col. 1 (Henry Tanner).
47. S/4807.
48. S/4803 and S/4807.
49. S/4807; compare this with the 273 mercenaries deported and the 65 awaiting deportation at the end of August, 1961 (S/4940, Add. 1, Annex III, p. 5).
50. S/4807, Annex II, para. 4.
51. CO/153 and Corr. 1.
52. *The New York Times*, May 7, 1961, sec. IV, p. 2, col. 2.
53. S/4841, Annex III.
54. *The New York Times*, June 12, 1961, p. 2, col. 3.
55. *Ibid.*, June 22, 1961, p. 9, col. 1 (Henry Tanner).
56. *Ibid.*, May 21, 1961, sec. IV, p. 2, col. 3.
57. *Ibid.*, July 1, 1961, p. 4, col. 5 (Henry Tanner).
58. *Ibid.*, July 4, 1961, p. 1, col. 2; *ibid.*, p. 2, col. 3 (Henry Tanner).
59. *Ibid.*, June 25, 1961, sec. IV, p. 2, col. 2.
60. *Ibid.*, July 1, 1961, p. 4, col. 5 (Henry Tanner).
61. *Ibid.*, June 25, 1961, sec. IV, p. 2, col. 2.

62. *U.N. Review*, VIII, No. 8 (August, 1961), 5; and S/4841, Add. 2.
63. *The New York Times*, July 2, 1961, sec. I, p. 2, col. 1; *ibid.*, July 5, 1961, p. 12.
64. *Ibid.*, July 4, 1961, p. 1, col. 2.
65. *Ibid.*, July 6, 1961, p. 2, col. 2; S/4841, Add. 2.
66. *The New York Times*, August 6, 1961, sec. IV, p. 2, cols. 3–4.
67. *Ibid.*, August 16, 1961, p. 12, cols. 3–4; and S/4923(b).
68. *The New York Times*, August 4, 1961, p. 6, col. 1 (Henry Tanner).
69. *Ibid.*, August 20, 1961, sec. IV, p. 2, col. 2.
70. A/4800, p. 14, col. 2, citing G. A. Resn. 1474 (ES-IV).
71. *The New York Times*, August 8, 1961, p. 1, cols. 4–5 (Henry Tanner).
72. *Ibid.*, August 19, 1961, p. 1, col. 6; ibid., p. 5, col. 1.
73. *Ibid.*, August 31, 1961, p. 9, col. 1.
74. S/4911, Adds. 1 and 2.
75. *The New York Times*, September 17, 1961, sec. IV, p. 5, col. 2 (Henry Tanner).
76. *Ibid.*, September 4, 1961, p. 2, cols. 7–8.
77. *Ibid.*
78. *Ibid.*
79. *Ibid.*, September 14, 1961, p. 3, col. 6.
80. S/4940, September 14, 1961, Annex I, p. 2.
81. *Ibid.*, p. 1.
82. *The New York Times*, August 26, 1961, p. 3, col. 8.
83. *Ibid.*, August 27, 1961, p. 20, cols. 4–5. The statement was confirmed in *The Sunday Telegraph* (London), November 11, 1962, p. 4, in a series of extracts from O'Brien's *To Katanga and Back*.
84. *The Observer* (London), December 3, 1961, p. 1; *ibid.*, December 10, 1961, p. 21; *ibid.*, December 17, 1961, p. 17.

CHAPTER VII
The First Action at Elisabethville:
August–September, 1961
(pp. 100–31)

1. S/4940, September 14, 1961, para. 3.
2. *The New York Times*, August 29, 1961, p. 1, col. 7; S/4940, para. 3.
3. S/4940, para. 3.
4. S/4940; *The New York Times*, September 15, 1961, p. 14, col. 1.
5. *The New York Times*, August 30, 1961, p. 5, cols. 4–6.
6. S/4940, paras. 5–7.
7. *Ibid.*, para. 8.
8. *The New York Times*, September 14, 1961, p. 3, col. 6.
9. S/4940, paras. 9–12.
10. *The New York Times*, September 10, 1961, sec. I, p. 23, col. 2 (Henry Tanner).
11. *Ibid.*, September 12, 1961, p. 11, col. 1 (David Halberstam).
12. *The Observer*, December 17, 1961, p. 17.
13. *Ibid.* Dr. O'Brien now adds that on September 10, Mr. Khiari had claimed quite specific instructions from the Secretary-General:

As regards the timing, Khiary said that the operation should be carried out either *before* three o'clock on the afternoon of Wednesday, September 13—

the time that Hammarskjoeld was due to arrive in Leopoldville—or after Hammarskjoeld's departure, estimated for three days later. Hammarskjoeld had given authority for these operations, but it would be embarrassing for him if fighting were actually going on in Katanga while he was in Leopoldville. (*The Sunday Telegraph* [London], November 4, 1962, p. 5.)

This, of course, may be a fabrication of O'Brien's; more plausibly, however, he is correctly reporting Khiari. But if Khiari were simply reporting Hammarskjöld, then responsibility for the September action would clearly be Hammarskjöld's. It seems most likely, however, that Khiari, and perhaps other U.N. authorities in Léopoldville, had of their own initiative determined upon U.N. military action in Elisabethville, and were anxious that it should be an accomplished fact before Hammarskjöld could intervene on his arrival in Leopoldville.

Dr. Linner is also implicated by Dr. O'Brien:

According to statements subsequently made by Dr. Linner, my chief in Leopoldville, Hammskjoeld did *not* know the plans for "Morthor" in advance. The operation was undertaken on Dr. Linner's own responsibility, in the light of his general instructions and knowledge of Hammarskjoeld's wishes. Presumably Dr. Linner and Khiary [Dr. Linner's Tunisian deputy] informed Hammarskjoeld, on his arrival, of what had been ordered.

(My present interpretation, as regards responsibilities in Leopoldville, is different from that in my articles in the *Observer* of last December 10 and 17; it is the result of a new information, further thought, and more attentive reading of a remarkable U.N. document, S/4940. Written too close to the events they deal with, the articles were at variance, on a number of points of interpretation, with my considered opinion. They placed what I now feel to be an undue emphasis on a single personal factor—Khiary's role.)

Dr. Linner has informed inquirers that he was not aware of the transmission to me, by Khiary and Fabry [legal adviser to the U.N. Operation in the Congo] of the arrest warrants and, if that is so, he (and perhaps also Hammarskjoeld) was kept in ignorance, by two of his trusted collaborators, of an extremely important fact. In any case, whatever gaps there may have been in Linner's or Hammarskjoeld's knowledge of the *instructions* given to us, they received an early and clear military report as to the *action* taken on September 13 (*The Sunday Telegraph* [London], November 11, 1962, p. 4 col. 3–4).

Thus Dr. O'Brien's evidence for Dr. Linner's implication is at best indirect; and his hypothesis that Hammarskjöld knew of "Morthor" depends upon Linner's having known. But he also endeavors to show that the Secretary had been committed, since February 21, to ending Katanga's secession by force:

He was involved, here, in a concealed contradiction. An essential element of his policy, in the early days, was *not* to use the U.N. force to end the secession —which was the object for which the Congo Government had invited the force in. The Afro-Asian Government had criticised this severely, and ultimately carried the February resolution which, as they interpreted it, provided a means in effect, of using the force to end the secession. And Hammarskjoeld had bound himself to seek their guidance on how to apply the resolution (*The Sunday Telegraph* [London], November 11, 1962, p. 5).

But as we have shown above, pp. 82–83 in Chapter V, after February 21

Hammarskjöld continued to distinguish sharply between the U.N.'s using force to end secession (which he repudiated) and its using force as a last resort to prevent civil war.

14. *The New York Times,* September 17, 1961, sec. IV, p. 11, col. 7 (Thomas J. Hamilton).

15. *Ibid.,* September 26, 1961, p. 4, cols. 5–6.

16. S/4940, para. 40.

17. *The New York Times,* September 15, 1961, p. 3, col. 1 (David Halberstam).

18. *Ibid.,* September 20, 1961, p. 11, col. 1.

19. *Ibid.,* September 14, 1961, p. 1, col. 8, and p. 2, col. 2.

20. *The Times,* September 14, 1961, p. 12, col. 1; *The New York Times,* September 21, 1961, p. 6, col. 1 (David Halberstam).

21. *The New York Times,* September 17, 1961 sec. IV, p. 11, col. 7 (Thomas J. Hamilton).

22. *The Observer,* December 10, 1963, p. 1.

23. S/4940, September 14, 1961.

24. *The Times,* September 14, 1961, p. 1, col. 1.

25. S/4939—a denial reiterated by M. Spaak in the Security Council debates of November 17–24, 1961. In *The Sunday Telegraph* (London), November 11, 1962, p. 4, Dr. O'Brien maintains that the "garage" incident was invented by the author of S/4940, in order to make the U.N. action appear defensive.

26. *The New York Times,* September 8, 1961, p. 17, col. 1 (David Halberstam).

27. *Ibid.,* September 21, 1961, p. 6, col. 1 (David Halberstam).

28. *Ibid.,* September 19, 1961, p. 1, col. 7, and p. 14, col. 6; S/4940, Adds.

29. *The New York Times,* September 24, 1961, sec. IV, p. 2, col. 1; S/4940, Adds.

An interesting comment on the military situation has been offered by Dr. O'Brien:

After the surrender of the Irish company at Jadotville it is possible to argue that the sooner Morthor was put out of its misery the better. The only argument against that is that it might have been better to await the arrival of the Ethiopian jets—for the passage of which the Uganda authorities were refusing clearance on technical grounds—before coming to terms with Tshombe. The terms then would, I think, have been better. If the Uganda authorities, and the British Government, had been made aware that the U.N. would not agree to a cease-fire before it had its jets, the technical difficulties at Entebbe might not have proved insoluble for long.

It has been argued retrospectively that an immediate cease-fire was necessitated by the military situation. That has been argued by civilians. It was not, I believe, the view of the U.N. Command. In some of our despatches from Elisabethville we did paint the military situation in sombre colours, as a means of putting on pressure for the jets.

(This was a mistaken tactic, but General McKeown, the Irish Commander of U.N. troops in the Congo, knew the situation in Elisabethville at first hand, and was not, I believe, unduly alarmed.)

The reasons that caused the operation to end in stalemate were fundamentally not military: they were political (*The Sunday Telegraph* [London], November 18, 1962, p. 4, col. 4).

30. *Ibid.*, November 26, 1961, sec. IV, p. 1, col. 6.
31. *Ibid.*, September 24, 1961, sec. I, p. 20, col. 4 (Henry Tanner).
32. *Ibid.*, September 16, 1961, p. 3, col. 4 (David Halberstam).
33. *Ibid.*, September 24, 1961, sec. I, p. 20, col. 4 (Henry Tanner).
34. *Ibid.*, p. 1, col. 6 (Henry Tanner).
35. *Ibid.*, December 17, 1961, sec. I, p. 4, cols. 4–5.
36. *Ibid.*, October 15, 1961, sec. I, p. 8, col. 7.
37. *Ibid.*, December 10, 1961, sec. I, p. 3, col. 6.
38. *Ibid.*, September 16, 1961, p. 1, col. 4.
39. *Ibid.*, p. 4, col. 4.
40. *Ibid.*, p. 1, col. 4.
41. *Ibid.*, September 22, 1961, p. 1, col. 7 (Robert Conley).
42. *Ibid.*, December 3, 1961, sec. I, p. 32, cols. 1–2.
43. *Ibid.*, December 17, 1961, sec. IV, p. 1, col. 2.
44. *Ibid.*, September 21, 1961, p. 6, col. 6.
45. *Ibid.*, September 16, 1961, p. 4, col. 4.
46. *Ibid.*, September 20, 1961, p. 11, col. 5 (David Halberstam).
47. *Ibid.*, September 21, 1961, p. 1, col. 8 (David Halberstam).
48. S/4940, Add. 7, para. 4; *ibid.*, Add. 11, Annex I, pp. 1–3.
49. *The New York Times*, October 29, 1961, sec. I, p. 21, col. 3 (David Halberstam).
50. *Ibid.*, September 21, 1961, p. 6, col. 4.
51. *Ibid.*, September 20, 1961, p. 10, col. 7.
52. *Ibid.*, cols. 7–8.
53. *Ibid.*, September 21, 1961, p. 6, cols. 5–6.
54. *Ibid.*, p. 1, col. 8, and p. 6, col. 2.
55. *Ibid.*, November 4, 1961, p. 1, col. 5 (Sam Pope Brewer).
56. *Ibid.*, November 13, 1961, p. 1, col. 1.
57. *The Observer*, December 10, 1961, p. 10.
58. The "Congo Club": Andrew W. Cordier (U.S.), Under-Secretary of General Assembly Affairs; Ralph J. Bunche (U.S.), Under-Secretary for Special Political Affairs; C. V. Narasimhan (India), Staff Aide to Hammarskjöld; Brigadier I. J. Rikhye (India), Military Adviser to the Secretary-General; Sir Alexander MacFarquhar (U.K.), Special Adviser on civilian operations in the Congo; and Robert W. Gardiner of Ghana, an economic- and social-affairs officer (*The New York Times*, October 19, 1961, p. 7, col. 1).
59. S/4940, Add. 12, para. 16.
60. *The New York Times*, October 17, 1961, p. 1, col. 6.
61. *Ibid.*, November 12, 1961, sec. IV, p. 9, cols. 6–8.
62. *Ibid.*, October 22, 1961, sec. IV, p. 2, col. 1.
63. *Ibid.*, October 25, 1961, p. 1, col. 8 (Robert Conley).
64. *Ibid.*, October 31, 1961, p. 2, cols. 5–6.
65. S/4940, Add. 11, Annex II, p. 1.
66. *Ibid.*, p. 5, para. 13.
67. *Ibid.*, Annex II, p. 1.
68. *Ibid.*, Add. 12, para. 12.
69. *The New York Times*, September 23, 1961, p. 1, col. 6 (Robert Conley).
70. *Ibid.*, November 12, 1961, sec. IV, p. 9, col. 8.

71. S/4940, Add. 13, pp. 1–2, para. 4.
72. *Ibid.*, Add. 12, p. 5, para. 14.
73. *The Observer*, December 17, 1961, p. 17, col. 1.
74. S/4940, Add. 11, paras. 2–11.
75. *The New York Times*, October 15, 1961, sec. I, p. 25, col. 4 (David Halberstam).
76. S/4940, Add. 11, Annex I, paras. 1–13.
77. *The New York Times*, October 16, 1961, p. 10, col. 5 (David Halberstam).
78. *Ibid.*, October 22, 1961, sec. IV, p. 2, col. 1.
79. *Ibid.*, October 19, 1961, p. 7, col. 1 (Robert Conley).
80. *Ibid.*, October 25, 1961, p. 12, col. 4 (Robert Conley).
81. S/4940, Add. 12., para. 19.
82. *The New York Times*, October 3, 1961, p. 3, col. 5.
83. S/4940, Add. 12, para. 2. The prisoners were as follows: Irish, 184 military personnel and 2 civilians; Swedish, 2 military; Norwegian, 1 military; British, 1 civilian. The U.N. had 240 Katangese prisoners.
84. *The New York Times*, October 17, 1961, p. 14, col. 5 (Robert Conley).
85. *Ibid.*, October 19, 1961, p. 1, col. 4 (Robert Conley).
86. *Ibid.*, October 22, 1961, sec. I, p. 20, col. 4 (Kenneth Love).
87. *Ibid.*
88. *Ibid.*, October 31, 1961, p. 1, col. 8, and p. 2, cols. 3–5 (David Halberstam); and S/4940, Add. 12.
89. *The New York Times*, November 1, 1961, p. 10, cols. 3–4 (David Halberstam).
90. *Ibid.*, November 3, 1961, p. 1, cols. 2–3 (David Halberstam).
91. *Ibid.*, November 5, 1961, sec. I, p. 1, col. 5 (David Halberstam).
92. See above, pp. 00.
93. *The New York Times*, November 4, 1961, p. 3, col. 2.
94. S/4940, Add. 12, p. 4, paras. 9–10.
95. *The New York Times*, November 1, 1961, p. 10, col. 3 (David Halberstam).
96. S/4940, Add. 12, p. 4, para. 9.
97. *The New York Times*, November 5, 1961, sec. IV, p. 2, col. 1.
98. S/4940, Add. 12, p. 4, para. 9.
99. *The New York Times*, October 14, 1961, p. 8, col. 5.
100. *Ibid.*, November 13, 1961, p. 2, col. 5 (David Halberstam).
101. *Ibid.*, col. 6.
102. *Ibid.*, November 8, 1961, p. 5, col. 6.
103. *Ibid.*, October 15, 1961, sec. IV, p. 2, col. 2.
104. S/4940, Add. 13, paras. 2–4.
105. *Ibid.*, paras. 2–5.
106. *The New York Times*, November 7, 1961, p. 1, col. 2 (David Halberstam).
107. *Ibid.*, November 9, 1961, p. 1, col. 3, and p. 6, cols. 3–6 (David Halberstam).
108. S/4940, Add. 13, paras. 6–23.
109. S/5053, Add. 1, paras. 3–4.
110. *The New York Times*, November 17, 1961, p. 1, col. 7, and p. 4, cols. 2–3 (Thomas J. Hamilton).

111. *Ibid.*, November 16, 1961, p. 1, col. 8 (David Halberstam).
112. S/4940, Add. 13, pp. 24–34.
113. *Ibid.*, p. 11, paras. 40–41.
114. *The New York Times*, November 26, 1961, sec. I, p. 1, col. 6, and p. 28, col. 1 (David Halberstam).
115. *Ibid.*, sec. IV, p. 1, col. 6.
116. *The Times*, December 4, 1961, p. 10, col. 7.
117. *The New York Times*, November 26, 1961, sec. I, p. 1, col. 6, and p. 28, col. 1 (David Halberstam).
118. *Ibid.*, January 12, 1962, p. 2, col. 5 (David Halberstam).
119. *Ibid.*, January 21, 1962, sec. I, p. 4, col. 1 (David Halberstam).
120. *Ibid.*, November 9, 1961, p. 6, col. 3.
121. S/4940, Add. 13, pp. 4–7.
122. S/PV 973, November 13, 1961, *passim*.
123. S/PV 974, November 15, 1961, *passim*.
124. S/PV 975, November 16, 1961, *passim*.
125. S/PV 976, November 17, 1961, para. 67–72.
126. S/5002, November 24, 1961. For the full text of this resolution, see Appendix B of this study.
127. S/4940, Add. 14, November 13, 1961, Ordinance No. 83, Article 2.
128. S/PV 976, November 17, 1961, pp. 67–72; and S/PV 982, November 24, pp. 81–86.
129. S/4989, Rev. 1, paras. 4–5.
130. S/PV 979, November 21, 1961, *passim*.
131. S/PV 976, November 17, 1961; and S/PV 982, November 24, 1961, *passim*.
132. *Ibid.*, paras. 71–80.
133. See S/5002 in Appendix B of this study.
134. S/PV 976, November 17, 1961, pp. 99–100.
135. U.N. Information Centre, London, Release No. 41/61.
136. *The New York Times*, November 14, 1961, p. 17, col. 3 (Thomas J. Hamilton).
137. S/4940, Add. 15, paras. 5 and 6.
138. *Ibid.*, Annex I.
139. *Ibid.*, paras. 11–19.
140. *Ibid.*, Add. 16, paras. 3–7.
141. *Ibid.*, Add. 15–16.
142. *Ibid.*, paras. 9–19.
143. U.N. Information Centre, London, Release No. 43/61, December 12, 1961, p. 1.
144. *The Times*, December 6, 1961, p. 14, cols. 1 and 2.

Chapter VIII
The Second Action at Elisabethville and Its Aftermath
(pp. 132–60)

1. S/4940, Adds. 15–17.
2. *The Times*, December 22, 1961, p. 10.
3. *Ibid.*
4. U.N. Information Centre, London, Releases No. 42/61, December 5, 1961, and No. 43/61, December 12, 1961.

5. See Krishna Menon in Security Council debate on November 17, 1961; S/PV 976, pp. 36–37.

6. S/4940, Add. 16, para. 27.

7. *The Times*, December 12, 1961, p. 10; and S/4940, Add. 18, paras. 4–5.

8. *The Times*, December 11, 1961, p. 12, col. 2.

9. S/4940, Add. 17, paras. 4 and 12, and Add. 18, paras. 5, 8, 19, and 23.

10. *Ibid.*, Add. 18, para. 12.

11. *Ibid.*, paras. 17 and 18.

12. *The New York Times*, December 17, 1961, sec. I, p. 1, col. 8.

13. *Ibid.*, December 19, 1961, p. 1, col. 1.

14. *Ibid.*, and S/4940, Add. 19, paras. 6 and 7.

15. *The New York Times*, December 8, 1961, p. 4, col. 2.

16. *The Times*, December 11, 1961, p. 8; and U.N. Information Centre, London, SPL/ 21, December 11, 1961, transmitting the entire statement from New York.

17. S/PV 976, p. 72.

18. *The Observer*, December 17, 1961, p. 1; and *The New York Times*, December 24, 1961, sec. IV, p. 1.

19. *Ibid.*, December, 1961, sec. IV, p. 1, col. 1.

20. *Ibid.*, December 7, 1961, p. 3, quotes fifteen jets alone. There were other planes.

21. *Ibid.*, December 10, 1961, sec. IV, p. 1.

22. S/4940, Add. 18, para. 17.

23. *The New York Times*, December 10, 1961, sec. IV, p. 1, col. 4.

24. *Ibid.*, col. 5.

25. S/4940, Add. 18, para. 9.

26. *The New York Times*, December 10, 1961, sec. I, p. 3; cf., however, U Thant's reprobation in his statement of the same day (see note 16 above) of press reports that he had given his officials "a completely free hand."

27. *Ibid.*, December 21, 1961, p. 1, col. 7.

28. S/5002. For the full text, see Appendix B of this study.

29. S/PV 974, November 15, 1961, p. 28.

30. *The Times*, November 27, 1961, editorial.

31. *The New York Times*, December 7, 1961, p. 4, cols. 3–7.

32. *Ibid.*, December 10, 1961, sec. IV, p. 1, col. 4.

33. *Ibid.*, December 17, 1961, sec. IV, p. 1, col. 2.

34. *The Times*, December 12, 1961, p. 10.

35. *Ibid.*, December 14, 1961, editorial p. 13.

36. *Ibid.*, December 8, 1961, p. 14.

37. *Ibid.*, December 9, 1961, p. 8.

38. *The Observer*, December 10, 1961, p. 2 (Colin Legum).

39. *The Times*, December 9, 1961, p. 8.

40. *The Observer*, December 24, 1961, p. 1.

41. *The Times*, December 12, 1961, p. 10.

42. *Ibid.*, December 9, 1961, p. 8.

43. *Ibid.*, December 13, 1961, p. 12.

44. *The New York Times*, December 17, 1961, sec. IV, p. 1, col. 4.

45. *The Observer*, December 17, 1961, p. 1.

46. *The New York Times*, December 15, 1961, p. 2, col. 6.

47. *Ibid.*, December 22, 1961, p. 2, col. 4.

48. *Ibid.*, December 17, 1961, sec. IV, p. 4, col. 5.
49. *Ibid.*, sec. IV, p. 1, col. 4.
50. *Ibid.*, December 21, 1961, p. 6, col. 4.
51. *The Observer*, December 17, 1961, p. 2.
52. *The Times*, December 15, 1961, p. 20.
53. *The New York Times*, December 19, 1961, p. 1.
54. *The Observer*, December 31, 1961, p. 28, col. 6.
55. *Ibid.*, December 24, 1961, p. 1, cols. 1–2.
56. *The New York Times*, January 1, 1962, p. 1, col. 5.
57. *Ibid.*, December 7, 1961, p. 4, col. 4.
58. *Ibid.*, December 9, 1961, p. 6, col. 1.
59. *Ibid.*, December 21, 1961, p. 6, col. 7.
60. *Ibid.*, December 15, 1961, p. 2, col. 4.
61. *Ibid.*, December 22, 1961, p. 2, col. 4.
62. *Ibid.*, December 7, 1961, p. 4, cols. 3–7.
63. *The Observer*, December 17, 1961, p. 1.
64. *The New York Times*, December 7, 1961, p. 4, col. 5, and p. 1, col. 7; *ibid.*, December 15, 1961, p. 1, col. 8.
65. *Ibid.*, December 7, 1961, p. 4, col. 5.
66. *Ibid.*, December 16, 1961, p. 1, col. 6.
67. S/4940, Add. 19, para. 1.
68. *Ibid.*, December 22, 1961, p. 2, cols. 3–4.
69. *Ibid.*, December 17, 1961, p. 1, col. 5.
70. *Ibid.*, December 18, 1961, p. 1, col. 5.
71. *Ibid.*, December 16, 1961, p. 3, cols. 1–2.
72. *Ibid.*, December 20, 1961, p. 5, col. 6.
73. *Ibid.*, December 22, 1961, p. 2, cols. 4–5.
74. *Ibid.*
75. *U.N. Review*, IX, No. 1 (January, 1962), 6. (The U.N. group consisted of Dr. Bunche, Robert Gardiner of Ghana, George Dumontet, and Mahmoud Khiari, and the American team included Ambassador Gullion, Hugh Greene, the public-affairs officer, and G. MacMurtrie Godley, embassy counselor.
76. *The New York Times*, December 22, 1961, p. 2, cols. 4–5, and p. 3, col. 5.
77. *U.N. Review*, IX, No. 1 (January, 1962), 45.
78. *Ibid.*, p. 6.
79. *The New York Times*, December 24, 1961, sec. IV, p. 7, cols. 1–2 (Arthur Krock).
80. *The Hindu Weekly Review*, December 4, 1961, p. 7.
81. *Ibid.*, editorial, "Another Shot at Katanga."
82. *The New York Times*, December 8, 1961, p. 4, cols. 4–5.
83. PR/SG/107.
84. *The New York Times*, January 21, 1962, sec. IV, p. 3, col. 8.
85. U.N. Information Centre, London, SPL/29, December 19, 1961.
86. *The New York Times*, December 24, 1961, sec. IV, p. 3, col. 1.
87. *Ibid.*, December 21, 1961, p. 6, col. 3; and S/4940, Add. 19.
88. *U.N. Review*, IX, No. 2 (February, 1962), 5, col. 3.
89. *The New York Times*, December 22, 1961, p. 2, col. 3.
90. *Ibid.*, December 24, 1961, sec. I, p. 10, col. 4.
91. *Ibid.*, col. 5.

92. *Ibid.*, December 24, 1961, sec. IV, p. 1, col. 3.
93. *Ibid.*, sec. IV, p. 1, col. 2.
94. S/5053.
95. *The New York Times*, February 18, 1962, sec. IV, p. 2, col. 3.
96. *Ibid.*, February 24, 1962, p. 1, col. 1, and p. 6, cols. 3–6. Although it was written in April, 1962, this sentence also described the situation in December, 1962.
97. *The Observer*, December 24, 1961, p. 1, cols. 4–5.
98. S/4426, August 9, 1960.
99. Chapter I, Article 2, para. 7.
100. *U.N. Review*, IX, No. 1 (January, 1962), 2, col. 1.
101. *The New York Times*, December 23, 1961, p. 2, col. 1.
102. *Ibid.*, January 11, 1962, p. 9, col. 1.
103. S/5053.
104. S/5064.
105. S/5053, Add. 1, para. 32.
106. *The New York Times*, February 16, 1962, p. 1, col. 3.
107. *Ibid.*, February 21, 1962, p. 12, cols. 3–4.
108. *U.N. Review*, IX, No. 2 (February, 1962), 5, col. 3.
109. *The New York Times*, January 11, 1962, sec. I, p. 9, col. 1.
110. S/5066.
111. S/5069.
112. *The New York Times*, January 31, 1962, p. 1, cols. 6–7, and p. 6, col. 4.
113. *Ibid.*, December 30, 1961, p. 2, col. 4 (Henry Tanner).
114. *Ibid.*, January 7, 1962, sec. IV, p. 11, col. 7 (Sam Pope Brewer).
115. *The Hindu Weekly Review*, February 5, 1962, p. 11, col. 5.
116. *The New York Times*, January 7, 1962, sec. I, p. 1, cols. 6–7.
117. *Ibid.*, December 20, 1961, p. 6, col. 4 (Harry Gilroy).
118. S/PV 973, pp. 71 and 36.
119. S/PV 976, November 17, 1961, pp. 57–63.
120. *The Observer*, December 17, 1961, p. 1, col. 1.
121. *The New York Times*, December 24, 1961, sec. I, p. 1, col. 5, and p. 9, cols. 1–4.
122. *Ibid.*, January 27, 1962, p. 1, col. 8.
123. S/5053, p. 4, para. 14.
124. *Ibid.*, para. 16.
125. *The New York Times*, January 3, 1962, p. 3, col. 5.
126. *Ibid.*, January 10, 1961, p. 6, col. 4.
127. *U.N. Review*, IX, No. 2 (February, 1962), 5.
128. *The New York Times*, January 11, 1962, p. 9, col. 1.
129. *Ibid.*, January 18, 1962, p. 4, cols. 3–4.
130. S/PV 974, November 15, 1961, p. 12.
131. Mr. Loufti, *ibid.*, p. 27.
132. S/PV 973, November 13, 1961, pp. 63–65.
133. *Ibid.*, p. 42.
134. S/PV 974, November 15, 1961, p. 77.
135. *The New York Times*, December 10, 1961, sec. IV, p. 1, col. 5.
136. S/4940, Add. 18, paras. 19–28, and Add. 19, paras. 5–6.
137. *Ibid.*, Add. 18, para. 23.
138. *The New York Times*, December 20, 1961.

139. *Ibid.*, Add. 19, para. 7.
140. *The New York Times*, December 10, 1961, sec. I, p. 1, col. 8, and p. 2, col. 5.
141. *Ibid.*, January 4, 1962, p. 10, col. 3.
142. *Ibid.*, January 14, 1962, sec. I, p. 19, col. 1 (Henry Tanner).
143. *Ibid.*, January 2, 1962, p. 1, col. 2, and p. 5, cols. 3–5.
144. *Ibid.*, January 2, 1962, sec. IV, p. 5, col. 3.
145. *Ibid.*, February 8, 1962, p. 1, col. 7.
146. S/5053, Add. 1, p. 1, paras. 1–4.
147. E.g., *The New York Times*, November 14, 1961, p. 17, col. 2; *ibid.*, January 10, 1962, p. 46, cols. 3–4 (editorial); *ibid.*, November 12, 1961, sec. IV, p. 9, col. 3.
148. S/5053, Add. 1, paras. 4–5.
149. *Ibid.*, p. 2, paras. 5–8.
150. *The New York Times*, January 12, 1962, p. 2, col. 5.
151. S/5053, Add. 1, paras. 10–16.
152. S/4940, Add. 13, para. 15.
153. S/5053, Add. 1, paras. 13–15.
154. *The New York Times*, January 12, 1962, p. 34, col. 6.
155. S/5053, Add. 1, para. 16.
156. *Ibid.*, Annex VII, p. 1.
157. *Ibid.*, paras. 20–24.
158. S/4389, p. 5.
159. S/4426, para. 4.
160. S/PV 975, November 16, 1961, p. 26.
161. *Ibid.*, pp. 24–25.
162. *Ibid.*, p. 26.
163. *The New York Times*, November 21, 1961, p. 1, col. 7 (Thomas J. Hamilton).
164. S/PV 982, November 24, 1961, pp. 62–65.
165. *Ibid.*, p. 61.
166. S/PV 978, November 21, 1961, p. 4.
167. *Ibid.*, p. 7.
168. S/PV 982, November 24, 1961, pp. 62–65.
169. *The New York Times*, November 22, 1961, p. 11, cols. 5–6 (Thomas J. Hamilton).
170. S/5053, Add. 1, paras. 20–23.
171. S/4940, Add. 16, para. 9.
172. *The New York Times*, November 13, 1961, p. 2, col. 6 (David Halberstam).
173. S/5053, Add. 1, para. 22.
174. *The New York Times*, November 15, 1961, p. 1, col. 8; and p. 14, cols. 4–5.
175. *Ibid.*, January 28, 1962, sec. I, p. 17, cols. 1–2.
176. S/5053, Add. 1, para. 22; *The New York Times*, January 14, 1962, p. 1, col. 8.
177. *Ibid.*, para. 24.
178. *Ibid.*, paras. 26–27.
179. *The New York Times*, January 21, 1962, sec. I, p. 1, col. 5.

180. *Ibid.*, sec. IV, p. 1, col. 5.
181. S/5053, Add. 2.
182. *The Observer*, January 21, 1962, p. 1, col. 4.
183. S/5053, Add. 2, para. 18.
184. *The New York Times*, January 24, 1962, p. 3, col. 1; *ibid.*, February 9, 1962, p. 5, cols. 4–5.

CHAPTER IX
U.N. Forces: Their Limitations and Possibilities
(pp. 161–92)

1. Dyason Lectures, Australia, March–April, 1962 (to be published in *Australian Outlook*, 1962–63).

POSTSCRIPT
Operations of the U.N. Force: December, 1962–February, 1963
(pp. 193–224)

1. The build-up—especially of air strength—becomes evident at the beginning of October, 1962. The number of mercenaries was estimated at 300–500. S/5053, Add. 12, paras. 1–36, Annex. V.
2. S/5053, Add. 12, paras. 37–54, Annexes IX–XX; S/5053, Add. 14, paras. 3–10, Annexes I–V; Bombings of North Katanga, paras. 12–15, and Annexes VI–XI.
3. *The New York Times*, November 28, 1962, p. 12, col. 1.
4. *Ibid.*
5. *Ibid.*, October 12, 1962, p. 4, cols. 5–6.
6. *Ibid.*, October 13, 1962, p. 2, col. 5.
7. *Ibid.*, October 15, 1962, p. 1, col. 15.
8. *Ibid.*, October 22, 1962, p. 1, col. 7, and p. 4, col. 3.
9. *Ibid.*, p. 4, col. 3.
10. S/5053, Add. 14, Annex XXXIV, Part A, paras. 7–8.
11. S/5053, Add. 12.
12. *The New York Times*, October 10, 1962, p. 1, col. 1.
13. *Ibid.*, October 13, 1962, p. 2, col. 4–6.
14. *Ibid.*, October 16, 1962, p. 2, col. 3.
15. *Ibid.*, p. 1, col. 5, and p. 2, col. 3–5.
16. *Ibid.*, November 7, 1962, p. 10, col. 1.
17. *Ibid.*, November 15, 1962, p. 19, cols. 3–4.
18. *Ibid.*, November 18, 1962, sec. IV, p. 11, col. 7–8.
19. S/5053, Add. 14, para. 1 and para. 16.
20. *The New York Times*, International Edition, News of the Week, December 3, 1962, p. 1, col. 7. (Henceforth the International Edition is referred to as "Int.") See also *ibid.*, December 8, 1962, p. 1, col. 6, and p. 3, col. 6.
21. *The New York Times*, October 23, 1962, p. 1, col. 2, November 18, 1962, sec. IV, p. 11, col. 7.
22. *Le Soir*, December 5, 1962, p. 3, col. 1; *ibid.*, December 8, 1962, p. 1, cols. 7–8.
23. Belgium, France, and West Germany are the principal purchasers of Katanga's copper. Britain, like the U.S., buys only a small amount but has a large investment in the Union Minière. The U.S. buys most of the Katangese cobalt. *The New York Times*, October 13, 1962, p. 2, cols. 4–5.
24. *Ibid.*, November 18, 1962, sec. IV, p. 11, col. 7.

25. *Ibid.*, October 20, 1962, p. 6, cols. 5–6.
26. *Ibid.*, October 23, 1962, p. 1, col. 2.
27. *Ibid.*, November 12, 1962, p. 1, col. 4, and *ibid.*, November 17, 1962, p. 11, cols. 5–6.
28. *Ibid.*, November 30, 1962, p. 1, cols. 2–3, and p. 12, cols. 3–4; *ibid.* (Int.), December 3, 1962, p. 3, col. 4.
29. *Le Soir*, December 14, 1962, p. 3, cols. 1–3.
30. *The New York Times*, November 27, 1962, p. 12, cols. 3–4.
31. *Ibid.*, November 24, 1962, p. 1, col. 3.
32. *Ibid.*, October 23, 1962, p. 8, cols. 3–4.
33. *Ibid.*, November 28, 1962, p. 1, col. 8, and p. 12, col. 1, and *ibid.* (Int.), December 3, 1962, sec. IV, p. 1, col. 7, p. 8, col. 1; p. 3, col. 4.
34. *Le Soir*, December 5, 1962, p. 3, col. 1.
35. *Ibid.*, December 14, 1962, p. 3, col. 3.
36. *The New York Times*, November 20, 1962, p. 34, col. 6 (Arthur Krock).
37. *Ibid.*, November 30, 1962, p. 12, cols. 3–6.
38. *Ibid.* (Int.), December 3, 1962, p. 1, col. 7.
39. *Le Soir*, December 14, 1962, p. 3, cols. 1–3, and *The New York Times* (Int.), December 11, 1962, p. 4, col. 3 (Arthur Krock).
40. *The New York Times*, November 29, 1962, p. 8, cols. 3–4.
41. *Ibid.* (Int.), December 4, 1962, p. 5, col. 4.
42. *Le Soir*, December 8, 1962, p. 1, cols. 7–8.
43. S/5053, Add. 14, para. 17, and Annex XII.
44. *Ibid.*, para. 18, and Annex XIII.
45. *Ibid.*, para. 19, and Annex XIV and XV.
46. *Ibid.*, para. 21, and Annex XVII.
47. *Ibid.*, para. 20, and Annex XVI.
48. *La Libre Belgique*, January 7, 1963, p. 3, cols. 1–3.
49. *The New York Times* (Int.), December 13, 1962, p. 1, col. 4.
50. *The Times* (London), December 15, 1962, p. 6, col. 7.
51. *Le Soir*, December 14, 1962, p. 3, cols. 1–3.
52. S/5053, Add. 14, para. 23, and Annex XX.
53. *Ibid.*, para. 24, and Annex XXI.
54. *The Times* (London), December 15, 1962, p. 6, col. 7.
55. *Le Soir*, December 19, 1962, p. 1, cols. 5–8.
56. *Ibid.*, December 13, 1962, p. 3, col. 3.
57. *Ibid.*, December 14, 1962, p. 3, cols. 1–3, and *The Times* (London), December 13, 1962, p. 10, col. 6.
58. *The New York Times* (Int.), December 17, 1962, p. 6, cols. 7–8.
59. *Ibid.*, December 19, 1962, p. 2, col. 3.
60. *The New York Times*, October 13, 1962, p. 2, cols. 4–5.
61. S/5053, Add. 14, Annex XIII, p. 2 (Letter dated December 11, 1962, from the Secretary-General to the Foreign Minister of Belgium; similar statement in Annex XIV, p. 2, to Portugal and South Africa; Annex IV, p. 2 to the U.K.)
62. *Le Soir*, December 20, 1962, p. 3, col. 3.
63. *The New York Times* (Int.), December 19, 1962, p. 2, col. 5.
64. S/5053, Add. 14, para. 25, and Annex XXII.
65. *The New York Times* (Int.), December 20, 1962, p. 3, cols. 3–4, and *ibid.*, December 24, 1962, p. 1, col. 1, and p. 2, col. 4.

66. S/5053, Add. 14, para. 26, Annex XXIII.
67. *The New York Times* (Int.), December 22, 1962, p. 2, col. 2.
68. *The Times* (London), December 21, 1962, p. 8, col. 2.
69. *The New York Times* (Int.), December 20, 1962, p. 1, col. 5.
70. *Ibid.*, December 19, 1962, p. 2, col. 3.
71. *Ibid.*, December 20, 1962, p. 1, col. 5, and December 21, 1962, p. 1, cols. 7–8.
72. *Le Soir*, December 14, 1962, p. 3, cols. 1–3.
73. *Ibid.*, December 23–24, 1962, p. 3, col. 5.
74. *The New York Times* (Int.), December 24, 1962, p. 2, col. 4.
75. *Ibid.*, December 20, 1962, p. 3, cols. 3–4, and *The Times* (London), December 20, 1962, p. 6, cols. 1–3.
76. *The New York Times* (Int.), December 19, 1962, p. 2, col. 3.
77. *The Times* (London), December 20, 1962, p. 6, col. 1, and *The New York Times* (Int.), December 20, 1962, p. 1, cols. 2–3.
78. *Le Soir*, January 9, 1963, p. 3, cols. 1–3.
79. S/4405, July 22, 1960, para. 2, and S/4722, February 21, 1961, para. A-2 and 3; also a General Assembly resolution may be mentioned, A/Res 1474, Rev. 1 (ES-IV), para. 5a, September 20, 1960.
80. *Le Soir*, December 26, 1962, p. 3, col. 2.
81. *The New York Times* (Int.), December 22, 1962, p. 1, cols. 4–5.
82. *Le Soir*, December 21, 1962, p. 3, cols. 1–3.
83. *Ibid.*, December 20, 1962, p. 1, cols. 5–8, and *ibid.*, December 28, 1962, p. 1, cols. 1–4.
84. *Ibid.*, December 21, 1962, p. 3, cols. 1–3.
85. *The New York Times* (Int.), December 21, 1962, p. 1, cols. 7–8.
86. *Ibid.*, December 27, 1962, p. 1, col. 7, and p. 2, col. 3.
87. *Ibid.*, December 22, 1962, p. 1, cols. 4–5.
88. *Ibid.*, December 27, 1962, p. 1, col. 7.
89. *Ibid.*, December 24, 1962, p. 1, col. 1, and p. 2, col. 4.
90. S/5053, Add. 14, paras. 27–29.
91. S/5053, Annex XIV, part A, para. 7.
92. *Ibid.*
93. S/5002, op. para. 4, and paras. 1 and 2.
94. S/5053, Add. 14/E, para. 30.
95. *La Libre Belgique*, December 25, 1962, p. 1, col. 1.
96. *The New York Times* (Int.), January 8, 1963, p. 1, cols. 7–8.
97. S/5053, Add. 14/E, paras. 31–35.
98. *Ibid.*, paras. 35–38.
99. *Ibid.*, Annex XXV.
100. *Ibid.*, Annex XXVI.
101. *Ibid.*, Add. 14/E, para. 38.
102. *Ibid.*, Add. 14/H, para. 75.
103. *Ibid.*, paras. 75–81.
104. *Ibid.*, paras. 40–43, and Annex XXVII.
105. *Ibid.*, para. 44.
106. *Ibid.*, para. 45, and Annex XXVIII.
107. *Ibid.*, paras. 46–59.
108. *Ibid.*, paras. 59–61.
109. *Ibid.*, Add. 14/G, para. 69.

110. *Ibid.*, Add. 14, Annex XXXIV, Part A, para. 1.
111. *Ibid.*, Annex XXXIII.
112. *Ibid.*, Annex XXXIV, Part B, para. 13.
113. *Ibid.*, para. 5.
114. *Ibid.*, Part A, para. 7.
115. *Ibid.*, para. 8.
116. *Ibid.*, para. 10.
117. *Ibid.*, and Add. 14/G, para. 63.
118. *Ibid.*, Add. 14, Annex XXXI, para. 7 (the Secretary-General's own statement of December 31, 1962).
119. *Ibid.*, Add. 14/G, paras. 64–66.
120. *Ibid.*, and Add. 14, Annex XXXIV, Part B, paras. 5–8.
121. *La Libre Belgique*, January 1, 1963, p. 4, col. 1; *Le Soir*, December 30–31, 1962, p. 3, col. 2.
122. S/5053, Add. 14, Annex XXXI, para. 1.
123. *Ibid.*, para. 2.
124. *Ibid.*, paras. 4–5.
125. *The Times* (London), January 2, 1963, p. 8, cols. 6–7.
126. *Ibid.*
127. *La Libre Belgique*, January 11, 1963, p. 1, cols. 7–8.
128. *The New York Times* (Int.), January 2, 1963, p. 1, col. 8, and p. 2, col. 5.
129. *Ibid.*, p. 2, col. 5.
130. S/5053, Add. 14, Annex XXXIV, Part B, paras. 11–12.
131. *The New York Times* (Int.), January 4, 1963, p. 3, col. 3; *ibid.*, January 5, 1963, p. 1, col. 6; and *ibid.*, January 8, 1963, p. 1, col. 6.
132. *Ibid.*, January 9, 1963, p. 1, col. 1, and p. 3, col. 3.
133. S/5053, Add. 14, Sec. I, paras. 82–83.
134. *The New York Times* (Int.), January 8, 1963, p. 3, col. 2.
135. *Ibid.*, and *The Times* (London), January 12, 1963, p. 6, col. 4.
136. *The Times*, January 11, 1963, p. 10, cols. 1–2.
137. *The New York Times* (Int.), January 9, 1963, p. 1, col. 1.
138. *La Libre Belgique*, January 11, 1963, p. 1, cols. 6–8.
139. *The New York Times* (Int.), January 11, 1963, p. 2, col. 5.
140. *Ibid.*, p. 2, cols. 6–7.
141. *Ibid.*, January 14, 1963, p. 1, col. 7.
142. *Ibid.*, January 16, 1963, p. 1, col. 8.
143. *Ibid.*, January 17, 1963, p. 1, col. 2.
144. *Ibid.*
145. *Ibid.*, January 18, 1963, p. 1, col. 2.
146. *Ibid.*, January 22, 1963, p. 1, col. 4, and p. 3, col. 6.
147. *Ibid.*, January 24, 1963, p. 1, col. 3; *ibid.*, February 2, 1963, p. 1, col. 5, and p. 2, col. 7; *ibid.*, February 4, 1963, p. 5 col. 2.
148. *Ibid.*, January 30, 1963, p. 2, col. 2.
149. Mr. Thant's inherited problems included the critical one of continuing to pay for the Congo operation. This issue is not dealt with in the present study, but for those interested, the following references may be helpful:
The New York Times (Int.), December 3, 1962, p. 1, col. 5, and p. 3, col. 6; *ibid.*, December 4, 1962, p. 1, col. 4; *ibid.*, December 20, 1962, p. 3, cols. 3–4; *ibid.*, December 24, 1962, p. 4, cols. 5–7, and p. 4, cols. 6–7.

APPENDIX A

Relevant Articles from the U.N. Charter

Chapter I, *Article 2*, paragraph 7

7. Nothing contained in the present Charter shall authorize the United Nations to intervene in matters which are essentially within the domestic jurisdiction of any state or shall require the Members to submit such matters to settlement under the present Charter; but this principle shall not prejudice the application of enforcement measures under Chapter VII.

Chapter VII, *Article 39*

The Security Council shall determine the existence of any threat to the peace, breach of the peace, or act of aggression and shall make recommendations, or decide what measures shall be taken in accordance with Articles 41 and 42, to maintain or restore international peace and security.

Article 40

In order to prevent an aggravation of the situation, the Security Council may, before making the recommendations or deciding upon the measures provided for in Article 39, call upon the parties concerned to comply with such provisional measures as it deems necessary or desirable. Such provisional measures shall be without prejudice to the rights, claims, or position of the parties concerned. The Security Council shall duly take account of failure to comply with such provisional measures.

Article 41

The Security Council may decide what measures not involving the use of armed force are to be employed to give effect to its decisions, and it may call upon the Members of the United Nations to apply such measures. These may include complete or partial interruption of economic relations and of rail, sea, air, postal, telegraphic, radio, and other means of communication, and the severance of diplomatic relations.

Article 42

Should the Security Council consider that measures provided for in Article 41 would be inadequate or have proved to be inadequate, it may take such action by air, sea, or land forces as may be necessary to maintain or restore international peace and security. Such action may include demonstrations, blockade, and other operations by air, sea, or land forces of Members of the United Nations.

Article 49

The Members of the United Nations shall join in affording mutual assistance in carrying out the measures decided upon by the Security Council.

Article 51

Nothing in the present Charter shall impair the inherent right of individual or collective self-defense if an armed attack occurs against a Member of the United Nations, until the Security Council has taken the measures necessary to maintain international peace and security. Measures taken by Members in the exercise of this right of self-defense shall be immediately reported to the Security Council and shall not in any way affect the authority and responsibility of the Security Council under the present Charter to take at any time such action as it deems necessary in order to maintain or restore international peace and security.

Chapter XV, *Article 99*

The Secretary-General may bring to the attention of the Security Council any matter which in his opinion may threaten the maintenance of international peace and security.

APPENDIX B

Resolutions on the Congo Adopted by the Security Council and General Assembly

S/4387, 14 July 1960
The Security Council,
Considering the report of the Secretary-General on a request for United Nations action in relation to the Republic of the Congo,

Considering the request for military assistance addressed to the Secretary-General by the President and the Prime Minister of the Republic of the Congo (document S/4382),

1. *Calls upon* the Government of Belgium to withdraw their troops from the territory of the Republic of the Congo;

2. *Decides* to authorize the Secretary-General to take the necessary steps, in consultation with the Government of the Republic of the Congo, to provide the Government with such military assistance as may be necessary, until, through the efforts of the Congolese Government with the technical assistance of the United Nations, the national se-

curity forces may be able, in the opinion of the Government, to meet
fully their tasks;

3. *Requests* the Secretary-General to report to the Security Council
as appropriate.

[This resolution was adopted by eight votes—Argentina, Ceylon,
Ecuador, Italy, Poland, Tunisia, the U.S.S.R., and the United States—
to zero, with three abstentions—China, France, and the United Kingdom.]

S/4405, 22 July 1960
The Security Council,

Having considered the first report by the Secretary-General on the
implementation of Security Council resolution S/4387 of 14 July 1960
(document S/4389),

Appreciating the work of the Secretary-General and the support so
readily and so speedily given to him by all Member States invited by him
to give assistance,

Noting that as stated by the Secretary-General the arrival of the troops
of the United Nations force in Leopoldville has already had a salutary
effect,

Recognizing that an urgent need still exists to continue and to in-
crease such efforts,

Considering that the complete restoration of law and order in the
Republic of the Congo would effectively contribute to the maintenance
of international peace and security,

Recognizing that the Security Council recommended the admission
of the Republic of the Congo to membership in the United Nations as
a unit,

1. *Calls upon* the Government of Belgium to implement speedily the
Security Council resolution of 14 July 1960, on the withdrawal of their
troops, and *authorizes* the Secretary-General to take all necessary action
to this effect;

2. *Requests* all States to refrain from any action which might tend to
impede the restoration of law and order and the exercise by the Government of the Congo of its authority and also to refrain from any action
which might undermine the territorial integrity and the political independence of the Republic of the Congo;

3. *Commends* the Secretary-General for the prompt action he has
taken to carry out resolution S/4387 of the Security Council and his first
report;

4. *Invites* the specialized agencies of the United Nations to render to
the Secretary-General such assistance as he may require;

5. *Requests* the Secretary-General to report further to the Security
Council as appropriate.

[This resolution was adopted unanimously.]

S/4426, 9 August 1960
  The Security Council,

Recalling its resolution of 22 July 1960 (S/4405) *inter alia,* calling upon the Government of Belgium to implement speedily the Security Council resolution of 14 July (S/4387) on the withdrawal of their troops, and authorizing the Secretary-General to take all necessary action to this effect,

Having noted the second report by the Secretary-General on the implementation of the aforesaid two resolutions and his statement before the Council,

Having considered the statements made by the representatives of Belgium and the Republic of the Congo to this Council at this meeting,

Noting with satisfaction the progress made by the United Nations in carrying out the Security Council resolution in respect of the territory of the Republic of the Congo other than the Province of Katanga,

Noting however that the United Nations had been prevented from implementing the aforesaid resolutions in the Province of Katanga although it was ready, and in fact attempted, to do so,

Recognizing that the withdrawal of Belgian troops from the Province of Katanga will be a positive contribution to and essential for the proper implementation of the Security Council resolutions,

1. *Confirms* the authority given to the Secretary-General by the Security Council resolutions of 14 July and 22 July 1960 and *requests* him to continue to carry out the responsibility placed on him thereby;

2. *Calls upon* the Government of Belgium to withdraw immediately its troops from the Province of Katanga under speedy modalities determined by the Secretary-General and to assist in every possible way the implementation of the Council's resolutions;

3. *Declares* that the entry of the United Nations force into the Province of Katanga is necessary for the full implementation of this resolution;

4. *Reaffirms* that the United Nations force in the Congo will not be a party to or in any way intervene in or be used to influence the outcome of any internal conflict, constitutional or otherwise;

5. *Calls upon* all Member States, in accordance with Articles 25 and 49 of the Charter, to accept and carry out the decisions of the Security Council and to afford mutual assistance in carrying out measures decided upon by the Security Council;

6. *Requests* the Secretary-General to implement this resolution and to report further to the Security Council as appropriate.

[This resolution was adopted by nine votes to zero, with two abstentions—France and Italy.]

A/4510, Resolution 1474, Rev. 1 (ES-IV), 20 September 1960
  The General Assembly,

Having considered the situation in the Republic of the Congo,

Taking note of the resolutions of 14 and 22 July and of 9 August 1960 of the Security Council,

Taking into account the unsatisfactory economic and political conditions that continue in the Republic of the Congo,

Considering that, with a view to preserving the unity, territorial integrity and political independence of the Congo, to protecting and advancing the welfare of its people, and to safeguarding international peace, it is essential for the United Nations to continue to assist the Central Government of the Congo,

1. *Fully supports* the resolution of 14 and 22 July and of 9 August of the Security Council,

2. *Requests* the Secretary-General to continue to take vigorous action in accordance with the terms of the aforesaid resolutions and to assist the Central Government of the Congo in the restoration and maintenance of law and order throughout the territory of the Republic of the Congo and to safeguard its unity, territorial integrity and political independence in the interests of international peace and security;

3. *Appeals* to all Congolese within the Republic of the Congo to seek a speedy solution by peaceful means of all their internal conflicts for the unity and integrity of the Congo, with the assistance, as appropriate, of Asian and African representatives appointed by the Advisory Committee on the Congo, in consultation with the Secretary-General, for the purpose of conciliation;

4. *Appeals* to all Member Governments for urgent voluntary contributions to a United Nations Fund for the Congo to be used under United Nations control and in consultation with the Central Government for the purpose of rendering the fullest possible assistance to achieve the objective mentioned in the preamble;

5. *Requests*

(a) All States to refrain from any action which might tend to impede the restoration of law and order and the exercise by the Government of the Congo of its authority and also to refrain from any action which might undermine the unity, territorial integrity and political independence of the Republic of the Congo;

(b) All Member States, in accordance with Articles 25 and 49 of the Charter, to accept and carry out the decisions of the Security Council and to afford mutual assistance in carrying out measures decided upon by the Security Council;

6. Without prejudice to the sovereign rights of the Republic of the Congo, *calls upon* all States to refrain from the direct and indirect provision of arms or other material of war and military personnel and other assistance for military purposes in the Congo during the temporary period of military assistance through the United Nations, except upon the request of the United Nations through the Secretary-General for carry-

ing out the purposes of this resolution and of the resolutions of 14 and 22 July and of 9 August 1960 of the Security Council.

[This resolution was adopted by 70 votes to 1, with 11 abstentions (Albania, Bulgaria, Byelorussia, Czechoslovakia, France, Hungary, Poland, Romania, the Ukraine, Union of South Africa, and the U.S.S.R.). Bolivia was absent.]

S/4741, 21 February 1961 [also in draft form, S/4722, 17 February 1961]

A

The Security Council,

Having considered the situation in the Congo,

Having learned with deep regret the announcement of the killing of the Congolese leaders, Mr. Patrice Lumumba, Mr. Maurice Mpolo and Mr. Joseph Okito,

Deeply concerned at the grave repercussions of these crimes and the danger of wide-spread civil war and bloodshed in the Congo and the threat to international peace and security,

Noting the Report of the Secretary-General's Special Representative (S/4691) dated 12 February 1961 bringing to light the development of a serious civil war situation and preparations therefor,

1. *Urges* that the United Nations take immediately all appropriate measures to prevent the occurrence of civil war in the Congo, including arrangements for cease-fires, the halting of all military operations, the prevention of clashes, and the use of force, if necessary, in the last resort;

2. *Urges* that measures be taken for the immediate withdrawal and evacuation from the Congo of all Belgian and other foreign military and para-military personnel and political advisers not under the United Nations Command, and mercenaries;

3. *Calls* upon all States to take immediate and energetic measures to prevent the departure of such personnel for the Congo from their territories, and for the denial of transit and other facilities to them;

4. *Decides* that an immediate and impartial investigation be held in order to ascertain the circumstances of the death of Mr. Lumumba and his colleagues and that the perpetrators of these crimes be punished;

5. *Reaffirms* the Security Council resolutions of 14 July, 22 July, and 9 August 1960 and the General Assembly resolution 1474 (ES-IV) of 20 September 1960 and reminds all States of their obligation under these resolutions.

B

The Security Council,

Gravely concerned at the continuing deterioration in the Congo, and the prevalence of conditions which seriously imperil peace and order, and the unity and territorial integrity of the Congo, and threaten international peace and security,

Noting with deep regret and concern the systematic violations of human rights and fundamental freedoms and the general absence of rule of law in the Congo,

Recognizing the imperative necessity of the restoration of parliamentary institutions in the Congo in accordance with the fundamental law of the country, so that the will of the people should be reflected through the freely elected Parliament,

Convinced that the solution of the problem of the Congo lies in the hands of the Congolese people themselves without any interference from outside and that there can be no solution without conciliation,

Convinced further that the imposition of any solution, including the formation of any government not based on genuine conciliation would, far from settling any issues, greatly enhance the dangers of conflict within the Congo and threat to international peace and security,

1. *Urges* the convening of the Parliament and the taking of necessary protective measures in that connection;

2. *Urges* that Congolese armed units and personnel should be reorganized and brought under discipline and control, and arrangements be made on impartial and equitable bases to that end and with a view to the elimination of any possibility of interference by such units and personnel in the political life of the Congo;

3. *Calls upon* all States to extend their full co-operation and assistance and take such measures as may be necessary on their part, for the implementation of this resolution.

[This resolution was adopted by nine votes to zero, with two abstentions—France, the U.S.S.R.]

S/5002, 24 November 1961
   The Security Council,
   Recalling its resolutions S/4387, S/4405, S/4426 and S/4741,
   Recalling further General Assembly resolutions 1474 (ES-IV), 1592 (XV), 1599 (XV), 1600 (XV) and 1601 (XV),
   Reaffirming the policies and purposes of the United Nations with respect to the Congo (Leopoldville) as set out in the aforesaid resolutions, namely:

   (a) To maintain the territorial integrity and the political independence of the Republic of the Congo;

   (b) To assist the Central Government of the Congo in the restoration and maintenance of law and order;

   (c) To prevent the occurrence of civil war in the Congo;

   (d) To secure the immediate withdrawal and evacuation from the Congo of all foreign military, para-military and advisory personnel not under the United Nations Command, and all mercenaries; and

   (e) To render technical assistance,

   Welcoming the restoration of the national Parliament of the Congo in accordance with the *Loi fondamentale* and the consequent formation of a Central Government on 2 August 1961,

Deploring all armed action in opposition to the authority of the Government of the Republic of the Congo, specifically secessionist activities and armed action now being carried on by the Provincial Administration of Katanga with the aid of external resources and foreign mercenaries, and *completely rejecting* the claim that Katanga is a "sovereign independent nation,"

Noting with deep regret the recent and past actions of violence against United Nations personnel,

Recognizing the Government of the Republic of the Congo as exclusively responsible for the conduct of the external affairs of the Congo,

Bearing in mind the imperative necessity of speedy and effective action to implement fully the policies and purposes of the United Nations in the Congo to end the unfortunate plight of the Congolese people, necessary both in the interests of world peace and international cooperation, and stability and progress of Africa as a whole,

1. *Strongly deprecates* the secessionist activities illegally carried out by the provincial administration of Katanga, with the aid of external resources and manned by foreign mercenaries;

2. *Further deprecates* the armed action against United Nations forces and personnel in the pursuit of such activities;

3. *Insists* that such activities shall cease forthwith, and *calls upon* all concerned to desist therefrom;

4. *Authorizes* the Secretary-General to take vigorous action, including the use of requisite measure of force, if necessary, for the immediate apprehension, detention pending legal action and/or deportation of all foreign military and para-military personnel and political advisers not under the United Nations Command, and mercenaries as laid down in paragraph A-2 of the Security Council resolution of 21 February 1961;

5. *Further requests* the Secretary-General to take all necessary measures to prevent the entry or return of such elements under whatever guise and also of arms, equipment or other material in support of such activities;

6. *Requests* all States to refrain from the supply of arms, equipment or other material which could be used for warlike purposes, and to take the necessary measures to prevent their nationals from doing the same, and also to deny transportation and transit facilities for such supplies across their territories, except in accordance with the decisions, policies and purposes of the United Nations;

7. *Calls upon* all Member States to refrain from promoting, condoning, or giving support by acts of omission or commission, directly or indirectly, to activities against the United Nations often resulting in armed hostilities against the United Nations forces and personnel;

8. *Declares* that all secessionist activities against the Republic of the

Congo are contrary to the *Loi fondamentale* and Security Council decisions and specifically *demands* that such activities which are now taking place in Katanga shall cease forthwith;

9. *Declares* full and firm support for the Central Government of the Congo, and the determination to assist that Government in accordance with the decision of the United Nations to maintain law and order and national integrity, to provide technical assistance and to implement those decisions;

10. *Urges* all Member States to lend their support, according to their national procedures, to the Central Government of the Republic of the Congo, in conformity with the Charter and the decisions of the United Nations;

11. *Requests* all Member States to refrain from any action which may directly or indirectly impede the policies and purposes of the United Nations in the Congo and is contrary to its decisions and the general purpose of the Charter.

[This resolution was adopted by nine votes to zero, with two abstentions—France, the United Kingdom.]